STALIN'S CHILDREN

Three Generations of Love and War

OWEN MATTHEWS

BLOOMSBURY

LONDON · BERLIN · NEW YORK

First published in Great Britain 2008

Copyright © Owen Matthews 2008

The right of Owen Matthews to be identified as Proprietor of this work has been
asserted by him in accordance with the Copyright, Designs and Patents Act 1988
No part of this book may be used or reproduced in any manner whatsoever
without written permission from the Publisher except in the case of brief
quotations embodied in critical articles or reviews

Every reasonable effort has been made to trace copyright holders of material
reproduced in this book, but if any have been inadvertently overlooked the
publishers would be glad to hear from them

Bloomsbury Publishing Plc
36 Soho Square
London W1D 3QY

www.bloomsbury.com

Bloomsbury Publishing, London, New York and Berlin

A CIP catalogue record for this book is available from the British Library

ISBN 978 0 7475 9181 8

10 9 8 7 6 5 4 3 2

Typeset by Hewer Text (UK) Ltd, Edinburgh
Printed in Great Britain by Clays Ltd, St Ives plc

The paper this book is printed on is certified by the © 1996 Forest Stewardship
Council A.C. (FSC). It is ancient-forest friendly. The printer holds
FSC chain of custody SGS-COC-2061

FSC

Mixed Sources
Product group from well-managed
forests and other controlled sources

Cert no. SGS-COC-2061
www.fsc.org
© 1996 Forest Stewardship Council

To my parents

CONTENTS

Prologue

The hand that signed the paper felled a city . . .
Doubled the globe of dead and halved a country.
Dylan Thomas

On a shelf in a cellar in the former KGB headquarters in Chernigov, in the black earth country in the heart of the Ukraine, lies a thick file with a crumbling brown cardboard cover. It contains about three pounds of paper, the sheets carefully numbered and bound. Its subject is my mother's father, Bibikov, Boris Lvovich, whose name is entered on the cover in curiously elaborate, copperplate script. Just under his name is the printed title, 'Top Secret. People's Commissariat of Internal Affairs. Anti-Soviet Rightist-Trotskyite Organization in the Ukraine.'

The file records my grandfather's progress from life to death at the hands of Stalin's secret police as the summer of 1937 turned to autumn. I saw it in a dingy office in Kiev fifty-eight years after his death. The file sat heavily in my lap, eerily malignant, a swollen tumour of paper. It smelled of slightly acidic musk.

Most of the file's pages are flimsy official onion-skin forms, punched through in places by heavy typewriting. Interspersed are a few slips of thicker, raggy scrap paper. Towards the end are several sheets of plain writing paper covered in a thin, blotted handwriting, my grandfather's confessions to being an enemy of the people. The seventy-eighth document is a receipt confirming that he had read and understood the death sentence passed on him by a closed court in Kiev. The scribbled signature is his last recorded act on earth. The final document is a clumsily mimeographed slip, confirming that the sentence was carried out on the following day, 14 October 1937. The signature of his executioner is a casual squiggle. Since the careful bureaucrats who compiled the file neglected to record where he was buried, this stack of paper is the closest thing to Boris Bibikov's earthly remains.

In the attic of 7 Alderney Street, Pimlico, London, is a handsome steamer trunk, marked 'W.H.M. Matthews, St Antony's College, Oxford, АНГЛИА' in neat black painted letters. It contains a love story. Or perhaps it contains a love.

In the trunk are hundreds of my parents' love letters, carefully arranged by date in stacks, starting in July 1964, ending in October 1969. Many are on thin airmail paper, others on multiple sheets of neat white writing paper. Half – the letters of my mother, Lyudmila Bibikova, to my father – are covered in looping, cursive handwriting, even yet very feminine. Most of my father's letters to my mother are typed, because he liked to keep carbon copies of every one he sent, but each has a handwritten note at the bottom above his extravagant signature, or sometimes a charming little drawing. But those which he wrote by hand are closely written in tight, upright and very correct Cyrillic.

For the six years that my parents were separated by the fortunes of the Cold War, they wrote to each other every day, sometimes twice a day. His letters are from Nottingham, Oxford, London, Cologne, Berlin, Prague, Paris, Marrakech, Istanbul, New York. Hers are from Moscow, from Leningrad, from the family dacha at Vnukovo. The letters detail every act, every thought of my parents' daily lives. He sits in a lonely bedsit on a smoggy night in Nottingham, typing about his curry dinners and minor academic squabbles. She pines in her tiny room off Moscow's Arbat Street, writing about conversations with her friends, trips to the ballet, books she's reading.

At some moments their epistolary conversation is so intimate that reading the letters feels like a violation. At others the pain of separation is so intense that the paper seems to tremble with it. They talk of tiny incidents from the few months they spent together in Moscow, in the winter and spring of 1964, their talks and walks. They gossip about mutual friends and meals and films. But above all the letters are charged with loss, and loneliness, and with a love so great, my mother wrote, 'that it can move mountains and turn the world on its axis'. And though the letters are full of pain, I think that they also describe the happiest period of my parents' lives.

As I leaf through the letters now, sitting on the floor of the attic which was my childhood room, where I slept for eighteen years not a yard from where the letters lay in their locked trunk, in the box room under the eaves of the house, and where I listened to my parents' raised voices drifting up the stairs, it occurs to me that here is where their love is. 'Every letter is a piece of our soul, they mustn't get lost,' my mother wrote during their first agonizing months. 'Your letters bring me little pieces of you, of your life, your breath, your beating heart.' And so they spilled their souls out on to paper – reams of paper, impregnated with pain, desire and love, chains of paper, relays of it, rumbling through the night on mail trains across Europe almost without interruption for six years. 'As our letters travel they take on a magical quality . . . in that lies their strength,' wrote Mila. 'Every line is the blood of my heart, and there is no limit to how much I can pour out.' But by the time my parents met again they found there was barely enough love left over. It had all been turned to ink and written over a thousand sheets of paper, which now lie carefully folded in a trunk in the attic of a terraced house in London.

*   *   *

We believe we think with our rational minds, but in reality we think with our blood. In Moscow I found blood all around me. I spent much of my early adult life in Russia, and during those years I found myself, time and again, tripping over the roots of experience which grew into recognizable elements of my parents' character. Echoes of my parents' lives kept cropping up in mine like ghosts, things which remained unchanged in the rhythms of the city which I had believed was so full of the new and the now. The damp-wool smell of the Metro in winter. Rainy nights on the backstreets off the Arbat when the eerie bulk of the Foreign Ministry glows like a fog-bound liner. The lights of a Siberian city like an island in a sea of forest seen from the window of a tiny, bouncing plane. The smell of the sea-wind at Tallinn docks. And, towards the end of my time in Moscow, the sudden, piercing realization that all my life, I had loved precisely the woman who was sitting by my side at a table among friends in a warm fug of cigarette smoke and conversation in the kitchen of an apartment near the Arbat.

Yet the Russia I lived in was a very different place from the one my parents had known. Their Russia was a rigidly controlled society where unorthodox thought was a crime, where everyone knew their neighbours' business and where the collective imposed a powerful moral terror on any member who dared defy convention. My Russia was a society adrift. During the seventy years of Soviet rule, Russians had lost much of their culture, their religion, their God; and many of them also lost their minds. But at least the Soviet state had compensated by filling the ideological vacuum with its own bold myths and strict codes. It fed people, taught and clothed them, ordered their lives from cradle to grave and, most importantly, thought for them. Communists – men like my grandfather – had tried to create a new kind of man, emptying the people of their old beliefs and refilling them with civic duty, patriotism and docility. But when Communist ideology was stripped away, so its quaint fifties morality also disappeared into the black hole of discarded mythologies. People put their faith in television healers, Japanese apocalyptic cults, even in the jealous old God of Orthodoxy. But more profound than any of Russia's other, new-found faiths, was an absolute, bottomless nihilism. Suddenly there were no rules, no holds barred, and everything went for those bold and ruthless enough to go out and grab as much as they could.

There were plenty of ashes, but few phoenixes. Mostly the *narod*, the people, retreated into themselves, continuing with their old routines, ignoring the seismic shocks which had shaken their world. Work, school, car, dacha, allotment, television, sausage and potatoes for dinner. Russia after the Fall often reminded me of a maze full of lab rats trapped in an abandoned experiment, still vainly nuzzling the sugar-water dispenser long after the scientists had switched off the lights and emigrated.

Some of the Russian intelligentsia called it the *revolutsiya v soznanii*, the revolution in consciousness. But that didn't begin to describe it. It wasn't really a revolution, because only a small minority chose or had the imagination to seize the day, to reinvent themselves and adapt to the brave new world. For the rest, it was more like a quiet implosion, like a puffball mushroom collapsing, a sudden telescoping of life's possibilities, not a revolution but a slow sagging into poverty and confusion.

For most of my time in Russia, I thought I was in a story without a narrative, a constantly changing slideshow of phantasmagoria which Moscow was projecting on to my life for my personal delectation. In fact I was caught in a cool web of blood knowledge which was slowly winding me in.

I came to Moscow to get away from my parents. Instead, I found them there, though for a long time I didn't know it, or refused to see it. This is a story about Russia and my family, about a place which made us and freed us and inspired us and very nearly broke us. And it's ultimately a story about escape,

about how we all escaped from Russia, even though all of us –
even my father, a Welshman, who has no Russian blood, even
me, who grew up in England – still carry something of Russia
inside ourselves, infecting our blood like a fever.

1

The Last Day

I believe in one thing only, the power of human will.
Iosif Stalin

I spoke Russian before I spoke English. Until I was sent to an English prep school, dressed up in a cap, blazer and shorts, I saw the world in Russian. If languages have a colour, Russian was the hot pink of my mother's seventies dresses, the warm red of an old Uzbek teapot she had brought with her from Moscow, the kitschy black and gold of the painted Russian wooden spoons which hung on the wall in the kitchen. English, which I spoke with my father, was the muted green of his study carpet, the faded brown of his tweed jackets. Russian was an intimate language, a private code I would speak to my mother, warm and carnal and coarse, the language of the kitchen and the bedroom, and its smell was warm bed-fug and steaming mashed potatoes. English was the language of formality, adulthood, learning, reading *Janet and John* on my father's lap, and its smell was Gauloises and coffee and the engine oil on his collection of model steam engines.

My mother would read me Pushkin stories like the extraordinary folk epic 'Ruslan and Lyudmila'. The supernatural world of dark Russian forests, of brooding evil and bright, shining heroes conjured on winter evenings in a small London drawing room and punctuated by the distant squeal of trains coming into Victoria station, was infinitely more vivid to my childhood self than anything my father could summon. 'There is the Russian spirit, it smells of Russia there,' wrote Pushkin, of a mysterious land by the sea where a great green oak stood; round the oak was twined a golden chain, and on the chain a black cat paced, and in its tangled branches a mermaid swam.

At the end of the scorching summer of 1976 my grandmother Martha came to visit us in London. I was four-and-a-half years old, and the lawns of Eccleston Square garden were scorched yellow by a heatwave. It was a summer of baking pavements, the flavour of strawberry lollipops, a favourite pair of beige corduroy dungarees with a large yellow flower sewn on the leg. I remember my grandmother's heaviness, her musty Russian smell, her soft, pudgy face. In photographs she looks uncomfortable, large and angry and masculine, holding me like a wriggling sack while my mother smiles nervously. She scared me with her brusque scolding, her unpredictability, a sensed tension. She would sit for hours, alone and silent in an armchair by the drawing room window. Sometimes she pushed me away when I tried to climb on her lap.

One afternoon we were in Eccleston Square, my mother chatting with other mothers, my grandmother sitting on a bench. I was playing cops and robbers with myself, wearing a plastic policeman's helmet and touting a cowboy pistol, running around the garden. I crept up behind my grandmother, jumped out from behind the bench and tried to put a pair of toy handcuffs on her wrists. She sat there motionless as I struggled to close the handcuffs, and when I looked up she was crying. I ran to my mother, who came over and they sat together for a long time while I hid in the bushes. Then we went home, my grandmother still silently weeping.

'Don't be upset,' my mother said. 'Granny is crying because the handcuffs reminded her of when she was in prison. But it was a long time ago and it's all right now.'

For most of her life my mother lived for an imaginary future. Her parents were taken away to prison when she was three. From that moment, she was raised by the Soviet state, which moulded her mind, if not her spirit, in its ways. A bright dawn was just over the horizon, her generation was told, but could only be attained, Aztec-like, by the spilling of blood and by the sacrifice of individual will to the greater good. 'Simple Soviet people are everywhere performing miracles,' is a phrase from a popular 1930s song my mother often cites, always with heavy irony, when she is confronted by an example of bureaucratic stupidity or crassness. But in a profound sense, the idea that the individual could overcome seemingly impossible obstacles shaped her life.

Her father Boris Bibikov believed the same. He inspired – and terrified – thousands of men and women to raise a giant factory quite literally from the mud on which it stood. In her turn, my mother performed a scarcely less remarkable miracle. Armed with nothing but her unshakeable conviction, she took on the whole behemoth of the Soviet state, and won.

I never think of my mother as small, though she is in fact tiny, a shade under five feet tall. But she is a woman of gigantic character; the kinetic field of her presence fills large houses. I have often seen her crying, but never at a loss. Even at her weakest moments, she is never in doubt of herself. She has no time for navel-gazing, for the self-indulgent lives that my generation have led, though for all her iron self-discipline she possesses a vast fund of forgiveness for human failure in others. From my earliest childhood, my mother has insisted that everything in life must be fought for, that any failure is primarily a failure of will. All her life she imposed uncompromising demands on herself, and met them. 'We must be worthy of their belief in us, we must fight,' she wrote to my father. 'We have no right to be weak . . . Life will crush us in a minute and no one will hear our cries.'

She is also ferociously witty and intelligent, though I usually only see this side of her when she is in company. At the dinner table with guests her voice is clear and emphatic, pronouncing her opinions with unfashionable certainty in roundly enunciated English.

'Everything is relative,' she will say archly. 'One hair in a bowl of soup is too much, one hair on your head is not enough.' Or she will declare: 'Russian has so many reflexive verbs because Russians are pathologically irresponsible! In English you say, "I want", "I need". In Russian it's "want has arisen", "need has arisen". Grammar reflects psychology! The psychology of an infantile society!'

When she speaks she slips effortlessly from Nureyev to Dostoyevsky to Karamzin and Blok, her snorts of derision and dismissive hand-waves interspersed with gasps of admiration and hands rapturously clapped to the chest as she swerves on to a new subject like a racing driver taking a corner. 'Huh, Nabokov!' she will say with pursed lips and a raised eyebrow, letting all present know that she finds him an incorrigible show-off and a cold, heartless and artificial individual. 'Ah, Kharms,' she says, raising a palm to the sky, signalling that here is a man with a true understanding of Russia's absurdity, its pathos and everyday tragedy. Like many Russian intellectuals of her generation, she is utterly at home in the dense kasbah of her country's literature, navigating its alleys like a native daughter. I have always admired my mother, but at these moments, when she holds a table in awe, I am intensely proud of her.

Milan Kundera wrote that 'The struggle of man against power is the struggle of memory against forgetting.' And so it is for my mother, in telling this story. She rarely spoke to me about her childhood when I was myself a child. But as an adult, when I asked, she began to speak about it freely, without melodrama. Now, she recalls her own life with striking dispassion and candour. But at the same time, she worries that when I tell the story it will be too grim, too depressing. 'Write about the good people, not just about the darkness,' my mother has said to me when describing her childhood. 'There was so much human generosity, so many wonderful, soulful people.'

One final image of my mother, before we begin her story. Aged seventy-two, she is sitting at a lunch table spread with food and dappled with sunlight. We are at a friend's house on an island near Istanbul, on a cool terrace overlooking the Sea of Marmara. My mother perches sideways on a dining chair, as she has always done because of her hip, crippled by tuberculosis in childhood. Our host, a Turkish writer, is tanned as golden brown as an ancient sea god. He pours wine, passes plates of mussels he has gathered himself and plates of food that his excellent cook has prepared.

My mother is relaxed, at her most charming. Among the guests is a Turkish ballet dancer, a tall, beautiful woman with a dancer's rangy physicality. She and my mother are talking ballet with great passion. I am at the end of the table, talking to our host, when I hear the tone of my mother's voice change; nothing dramatic, a modulation only. But the tiny shift cuts across the various conversations at the table and we turn to listen.

She is telling a story about Solikamsk, a wartime town of lost children to which she was evacuated in 1943. The teacher at the overcrowded school she attended would bring a tray of plain black bread at lunchtime with which to feed her class. She would tell the local children to leave their pieces for the orphans, though they were all close to starving.

My mother tells the story simply, with no great pathos. She looks at no one. On her face is what I can only describe as a smile of pain. With a small gesture of her two index fingers she shows us the size of the pieces of bread on the tray. Her eyes stream with tears. The dancer begins to cry too, and hugs my mother. I, though I have heard the story before, am struck by the ordinary miracle of human life and fate – that the hungry child in that wartime winter schoolroom is the very same person sitting among us on that hot afternoon, as though she has joined our carefree modern lives from another, distant world of war and hunger.

My aunt Lenina's kitchen on Frunzenskaya Embankment, on a luminous Moscow summer evening in the late 1990s. I am sitting on my aunt's wide window sill, smoking a cigarette after a gargantuan, greasy dinner which I have been forced to praise at least five times before she is satisfied that I am content. Lenina is boiling water in her old enamel kettle, disdaining the German electric kettle her daughters have given her.

Lenina, my mother's sister, is as heavy-set as their mother Martha was, wide-hipped and large-breasted, her back bowed with the weight of the world's troubles. She has Martha's piercing blue eyes. So does my mother, so do I, so does my son Nikita. But in temperament Lenina seems to be more like her gregarious father, Boris Bibikov. She loves gathering friends around the kitchen table, chatting, gossiping, intriguing. She likes to pull strings and to organize other people's lives by means of epic telephone conversations. She is highly skilled at terrorizing television presenters during phone-ins and shop managers in person. She is a big woman with a powerful voice, and suffers from many, many near-fatal illnesses which she loves to talk about.

As she pours the tea, Lenina launches into her favourite subject, her nephew's variegated love life. Her eye gleams with a girlish prurience. I have seen through Lenina's stern old lady act long before. That is just one weapon in the formidable arsenal she deploys in the daily drama of struggle, conflict and scandal with the outside world. What she really wants to do is sit forward on her stool at the corner of the table, put an elbow on the table, fix her nephew with a beady eye and hear the latest details. At the naughty bits she cackles like a fishwife.

'You're lucky I don't tell your mother any of this,' she chortles. Strangely, though she never tires of scolding her own daughters, she seldom criticizes me during our weekly gossip sessions. Instead, she chips in with worldly-wise and often rather cynical advice. My aunt Lenina is, despite the half-century's difference in our ages, a true friend and confidante.

Lenina has a phenomenal memory for detail. Our conversations always start in the present, but that is transient and quickly dealt with, insufficiently colourful and dramatic to hold her attention for long. She drifts back into the past, quite seamlessly, from one sentence to the next, setting off on a nightly ramble through the paths of her memory, her attention pulled this way and that, like a glass on a Ouija board, by different stories and voices.

As she gets older, less mobile and blinder, her imagination seems to become clearer and clearer. The past is becoming more immediate to her than the present. At night the dead visit her, she complains. They won't leave her alone – her husband, her parents, her friends, her granddaughter Masha, dead of cancer at twenty-six, all arguing, cajoling, laughing, nagging, getting on with the business of life as though they don't realize that they're dead. She sees the past in her dreams, incessantly. 'It's like a cinema,' she says. As she approaches the end of her life, its beginning seems to her ever more vivid. Details float up, conversations, incidents, stories, snippets of life seen as tiny film clips, which she notes down in order to tell me the next time I come over. She knows I know the dramatis personae so well by now that they need no introduction.

'Did I tell you what I remembered about Uncle Yasha and the girls he picked up in his Mercedes? What Varya said?' she asks over the phone, and I know immediately that she's talking about a famously immoral automobile my great-uncle Yakov shipped back from Berlin in 1946, and the fury that this invoked in my great-aunt. 'She was so furious that she threw all the flowerpots in the house at him, and the crockery from the kitchen. Yasha couldn't stop laughing, even as the plates smashed around him. That's what made her most angry!'

Lenina sees the world in terms of conversations, tones of voice, people. She doesn't read much, unlike her sister, my bookish mother. She's a performer, with the kitchen table as her auditorium and an ever-changing set of friends, supplicants, former students, neighbours and relatives as the audience.

Lyudmila and Lenina's story begins in another kitchen in a handsome, high-ceilinged apartment in the centre of Chernigov in midsummer 1937. The tall windows stood wide open to catch the breeze off the River Desna. In a corner, my three-year-old mother was playing with a rag doll. My aunt Lenina leaned on the wide window sill, watching the street for the sleek silhouette of her father's big black official Packard. She was twelve years old, round-faced with large, intelligent eyes. She was fashionably dressed in her favourite white cotton tennis skirt, copied from a Moscow magazine. Outside, across the tops of the plane trees of Lermontov Street, she could see the golden domes of the cathedral of Chernigov's medieval Kremlin.

At the kitchen table her mother Martha fussed over a packed lunch for her husband Boris: roast chicken, boiled eggs and cucumber, some biscuits, a pinch of salt wrapped in newspaper, all packed in greaseproof paper. Boris was due to stop by on his way to the station to pick up his luggage before setting off to go on holiday at a Party sanatorium in Gagry, on the Black Sea coast. It was to be his first holiday in three years.

Martha was complaining to no one in particular that her husband was late again, which was typical, just typical. Boris was so obsessed with work that he couldn't even take the morning off on the day his holiday was due to begin. He always seemed to have more time for his Party committees than for his family.

Martha was a tall, sturdy woman, already running to the plumpness Russian peasant women often acquire along with motherhood. She was wearing a dress of imported cotton and carefully applied make-up. Her voice seemed always to be nagging, or so it seemed to Lenina, who was dreading the idea of a week alone with her mother without her father to intercede. At the sink stood Varya, the family's long-suffering housemaid, a sturdy country girl who wore a wide *sarafan*, the Russian peasant woman's traditional dress, with a starched apron pinned to the front. Varya slept in a kind of cupboard at the end of the hall, but she earned money and was fed, so she put up with Martha, and worse. She winked at Lenina when they caught each other's eye as Martha rushed out of the kitchen, grumbling, to check Boris's luggage, which was standing in the wide hallway.

Lyudmila – or Mila for short – was as devoted to her elder sister Lenina as a little dog, and preferred not to let her sibling out of her sight. The girls had a complicity with their father, a mutual defence pact which Martha disliked and didn't understand.

Lenina, at the window, saw her father's big black car round the corner and roll to a halt in front of the apartment block. There was a clatter on the stairs and Boris bounded in to the apartment. He was a powerfully built man, running to fat, prematurely bald with a shaved head. He wore self-consciously proletarian clothes, plain linen shirts in summer and sailor's striped vests in winter. He looked much older than his thirty-four years. He was already the second most powerful man in the city, Secretary for Propaganda and Agitation of the Communist Party's Regional Committee. A noted political agitator, rising star within the Party, a holder of the Order of Lenin, Boris was serving his apprenticeship in a provincial administration as a prelude to a powerful post in

Kiev or even Moscow. He was a man going places. Ignoring his wife's tirade of scolding and advice, he quickly kissed his two daughters goodbye.

'Be good, look after your mother and sister,' he whispered to Lenina.

He silenced his wife with a quick embrace, exchanged a few parting words with her, grabbed his packed case and lunch and ran downstairs. Lenina rushed to the window and saw her father's driver standing by the car, smoking a cigarette, which he tossed away as he heard his boss coming down the stone staircase. Lenina waved frantically as her beloved Papa climbed into his car, and he waved back, quickly, a sweeping gesture more like a salute. It was the last time she ever saw him.

After she had seen her husband off, Martha went across the landing to see if anything was wrong with the neighbours. She hadn't heard the usual thud of their door closing as the family went to work in the morning, and nobody had come home for lunch. When Martha returned Lenina noticed she was pale and nervous. There had been no response when she rang their doorbell. Then she'd seen a stamped paper pasted on to the door bearing the seal of the People's Commissariat of Internal Affairs, the NKVD. She knew immediately what it meant. The Bibikovs' neighbours, the family of a colleague of her husband's, had been arrested in the night.

The next morning there was a tiredness in Martha's eyes as she dressed little Lyudmila, a peremptoriness in her tone as she dragooned the children for a shopping expedition, squashing cotton summer cloche hats on to their heads.

On the way to the market, Martha stopped to tie little Lyudmila's shoelace. As she crouched, a young girl about Lenina's age walked silently up to them. She leaned over to Martha's ear and whispered something, then walked hurriedly away. Instead of standing up, Martha sank down on to her knees on the pavement like a shot animal. Her children tried to help her up, alarmed. In a few moments she recovered, stood, and turned back home, dragging Lyudmila as she stumbled to keep pace. Years later, Martha told Lenina what the girl had said: 'Tonight they will come with a search warrant.' Nobody knew who the girl was, or who had sent her.

Back in the apartment, Martha began to cry. She had been parted from her husband only once in their twelve years of marriage, when he went away to serve in the Red Army soon after they had met. And now he was gone, and the world they had made was about to fly apart.

That night the children went to bed hungry after a supper of kitchen scraps their mother had hurriedly thrown together. Martha couldn't sleep, she told Lenina later, and spent half the night doing laundry. Then she sat by the open window listening for the sound of a car. She fell asleep just before dawn, and never heard it.

Martha was woken by a sharp knocking on the door. She looked at her watch; it was just after four in the morning. Martha pulled on a dressing gown and opened the door. Four men stood outside, all wearing black leather jackets with pistol belts, and leather boots. Their officer showed her a search warrant and an arrest warrant for her husband. He asked if Bibikov was at home. Martha said no, he was away, and began pleading for an explanation. The men pushed past her and started to search the apartment. The children were woken by the sound of voices. Lyudmila began crying. A man opened the door of their room, switched on the light briefly, looked around and told the children to be quiet. Lyudmila got into bed with Lenina and cried herself back to sleep. Their mother distractedly came in to comfort them to the sounds of drawers being rifled through and cupboards emptied in the next room.

The men stayed for twelve hours, systematically searching every book, every file in Boris's study. The men did not allow Martha to go to the kitchen to feed the children. Lenina remembers their faces, 'hard as their leather coats'. When they had finished the search, confiscating a boxful of documents they made Martha sign for, the NKVD officers sealed the apartment's four rooms and left Martha and her children in the kitchen, still in their nightdresses. As the door slammed shut, Martha collapsed on the floor in tears. Lyudmila and Lenina also began bawling, hugging their mother.

When Martha managed to pull herself together, she went into the bathroom and wrung out a wet dress. Wiping her face in the bathroom mirror, she told Lenina to look after her sister, and left the house. She ran to the local NKVD headquarters, sure that their family had been the victim of some terrible mistake. She came back to the children late that night, empty-handed and desperate. She had found out almost nothing, except that she was just one of dozens of panicking wives who had besieged the stony-faced receptionist with questions about their missing husbands, only to be told that the men were 'under investigation' and that the women would be kept informed.

Though Martha didn't know it at the time, her husband was still a free man, relaxing in a first-class sleeper coach heading south and innocently looking forward to his well-earned days of rest at the Party sanatorium.

2

'Not Men but Giants!'

Lads, let's fulfil the Plan!
Slogan chalked on the factory
toilet wall by Boris Bibikov

There are only two surviving photographs of Boris Bibikov. One is an informal group shot taken at the Kharkov Tractor Factory around 1932. He is sitting on the ground in front of two dozen fresh-faced, beaming young workers, his arm around the shoulder of a crew-cut young man. Bibikov is wearing a rumpled, open-necked shirt and his head is shaven, in the proletarian style affected by many of his generation of Party cadres. Unlike everyone else in the photo, there is no smile on his face, only a severe glare.

The other photo, from his Party card, was taken early in 1936. Bibikov is wearing a Party cadre's tunic, buttoned to the neck, and he once again stares purposefully from the frame. There is more than a hint of cruelty in his down-turned mouth. He is every inch the ruthless Party man. The formality of the pose and the fact that Bibikov was born in an age before one felt entirely unselfconscious in front of a camera mean that the mask is near perfect. There is no hint of the man in either picture, only of the man he wanted to be.

He died a man without a past. Like many of his age and class, Bibikov shed his former self like a shameful skin, to be

reborn as a Homo Sovieticus, a new Soviet man. He rein-
vented himself so effectively that even the NKVD investigators who painstakingly chronicled his passage through the
NKVD's 'meat grinder' in the summer and autumn of 1937
were able to unearth only the merest trace of his former
existence. There were no photos, no papers, no records of his
life before the Party.

His family were descended from one of Catherine the
Great's generals, Alexander Bibikov, who earned the Empress's favour and a noble title by putting down a peasant
uprising led by Emeliyan Pugachev in 1773. The revolt was
crushed with great brutality, just as the Empress ordered;
summary hangings and beatings were meted out to thousands
of rebels who had dared to defy the state.

Boris Bibikov was born in the Crimea in 1903 or 1904 – his
NKVD file says the former, his mother writes the latter. His
father Lev, a small landowner, died when Boris and his two
brothers, Yakov and Isaac, were very young. Bibikov never
talked about him. Their mother, Sofia, was a Jewess from a
well-to-do Crimean merchant family whose father Naum
owned a flour mill and a grain elevator, which could account
for the odd 'profession' Bibikov listed on his arrest form, 'mill
worker'. Boris knew English, he did not fight in the Civil War.
That is just about all we know of his early life. Yakov, the only
one of the Bibikov brothers to survive past the Second World
War, who lived until 1979, was similarly obsessive – he never
mentioned his background, or his executed brother. For the
Bibikov brothers there was only the future, no looking back.

I don't believe that my grandfather was a hero, but he lived in
heroic times, and such times brought out an impulse to
greatness in people large and small. The slogans of the
Bolshevik Revolution were Peace, Land and Bread; and at
the time this message must, to ambitious and idealistic men,
have seemed fresh, vibrant and couched in the language of

prophesy. The Party's cadres were to be nothing less than the avant-garde of world history. At some point soon after the October Revolution swept away the old Russia Bibikov seems, like many members of the 'former classes', to have had some sort of romantic epiphany. Or perhaps – who now knows – it was an impulse of ambition, vanity or greed. His inheritance, his maternal grandfather's minor Crimean flour-milling empire, was nationalized in 1918. Many of his grander relatives in Moscow and Petrograd had fled into exile or been arrested as class enemies. The Bolsheviks were Russia's new masters, and the route to advancement for an energetic and intelligent young man was to join the winning side, as quickly as possible.

But the only witness we have left is Lenina, and her testimony is that her father was a high-minded and selfless man. And even if that wasn't the case, Lenina's word has a kind of emotional truth of its own. So let us say that a new world was being built, and Boris's imagination was caught by the grandeur of the vision, fresh, new and beautiful, and so he and his two younger brothers, Yakov and Isaac, threw themselves wholeheartedly into it.

During the last year of the Civil War Boris enrolled in the newly opened Higher Party School in the Crimean port of Simferopol. The school was designed to train a new generation of commissars to rule the great empire which the Bolsheviks had recently won, much to their own surprise. After a year's training in theoretical Marxist-Leninism and the rudiments of agitation and propaganda, my grandfather was inducted into the Party in May 1924, a young firebrand of twenty-one, ready to serve the Revolution wherever it needed him.

As it turned out, the Revolution's most pressing immediate need was a prosaic one. Boris was sent to supervise the summer tomato and aubergine harvest at a fledgling collective farm in Kurman Kimilchi, a former Tatar settlement populated for two centuries by ethnic Germans, in the highlands of the Crimean peninsula. It was there, in the dusty summer fields, that he met his future wife, Martha Platonovna Shcherbak.

A few weeks before she met Boris, Martha Shcherbak had left her younger sister Anna to die on a train platform in Simferopol.

The two girls were on their way from their native village near Poltava, in the western Ukraine, to look for summer work on the farms of the Crimea. Martha, already twenty-three years old, was well past the age when peasant girls of her generation were expected to marry. They came from a family of eleven sisters; two brothers had died in infancy. There is little doubt that her father, Platon, considered having so many daughters nothing less than a curse and seems to have been only too glad to get rid of two of them.

Martha grew up amid the brooding suspicion and casual brutality of a dirt-poor village on the Ukrainian steppes. But even by the hard standards of Russian peasant life, her siblings found Martha quarrelsome, jealous and difficult. That may explain why she had failed to find a husband in her village, and why she and Anna were the two sisters deemed surplus to requirements and sent away to fend for themselves. Her father's rejection was the first, and perhaps deepest, of the many scars on her mind which were to develop into a deep, vicious streak.

By the time Anna and Martha reached Simferopol they had been living rough for at least a week, travelling on local trains and catching lifts on produce trucks. Anna had developed a fever, and in the crowds thronging the sweltering railway platform she fell into a dead faint. People gathered around the girl, who was turning blue and shivering. Someone shouted 'Typhus!' and panic spread. Martha stepped away from her sister, and turned to flee with the rest.

Martha was young, frightened, and alone for the first time after a life in the oppressive intimacy of the family's wooden farmhouse. Her fear of being quarantined in one of the notorious and deadly local typhus hospitals was perhaps rational enough. But her decision to abandon her sister was to haunt her for the rest of her life, an original sin for which she was cruelly punished. Driven by fear, no doubt, and confusion, Martha disclaimed all knowledge of the feverish teenager sprawled on the platform. She joined the crowd piling on to the first westbound train.

Many years later, after both mother and daughter had been through half a lifetime of horrors, Martha told her daughter Lenina the story of her sister's presumed death. But Martha mentioned the incident casually, pretending that it was perfectly normal. Something was broken inside her, or perhaps it had never been there.

Even as a small child, I feared my grandmother Martha. When she came to visit us in 1976 it was the first and only time she left the Soviet Union, and her first flight in an aeroplane. Before her trip to England, the longest journey she had made was as a Gulag prisoner in a train to Kazakhstan, and again on her way back. In the heavy suitcases she brought to London she had packed her own set of thick cotton bed sheets, as was the custom for Soviet travellers.

When Martha moved her limbs seemed impossibly cumbersome, as though her body were a burden to her. She wore the cheapest possible Soviet print dresses and heavy carpet slippers at home; when she went out she would put on a musty tweed twinset. She almost never smiled. At the family dinner table she would sit grim and impassive, as though disapproving of the bourgeois luxury in which her daughter lived. Once, when I pretended that my knife and fork were drumsticks, Martha scolded me with a sudden anger which made my eyes prick with tears. I wasn't sorry when she left. She dissolved into passionate tears as she said goodbye, which embarrassed me. 'I'll never see you again,' she said to my mother, and she was right. There was no time to say much more, as my father was waiting outside in his orange Volkswagen Beetle to take her to Heathrow.

I often think of Martha now, trying to strip away the layers of hearsay and adult knowledge which have grown around her image in my mind, to recall my own memories of her. I try to imagine the pretty, buxom girl that Boris Bibikov married. I wonder how she could have had a daughter as vivacious and full of positive energy as my own mother. After unravelling some of the story of Martha's broken life, I see that some twist in her soul turned all her energy and life force in on itself. She hated the world, and having been deprived of happiness, she tried to destroy it in everyone around her. I was a small child when I knew her. But even then, I sensed in the deadness of her eyes, the woodenness of her embrace, something eerie, and damaged.

The train from Simferopol carried Martha weswards to Kurman Kimilchi. People told her there was work to be had there, so she descended on to the dusty platform and walked to the collective farm office. She was given a cot in a jerry-built barracks for itinerant summer labourers. There she met the young commissar Boris Bibikov.

Martha and Boris's liaison was a revolutionary marriage. He was a fast-rising and educated member of the new revolutionary élite, she a simple farm girl with impeccable proletarian credentials. There may have been an element of calculation in Bibikov's choice. Or, perhaps more likely, it was a shotgun wedding, the result of a summer fling consummated in the high grass of a Crimean meadow on a hot summer night.

Their first daughter was born seven months after they 'signed' – the new jargon for civil marriage – in March 1925. Bibikov named her Lenina after the Revolution's recently deceased leader, Vladimir Ilyich Lenin. When Lenina was eight months old her father entered the Red Army for his military service. Martha would show Lenina the letters Bibikov sent home, would point to them and say, 'Daddy'.

When Bibikov returned home Lenina was two years old, and she cried as the strange man came into the house. Martha told her that her Daddy had come back. Little Lenina said no, that's not Daddy, and pointed to the tin box where Martha kept her husband's letters – that's Daddy in there. It was as if she had a childish premonition of the day when Boris would walk out of the door and out of their lives – and turn back into a stack of papers.

Boris Bibikov's life only really comes into focus in 1929, when Lenina's clearest memories of him begin, and the project to which he dedicated his career and which was to propel him to a kind of greatness was launched. In April of that year the Sixteenth Communist Party Conference approved the first Five Year Plan for the Development of the People's Economy. The Civil War was won, the Party's General Secretary Iosif Stalin had ousted his arch-rival Lev Trotsky, and the Plan was the Party's grand design for creating a socialist country out of the ruins of a Russia wrecked by war and revolution. It was not just an economic project – it was, to young believers like Bibikov, no less than the blueprint for a shining socialist future.

The key to the Plan was socializing the peasants, who made up over eighty per cent of the population and were considered by the Party to be dangerously reactionary. The Revolution was predominantly urban, educated, doctrinaire – like Bibikov himself. The peasants, with their blasphemous desire to own land, their strong attachment to family, clan and church, directly challenged the Party's monopoly over their souls. The aim was to turn the countryside into a 'grain factory', and the peasants into workers.

'A hundred thousand tractors will turn the *muzhik*, the peasant man, into a Communist,' wrote Lenin. As many peasants as possible were to be driven into the cities, where they would become good proletarians. Those who remained on the land were to work on vast, efficient, collective farms. And what was needed in order to make those farms efficient and free up labour for the cities was tractors. During the spring planting of 1929 there were only five tractors in use in the whole of the Ukraine. The rest of the labour was carried out by men and horses. The vast black-earthed land still moved, as it had for numberless generations, to the slow heartbeat of the seasons and the rhythms of human and animal labour.

This, the Party would change. Stalin personally ordered two giant tractor factories built in the heart of the grain belt of south-central Russia – one in Kharkov, in the Ukraine, the empire's bread basket, and another on the edge of the empty steppes of western Kazakhstan, in Chelyabinsk. The Party also coined a slogan: 'We will produce first-class machines, in order to more thoroughly plough up the virgin soil of the peasant consciousness!'

The Kharkov Tractor Factory, or KhTZ, was to be built on scrubland outside the city, in a bare field. The scale of the project, its sheer ambition, was staggering. For the first year of construction the Party allocated 287 million gold rubles, 10,000 workers, 2,000 horses, 160,000 tons of iron and 100,000 tons of steel. Bricks were to be made of the clay dug out for the foundations. The only machines on the site when the ground was broken were twenty-four mechanical concrete mixers and four gravel-crushers.

The vast majority of the labour force was made up of untrained peasants who had just been dispossessed of their land. Most had never seen a machine other than a horse-drawn thresher. Bricklayers knew how to build a Russian stove but had no idea how to construct a brick building, carpenters knew how to build an *izba*, a log cabin, with an axe, but not a barrack.

It seems appropriate to speak of these days in a heroic tone because that was certainly how Bibikov viewed himself and his mission. That the project got started, let alone finished in record time, is a testament to the ruthless faith and fanatical energy of its builders. Unlike later generations of Soviet bureaucrats, the Party men of the KhTZ were not desk-bound pen-pushers. Even discounting the hyperbole of the official accounts, reports that they worked in the mud among the bewildered, sullen and half-starved peasants are well-documented. More, they turned them not just into workers but into believers themselves. And in the absence of proper equipment or skilled workers, it was little more than pure faith – and pure fear – that turned a clay field into ninety million bricks, and from those bricks built an industrial behemoth. The whole project was to be a demonstration of how the Party's unshakeable will could triumph over impossible odds.

Bibikov and his family lived in a large communal apartment at 4 Kuybishev Street in central Kharkov, a grand-ish place in an old bourgeois building appropriate to his rank as a rising Party official. They shared the apartment with a childless Jewish couple, Rosa and Abram Lamper. Abram was an engineer, Rosa an excellent cook. Martha's jealous suspicion that her children preferred Rosa's cooking to hers was spiced with her peasant's reflexive anti-Semitism.

Bibikov would disappear for days at the factory; Lenina hardly ever saw him. An official car would arrive early in the morning to pick him up, and he would come back home very late, after Lenina had gone to bed. But he still made time at weekends to take German lessons from a beautiful and aristocratic young teacher. Because Martha suspected her husband was having an affair with this teacher, Bibikov would take Lenina with him to the lessons, walking hand in hand past the 'Gigant' technical university. On the way he would buy Lenina sweets. Bibikov would greet the teacher by kissing her hand – an unforgivably bourgeois gesture if performed in public. Then he would give Lenina a book to read and retire into the teacher's room, closing the door behind him.

Some evenings he would bring factory friends back to the apartment – men like Potapenko, the head of the factory's Party committee, and Markitan, head of the Kharkov Party. Even though he didn't drink or smoke, Lenina remembers her father as being the life and soul of the party. She describes him as a great *zavodilo* – literally, a great winder-upper, an agitator, from the word *zavodit*, to wind up a clock. 'I was proud to be the child of a leader – and he was a leader,' remembers Lenina. 'He had a magic power to enthuse people.'

Magic or not, Bibikov certainly seems to have worked with an enthusiasm bordering on the fanatical on the building of the great factory. One of his colleagues later told Lenina that her father would write, 'Lads, let's fulfil the Plan!' in chalk on the lavatory wall in an effort to encourage his workers. Bibikov was also in charge of recruitment drives into the countryside and to Red Army units who were demobilizing, his task to sign up more labour. On these whistle-stop tours in trains, charabancs and cars, Bibikov and a few hand-picked workers would give speeches in praise of the KhTZ, complete with vividly coloured storyboards for the benefit of their mostly illiterate audiences. Bibikov would return from these trips dirty and exhausted. Lenina remembers her mother complaining of the lice he'd picked up from sleeping in peasant huts, and boiling his underclothes in a great enamel pot on the gas stove.

The factory's official history was written, anonymously, in 1977. But its author, apparently a retired factory executive, was clearly an eyewitness to the momentous early days of the KhTZ. One of the history's heroines is Varvara Shmel, a peasant girl who came to Kharkov from a remote village to join her brother on the construction site. Her time at the factory becomes a metaphor for the progress of the proletariat under the influence of the *stroika*, or building project. Varvara, the history recalls, amazed by her first sight of a tractor, got her hands and face covered in grease as she was examining it. The scene was observed by 'a sardonic young man in yellow rubber boots', a foreign correspondent visiting the site who becomes an allegory of the scoffing West, convinced of the inalterable backwardness of Russia.

'Symbolic!' said the foreign journalist. 'The peasant Miss is inspecting a tractor. And what happened? She only got her face dirty. I repeat and will always repeat – that the building of this factory is an unrealistic project. I would heartily advise this Miss not to waste her time and go home to cook – what do you call it – *shchi* with cabbage.'

The official history claims that people 'came from all over the Union, many answering the call of the Party and the Komsomol [the Communist Youth League]. These were people who were passionately committed to their task, giving it all their strength, true enthusiasts. They formed the basic backbone of the building, the front line of the active fighters for the creation of a sturdy foundation for the socialist economy.'

The reality was different. Most of the peasants who flocked to the site were starving refugees from a war the fledgling Soviet state had unleashed against its own people.

'The Party is justified in shifting from a policy of restricting the exploiting tendencies of the kulaks [prosperous peasants] to a policy of liquidating the kulaks as a class,' read the Central Committee's decree of 5 January 1930. The Wannsee memorandum of 1942 which mapped out the Final Solution of the Jewish Problem is more famous – but the Soviet Communist Party's condemnation of the kulaks to extermination was to prove twice as deadly.

Army units were mobilized to drive the peasants from their land and confiscate their 'hoarded' grain for the cities and for export. Officers of the NKVD went with them to weed out suspected kulaks – which in practice meant any peasant who was a little harder working than his neighbours, or who

resisted the move to collective farms. The Red Army, brutalized by the horrors of the Civil War, set out on its war against
the peasants in the same spirit. There were summary execu-
tions, villages were burned and their inhabitants sent on
forced marches in midwinter or packed on to cattle trucks
for resettlement in great slave labour camps all over the Soviet
Union. The deportees were called 'white coal' by their guards.

'It was a second Civil War – this time against the peasants,'
wrote Alexander Solzhenitsyn in his epic history, *The Gulag
Archipelago*, a 'literary investigation' of the terror of this
period. 'It was indeed the Great Turning Point, or as the
phrase had it, the Great Break. Only we are never told what it
was that broke. It was the backbone of Russia.'

By early 1930, after a winter of virtual warfare – virtual
because one side was unarmed – half the farms of the Ukraine
had been forcibly collectivized. On 2 March 1930 Stalin
published an article in *Pravda*, the Party's newspaper, in
which he blamed the violence and chaos of the winter months
on local cadres who were 'Dizzy with Success'. The reality
was that local Party members were confused and demoralized,
the peasants had abandoned the new collective farms in
droves, and peasant resistance to the system and its repre-
sentatives had escalated to a level which caused even Stalin to
call a temporary halt.

Despite the horrors which were being played out in the
countryside all around, Bibikov and the other cadres selected
to build the great tractor factory pressed on.

'When flocks of swallows returned from distant warm
lands, when larks began buzzing in the air and the ground
thawed under the gentle sun, the steppe began to glint with
thousands of shovels,' writes the author of the official history,
in the ringing language of a *Pravda* editorial. But conditions
were grim. Teams of workers hauled loads of fresh-dug clay on
sleds because of a lack of horsepower – fully half the horses of
Russia were slaughtered by starving or vengeful peasants by

1934. Carpenters knocked together 150 rough-hewn barracks for the workers, and a makeshift underground kiln fired the first bricks to build the chimney of the brick factory proper. Two railway carriages were brought up on newly laid rails, one a bath-house and the other a mobile clinic. Liquid mud squirted up through the floorboards of the workshops, and every evening rows of mud-soaked bast shoes were laid outside the barracks to dry in the spring sunshine. Slowly, the walls of the factory began to rise out of the heavy clay fields from which they were built.

It was a miracle which was being repeated all over the Soviet Union. The giant steel cities of Magnitogorsk in the Urals and Tomsk in Siberia were ordered built on bare steppe; in Sverdlovsk there was the giant heavy machinery plant, Uralmash; the other great tractor factory in Chelyabinsk, known as the ChTZ, and a factory for combine harvesters, the 'ships of the steppe'. Across the Ukraine new metal works were going up in Krivy Rog and Zaporozhiye, new anthracite mines were being sunk in the Donetsk basin. Each day of the first Five Year Plan one new factory was founded and 115 new collective farms opened. All over the country the apparently fantastical projects handed down by the politburo in Moscow were being made a reality. Certainly, the state had proved its ruthlessness in punishing the Revolution's enemies, and the cost of failure would doubtless be severe. But it is hard to believe that these prodigies of industrialization were created by fear alone. Behind the deluge of propaganda photographs of happy, smiling workers, I believe there lay a spark of truth. For a brief but intense moment, a genuine and fierce pride in what they were creating flowered in the men and women involved in the great project.

By the late summer of 1930, less than a year into the Five Year Plan, the fabric of the factory was in place – the walls, acres of glass roofs, chimneys, furnaces, roads, rails. A factory newspaper was set up, called *Temp*, or 'pace', to urge workers to greater productiveness, to up the pace. Bibikov was its editor-in-chief, writing regular articles and teaching courses for aspiring journalists from among the more literate workers. He also had some pieces published in *Izvestiya*, the great Moscow daily founded by Lenin himself. Lenina remembers him excitedly buying several copies at the newsstand on the morning that his pieces appeared. Sadly, most of the articles at the time were published with no by-line and much of the paper's archives of the period were destroyed in the war, so what Bibikov wrote is a mystery.

Alexander Grigoryevich Kashtanyer, who worked as an intern at *Temp* in 1931, wrote to Lyudmila in 1963 of what he remembered of Bibikov. 'At that time your father's name rang around the factory. I heard the speeches of Comrade Bibikov on the factory floor, at meetings, at the building sites. I remember they were strong, pugnacious speeches. The time was turbulent, and the very name of the paper reflected the thoughts of the tractor factory workers: come on, there's no time to waste, keep up the pace! You can be proud of your father; he was a true soldier of Lenin's guard. Carry a bright memory of him in your hearts!'

Pravda, the Party's newspaper, published a story on the KhTZ in February 1966 (after Bibikov's official rehabilitation under Krushchev) which conjures the mood of its epic birth. 'I spent Sunday at the home of [the worker] Chernoivanenko, full of chat about the present day work of the factory,' writes the anonymous *Pravda* correspondent. 'But memory kept returning us to the thirties. What a time it was! The beginning of the epoch of industrialization in the USSR! We recalled the people of the KhTZ, how they were at that time. The stern-looking but supremely fair-minded director, Svistun, the Party mass-agitator Bibikov – he was a jolly and soulful comrade, who could inspire our young people to storm difficulties, whether it was glazing a roof in record time, or tarring the floors, or installing new machinery – not by an order but simply by the passion of his convictions. "They weren't just ordinary men," said Chernoivanenko in a hollow voice full of suppressed passion. "They were giants!" '

To keep the project on schedule, Bibikov championed the seemingly paradoxical system of 'Socialist competition' – essentially, races between different shifts of workers over who could do the most work. He also gave the workers heroes chosen from among themselves: 'Men, who by their example inspired the others to great deeds of labour and entered the history of the factory as real heroes. People of legends.'

The heroes created by Bibikov and the propaganda department of *Temp* were men like Dmitry Melnikov, who assembled an American 'Marion' fourteen-ton excavator in six days, not two weeks as the manufacturer's guide said. These and other prodigious deeds were publicized on *stengazety*, hand-stencilled wall newspapers posted around the works. Those who slacked, conversely, were denounced by their colleagues: 'I, concrete pourer of the Kuzmenko group, stood idle for three hours because of the incompetence of X,' read one public notice displayed on a *stengazeta* in late 1930. 'I demand that the hero-workers of our group are paid for these lost hours out of his pocket.'

But despite this cajoling, work had fallen behind as the thirteenth anniversary of the Revolution approached in October 1930 and the deadline for the factory's completion loomed. At the instigation of Bibikov's Party Committee, foremen organized 'storm nights' of labour, accompanied by a brass band, teams of workers racing each other.

The factory's workers and management quickly became obsessed with these competitions, in line with a national newspaper campaign which reported these miraculous (and increasingly bizarre) feats exhaustively. One of the leitmotifs of the endless *Pravda* coverage became wowing foreigners and confounding their forecasts. Not to be outdone, the KhTZ soon produced its own records:

'The [workers] also refuted the calculations of foreign experts of the productivity of the "Kaiser" cement mixer,' the KhTZ's history proudly records. 'Professor Zailiger, for instance, claimed that the machine could not produce more than 240 portions of concrete in one eight-hour shift. But the Communists of the Tractor Factory decided to exceed the norm.' Four hundred men come on the shift, heroically producing 250 mixtures. 'Foreign specialists and their theories are not a law to us,' foreman G.B. Marsunin boasted to the *Temp* correspondent.

The factory brass bands now played all night, every night, echoing in the machine hall and drowning the noise of the KhTZ's six Kaiser concrete mixers. The foremen rushed back and forth, inciting their men to work. Over the next few months new records were set at 360 mixtures, then at 452. An all-Union rally of concrete pourers met in Kharkov to celebrate the KhTZ's amazing records. The foreign concrete mixture specialist, the mysterious Professor Zailiger himself, came from Austria and watched in amazement – 'Yes, you work, it's a fact,' *Temp* records him as saying.

There were prodigies of bricklaying, too. Arkady Mikunis, a young enthusiast from the Komsomol, would stay behind after work to watch old hands lay bricks and read specialist bricklaying journals in his spare time; he quickly matched his teachers with their norm of 800 bricks per shift. On a specially organized 'storm night' Mikunis laid 4,700 bricks in a single shift; 'More,' *Temp* records proudly, 'than even America.' On a factory sponsored holiday in Kiev, he was invited to show the local bricklayers his skills and laid 6,800. Word spread through the bricklaying world and a German champion came from Hamburg to see for himself – after half a shift against Mikunis he gave up the competition. And still Mikunis didn't stop. His record rose to 11,780 bricks in one day, a somewhat improbable three times the previous world record. For his prodigious skills at speed bricklaying – apparently at the rate of a brick every four seconds for twelve straight hours – Mikunis was awarded the Order of Lenin.

As if setting new records wasn't enough, Bibikov also instigated evening classes to 'raise the level of socialist consciousness' of the factory's workforce. By the spring of 1931 most of the workers, who a year before had been starving peasants digging clay, were taking voluntary evening classes to qualify as machinists and engineers. After the end of the shifts there was a crush to get to the canteen and wash before the classes began. A lucky 500 workers were even sent to Stalingrad and Leningrad to learn how to work new specialist machine tools installed in factories there. One of the many excuses Bibikov gave his long-suffering wife for his constant lateness was that he personally conducted classes in Marxist-Leninism for an advanced group of foremen and managers, and mass meetings and lectures on political economy for the rank and file. One imagines lines of eager, and not-so-eager, listeners, looking up at the bald, animated figure at the lectern in his striped sailor's shirt, soaking up information as indiscriminately as sponges, Marx and Lenin slowly displacing the no less jealous old God of the Russias with whom they had grown up.

On 31 May 1931, the Politburo's industrial supremo Sergo Orzhonikidze was reverently shown around the nearly complete factory buildings. Orzhonikidze ordered the construction to be completed by 15 July, and the installation of the production lines to begin immediately afterwards. Unsurprisingly, given the unspoken penalties for failure, the job was done on time.

By 25 August 1931 the first trial tractors were coming off the assembly line. On 25 September the factory director sent a telegram to the Central Committee reporting that the KhTZ would be ready to start full production on 1 October as planned, just fifteen months after the ground had been broken.

Twenty thousand people assembled in the giant machine hall for the official opening. Demyan Bedny, the 'proletarian poet' whose pseudonym meant Demyan the Poor, was there to record the event in verse, as was a delegation of dignitaries from Moscow. A biplane flew over the site, scattering leaflets with a poem entitled 'Hail to the Giant of the Five Year Plan'. The foreign journalist with the yellow rubber boots was there too, 'just as sloppy, but less confident'. Varvara, the peasant girl whom he had scoffed at, had been to the factory school and was now a qualified steel-presser.

Grigori Ivanovich Petrovsky, head of the All-Ukraine Central Committee of the People's Economy, cut the ceremonial ribbon, walked inside the hall and rode out on a bright red tractor covered in carnations and driven by champion woman worker, Marusya Bugayeva, as the factory band played the 'Internationale'. It was followed by dozens of other tractors. One collective farm worker shouted, records the *Temp* special issue on the opening, 'Comrades – But it's a miracle!'

The Soviet satirical magazine *Krokodil* published the factory management's telegram verbatim: 'October First opening of Kharkov Tractor Factory invite editorial representative attend celebrations opening factory – Factory Director Svistun. Party Secretary Potapenko. Factory Committee Director Bibikov.' The magazine composed a special poem in honour of the event, 'To the Builders of the Kharkov Tractor Factory.'

> To all, to all, the builder-heroes,
> Participants of one of our great victories,
> Who have worked on the building of the Kharkov Tractor
> A Crocodile's flaming greeting!
> The Crocodile, overwhelmed with joy at the news,
> Bows its jaws to you:
> You fulfilled your task with Bolshevik honour,
> Kharkov did not betray the pace . . .
> A record! One year and three months!

But behind the universal jubilation, further catastrophe was unfolding in the countryside. The KhTZ's tractors came too late to make an impact on the 1931 harvest, which, after the ravages of collectivization, was disastrous. The projected 'grain factories' were producing little more than half of what the same countryside had yielded five years before. The peasants' only way to protest against the loss of their land and homes was to slaughter their animals and eat as much of their food supplies as they could before the commissars came. Eyewitnesses from the Red Cross reported seeing peasants 'drunk on food', their eyes stupefied by their mad, self-destructive gluttony, and the knowledge of its consequences.

Unsurprisingly, they worked unwillingly for the new state farms. Yet the state demanded grain not only to feed the cities but also to export for hard currency in order to buy foreign machinery for projects like the KhTZ. Soviet engineers were sent to the United States and Germany to buy steam hammers, sheet steel rolling machines and presses with trunkloads of Soviet gold, all earned from selling grain at Depression prices. The KhTZ's American steam hammer, which Bibikov was later accused of sabotaging, cost 40,000 rubles in gold, the equivalent of nearly a thousand tons of wheat, enough to feed a million people for three days.

In October 1931 the Soviet government requisitioned 7.7 million tons of a meagre total harvest of 18 million tons. Most went to feed the cities, strongholds of Soviet power, though two million tons was exported to the West. The result was one of the greatest famines of the century.

During the expropriations of 1929 and 1930 individual villages had starved if they resisted the commissars, who punitively confiscated all the food they could find. Now, as the winter of 1931 set in, hunger gripped the whole of the Ukraine and southern Russia. Millions of peasants became refugees, flocking to the cities, dying on the pavements of

Kiev, Kharkov, Lvov and Odessa. Armed guards were posted on trains travelling through famine areas so they wouldn't be stormed. One of the most haunting images of the Russian century is a photograph of hollow-faced peasants caught selling dismembered children for meat on a market stall in the Ukraine.

The new vast fields of collective farms had watchtowers on the perimeter, like those of the Gulags, to watch for corn thieves. A law was introduced mandating a minimum of ten years of hard labour for stealing corn – one court in Kharkov sentenced 1,500 corn gatherers to death in a month. The towers were manned by young Pioneers, the Communist Children's League (for children aged ten to fifteen). Fourteen-year-old Pavlik Morozov became a national hero in 1930 when he denounced his own father to the authorities for not handing over kulak property to the local collective farm. The tale-telling Pavlik was subsequently, perhaps not unreasonably, murdered by his grandfather. The story of this young revolutionary martyr became front-page news in *Pravda* and prompted books and songs about his heroism.

'There was such inhuman, unimaginable misery, such a terrible disaster, that it began to seem almost abstract, it would not fit within the bounds of consciousness,' wrote Boris Pasternak after a trip to the Ukraine. The young Hungarian Communist Arthur Koestler found the 'enormous land wrapped in silence'. The British socialist Malcolm Muggeridge took a train to Kiev, where he found the population starving. 'I mean starving in its absolute sense, not undernourished,' he wrote. Worse, Muggeridge found that the grain supplies that did exist were being given to army units brought in to keep starving peasants from revolting. Embittered, the idealistic Muggeridge left the Soviet Union, convinced he had witnessed 'one of the most monstrous crimes in history, so terrible that people in the future will scarcely be able to believe it ever happened.'

Even hardened revolutionaries like Politburo member Ni-kolai Bukharin were horrified. 'During the Revolution I saw things that I would not want even my enemies to see. Yet 1919 cannot be compared to what happened between 1930 and 1932,' Bukharin wrote shortly before he was shot in 1938 in the Purges. 'In 1919 we were fighting for our lives . . . but in the later period we were conducting a mass annihilation of completely defenceless men together with their wives and children.'

The famine was not just a disaster – it was a weapon deliberately used against the peasants. 'It took a famine to show them who is master here,' a senior Party official told Victor Kravchenko, a Party planning apparatchik who de-fected to the US in 1949. 'It has cost millions of lives . . . but we have won the war.'

Bibikov must have seen the hunger too – the pinched faces, the bloated bellies and the empty eyes. He travelled often on Party and factory business in his black Packard, or in first-class train carriages with guards in the corridors. He must have known that special trucks, on secret orders from the municipal authorities, patrolled the cities of the Ukraine at night to collect the corpses of peasants who had crawled there from the villages. Many must have made it to the barbed-wire perimeter of the KhTZ, on the outskirts of the city. By morning there was no trace, for those who chose not to see, of the horror which was unfolding all around. George Bernard Shaw declared, after a carefully stage-managed tour of the Ukraine in 1932, that he 'did not see a single under-nourished person in Russia'. Walter Duranty, the Pulitzer Prize-winning *New York Times* correspondent, dismissed reports of famine as anti-Soviet propaganda. To the Party, starving peasants were simply the waste-matter of revolu-tion, to be ignored until they obligingly died – and then forgotten. The Party's leaders wanted the world to see only the shining achievements, not the price which was being paid for them.

Bibikov made sure his family knew nothing. Lenina's memory of those years in Kharkov is of bazaars filled with fruits and vegetables, and her father coming home laden with sausages from the factory's canteen and boxes of sweets for the children. She doesn't remember wanting for anything. What did Bibikov think, as he tucked those paper-wrapped sausages into his briefcase as dusk fell, bringing the night and its crop of starved and desperate wanderers? He thought, I am quite sure, thank God it's them, instead of us.

The convulsions of collectivization two years previously could be explained away as a war against the Revolution's class enemies, the kulaks. But now those enemies had been liquidated and the collective farms of the future established. Yet even those blinded by ideology could scarcely fail to see that the Workers' and Peasants' State was, painfully obviously, failing to feed its own people. Moreover, for all the glorious achievements of industrialization, it was equally clear that the whole dream of Socialism was being held together increasingly by coercion. Already in October 1930 a law forbade the free movement of labour, tying peasants to their land and workers to their factories, as in the days of serfdom. In December 1932 internal passports were introduced in an effort to stem the exodus of the starving into the cities.

Does Bibikov's decision to continue believing, in the face of mounting evidence that the dream was becoming a nightmare, make him a cynical man? It's hard to know, since first and foremost he had little choice but to follow the Party line. The alternative was to join the starving, or worse. Yet he was clearly intelligent enough to understand that terrible cracks were appearing in the paradise he had spent his adult life fighting for.

Perhaps, like many of his generation, he convinced himself of that greatest of twentieth-century heresies: that bourgeois sentimentality had no place in the heart of a servant of a higher humanity. Maybe he believed that the Party would ultimately create a brave new world from all this chaos. Or perhaps, less self-righteously, he convinced himself that his duty was to do what he could to conquer the backwardness of Russia, with its famines and grinding poverty, by helping to forge it into a modern, industrial nation. Most likely, though, is a more human explanation: it was much easier to live by one's myths, and to continue to believe in the ultimate wisdom of the Party, than to speak out and risk disaster.

Yet the famine-ravaged country Bibikov saw during the winter of 1931–32 seems to have profoundly altered him. The Party was always right, yes – but the Party's tactics might at least be altered. Like many Party leaders in the Ukraine who had seen the horrors which Stalin's hard line produced first hand, Bibikov became convinced that Stalin's rule must be softened if further disaster was to be averted. His chance to speak out came eighteen months later, shortly before the birth of his second daughter, my mother, Lyudmila Borisovna Bibikova.

3

Death of a Party Man

It was a long time ago, and it never happened.
Yevgeniya Ginzburg

In the first days of January 1934 Bibikov left his heavily pregnant wife at home and travelled with several senior factory managers by special train to Moscow to attend the Seventeenth All-Union Party Congress as an ex officio observer. Because he never discussed politics with Martha, she had no idea that her husband had determined on an act of defiance which was to cost him his life.

The meeting was billed as the 'Congress of Victors', a celebration of the victory of collectivization, the triumphant fulfilment of the first Five Year Plan and the consolidation of the Revolution. But despite the official encomiums to the success of the Party, there was widespread exhaustion among the rank and file. Bibikov, like many, felt strongly that the famine which still continued over much of southern Russia had to be brought to an end. The Five Year Plan had been fulfilled, but the men and women of the grass roots who were more managers than ideologues saw with their own eyes that the insane pace of change couldn't be sustained. Yet Stalin, the desk-bound firebrand, called for greater production, higher yields, and more vigour in pursuing collectivization despite its manifestly disastrous consequences.

There was no open dissent at the congress. But there was talk of easing Stalin out of the position of power he had forged from the hitherto insignificant post of General Secretary and replacing him with the more moderate Sergei Kirov. Kirov, the secretary of the Leningrad Party, was, at that point, still more than a match for Stalin. He was a Civil War hero, a former close ally of Lenin and the greatest orator the Party had seen since Trotsky.

Bibikov, along with many of his colleagues from the Ukraine, was encouraged by an apparent spirit of openness, a sense that there was to be a robust ideological debate among equals over the future of the great experiment they were building together, and they wholeheartedly backed Kirov's plan to slacken the pace. It proved to be a fatal mistake. In Stalin's already paranoid mind, Kirov's attempt to soften the punishing pace of collectivization was an unpardonable insult and challenge to his ideological leadership of the Revolution. Stalin did not forget who voted and how, though his revenge was four years in the making. Of the 1,966 delegates to the Seventeenth Congress, 1,108 were to die in the Purges. The conference ended with the now customary standing ovations and exhortations to even greater triumphs in the future. Bibikov stood and applauded Stalin and the Politburo with the rest. But the outcome was politically inconclusive. Kirov had refused openly to challenge Stalin. Yet it was equally clear that Stalin was not yet undisputed master of the Party. The supposedly open debate over the Party's future was not to be repeated until Mikhail Gorbachev's time, when dissent was to rip the Party apart for ever.

Bibikov's second daughter, Lyudmila, was born on 27 January 1934, just after her father's return from the Congress. Though he named his elder daughter after Lenin, he pointedly did not name his second, as some sycophants were already beginning to do, Stalina.

*   *   *

The year passed in furious work on the factory, with no sign of the political apocalypse which Stalin was quietly plotting. But on the evening of 2 December 1934, Lenina remembers that her father came home from work in tears. He threw himself on to the leather sofa in the sitting room and stayed there motionless for a long time, his head in his hands.

'*My propali*,' Bibikov said quietly to his wife. 'We are lost.'

Lenina asked her mother what was wrong. Martha didn't answer and sent her to bed.

The previous night Sergei Kirov had been shot dead by a lone assassin in his office at the Party headquarters at the Smolny Institute in Leningrad. 'We are lost,' Bibikov said as he wept for the death of a man he admired. But was he also weeping for himself? Weeping with anger for the mistake he had made in identifying himself too closely with the losing side? For all his cultivated proletarian bluffness, Bibikov must have been a political animal, a committee man, with a rising star's sense of the way the wind was blowing. As Bibikov lay on the sofa weeping for Kirov, he must have turned over those now-dangerous January conversations in his mind, wondering whether he had said too much.

And yet the hammer did not fall at once. Stalin, too, wept in public at Kirov's funeral, and acted as chief pallbearer, leading the nation in mourning. There was time enough to take revenge on the enemies in the heart of the Party which Stalin had identified at the congress.

On a local level, the Party machine continued to run smoothly. The KhTZ's production levels climbed to greater heights and the famine mercifully abated – if only because the millions of dead no longer needed to be fed. Bibikov, along with three other members of the KhTZ's management, was awarded the Order of Lenin, number 301, in a plush velvet box. It was a recognized prelude to greater things. In late 1935, the expected promotion came, to Provincial Party Secretary of the Chernigov region in the rolling farm country of the northern Ukraine. Bibikov was just thirty-two years old, well on his way to a high-flying future – perhaps membership of the Ukrainian or national Party Central Committee. Maybe higher still.

After the belching factory smokestacks and screeching rail junctions of Kharkov, Chernigov must have seemed like a step back into a slower, older Russia. The Chernigov Kremlin, with its medieval cathedrals, stands on the high bank of the sluggish River Desna. Wooded parkland comes right up to the centre of the city, and in summer the air is filled with pollen from poplar trees which line the streets. The squat, ornamented houses built by Chernigov's wealthy merchants still stand, and the place has retained an air of pre-revolutionary bourgeois respectability. The town has many great churches which somehow escaped the Bolsheviks' dynamite. Chernigov was too out-of-the-way, perhaps, to warrant a thorough purge of religious buildings, too far from the great industrial heartlands of the eastern Ukraine where the future of Socialism was being forged. It was a backwater, but Bibikov was sure that if he made a success of his new Party job he would not be tarrying long.

The Bibikovs lived the life of the privileged. Already the Spartan Party ethic of the early thirties was slackening. The élite quickly accrued perks which set them above their fellow citizens. Martha shopped at exclusive Party grocers', and Bibikov was entitled to holidays in specially built sanatoriums on the Black Sea. Every month, Bibikov would give Martha a little book of coupons for imported food, textiles and shoes from the *Insnab*, or 'Foreign Supply' shop. The family moved into a large four-room apartment with handsome furniture, confiscated from a wealthy merchant family for the use of Chernigov's new rulers. There, Varya scrubbed the Bibikovs' pans with brick dust until they shone.

Boris installed shelves right up to the high ceiling of his study and filled them with books which he read in his big

leather armchair. On his way back from work he'd stop in to
the local bookshop and buy children's books for the girls and
ideological tomes for himself. When Martha shouted at Lenina she would tiptoe into Bibikov's study and climb into his
lap, sobbing. 'Let's not complain about her,' he would say.
'Let's strengthen our Union instead.' It was a joking reference
to the current Party-speak.

During their first winter in Chernigov the Bibikov girls
wowed the town with their wrought-iron sled, made for them
by their old neighbour in Kharkov, which drew crowds of
envious children to behold this wonder under the steep earth
ramparts of the Kremlin, perfect for tobogganing. In summer
Martha made the girls fashionable white cloche hats, copied
from Moscow fashion plates, and sewed them dresses from
imported printed cotton. In keeping with her new status as an
élite wife she began calling herself 'Mara' because she felt that
'Martha' sounded too peasant-like – an odd twist of social
snobbery in the land of proletarian dictatorship. Bibikov was
as much a workaholic as ever, but began to spend more time
chatting – but not drinking – in his kitchen with Party
comrades. He bought season tickets to the newly built theatre
for Martha and Lenina, though he himself couldn't go because
he worked until nine each night, by which time the play was
already nearly over.

Lenina had never been so happy as during those days of her
secret alliance with her beloved father. 'I see it now so clearly,'
she told me, nearly a lifetime later. 'I see it like a dream. It's
hard to believe it ever really happened.'

Bibikov even began to relax enough to philander – or at
least, to philander more openly. Lenina remembers Martha
screaming at him in the kitchen, berating him about his
various mistresses. It was during this time, January 1936,
when all Party members were required to renew their Party
cards so that unworthy elements could be weeded out, that
the portrait photo we have of him in his Party tunic was taken.

Perhaps the hard-set face also shows a trace of smugness, of self-congratulation.

But behind the outward normality of Ukrainian small-town life, the country was drifting into madness. The NKVD, now under the leadership of the ruthless and sadistic Nikolai Yezhov, was preparing to unleash yet another civil war. This time it was not to be on the Whites or the peasants, but against the most insidious enemy of all, traitors within the Party itself.

Old Bolsheviks whose long standing and moral authority could challenge Stalin's position went first. Lev Kamenev and Grigory Zinoviev, both members of Lenin's first Politburo, stood to attention at show trials in Moscow in August 1936 and confessed to being imperialist spies, while being hectored by the hysterical Prosecutor-General, Andrei Vyshinsky. 'Wreckers', or senior engineers blamed for sabotaging the industrialization drive, were also put on public trial. They confessed to being members of a counter-revolutionary organization determined to subvert the triumph of Socialism. Stalin's rival Lev Trotsky, the head of the alleged counter-revolutionary movement, had already fled into exile on the island of Buyukada, near Istanbul. The vocabulary and tactics of the coming Great Purge were being rehearsed and refined.

Until 1937 the Ukraine was a relative sanctuary from the show trials that were decimating the Moscow-based élite of the army, intelligentsia and government. But it was the Ukraine, perceived by Stalin to be a den of Trotskyism and potential opposition, which was to feel the full brunt of his wrath when he finally unleashed the might of the security machine he had so carefully constructed.

At the February–March 1937 plenum of top Party members, Stalin's opponents made a last, doomed stand, protesting against Stalin's monopoly of power. Immediately after the meeting a fifth of the Ukrainian Party leadership were expelled. Bibikov, reading the curt announcement in *Pravda*, must have feared that worse was to come. By early summer close colleagues began to be summoned for questioning by the NKVD. Few returned.

People instinctively drew into themselves, huddling into self-protective silence like pedestrians hurrying home during a summer rainstorm. Lenina noticed a sudden change in atmosphere. Her father was looking tired and had lost much of his usual jollity. The friendly gossip of the Party wives on the stairwell had become nervous pleasantries. It must have been with relief that Bibikov prepared for his summer trip to a Party sanatorium in Gagry, on the Georgian Black Sea coast, in July 1937.

I opened the brown cardboard cover of my grandfather's NKVD file, now disintegrating with age, on a grey December morning in a gloomy office in the former NKVD building in Kiev, now the headquarters of the Ukrainian Security Service. By now bloated to 260 pages, the file existed on that peculiarly Russian border between banal bureaucracy and painful poignancy. It was a compilation of the absurdly petty (confiscation of Komsomol card, confiscation of a Browning automatic and twenty-three rounds of ammunition, confiscation of Lenina's Young Pioneer holiday trip voucher) and the starkly shocking: long confessions, written in microscopic, crabbed writing, covered in blotches and apparently written under torture, the formal accusation signed by Prosecutor-General Vyshinsky, the slip with its scribbled signature verifying that the sentence of death had been carried out. Papers, forms, notes, receipts – all the paraphernalia of a nightmarish, self-devouring bureaucracy. A stack of paper that equalled one human life.

The first document, as fatal as any which followed, was a typed resolution by the Chernigov Regional Prosecutor sanctioning the arrest of 'Boris L– Bibikov, Head of Department of Management of Party Organs of the Chernigov Region' for suspected involvement in a 'counter-revolutionary Trotskyite organization and organized anti-Soviet activity'. It recommends that Bibikov be held in custody without bail for the duration of the investigation. His middle name is left blank, as though the name was copied from a list by somebody who did not know Bibikov or anything about his case. The civilian prosecutor's resolution was backed up the same day by an NKVD authorization of arrest, which, as the convoluted bureaucracy gathered momentum, became by 22 July a formal arrest warrant issued by the local prosecutor. Officer Koshichursin – or something like it, the name is written in barely legible, semi-literate handwriting – was charged with finding Bibikov 'in the town of Chernigov'. He failed – Bibikov was already on his way to Gagry. They finally caught up with him there on 27 July, and brought him back to Chernigov's NKVD jail.

What he thought at that moment when he passed over to the other side of the looking glass, from the world of the living to that of the condemned, what he said, no one will now know. It would have been easiest for him if he'd said nothing, and resignedly submitted, considering himself already a dead man. But that wasn't his character. He was a fighter, and he fought for his life, pitifully unaware that his death had already been ordained by the Party. As a Party man he should have known there was no way to resist its almighty will – though we know that at some point in the months that followed, he ceased to be the apparatchik and became just a man, refusing to live by lies for a few brief moments of misguided bravery.

Alexander Solzhenitsyn writes in *The Gulag Archipelago* of the loneliness of the accused at his arrest, the confusion and dislocation, the fear and indignation of the men and women who were rapidly filling the Soviet Union's jails to bursting point that summer. 'The whole apparatus threw its full weight on one lonely and uninhibited will,' writes Solzhenitsyn. 'Brother mine! Do not condemn those who turned out to be weak and confessed to more than they should have. Do not be the first to cast a stone at them.'

Yevgeniya Ginzburg's harrowing account of her own arrest
and eighteen-year imprisonment during the Purge, *Into the
Whirlwind*, describes the infamous NKVD 'conveyor'. Prisoners would be continually interrogated by teams of investigators,
deprived of food and sleep, harangued, beaten and humiliated
until they signed or wrote their confessions. The ones who
broke down first were confronted with those more resilient, in
order to break their solidarity. They were told that resistance
was useless; once one made a confession the rest could be shot
on that basis alone. Their wives and children were threatened.
Perversely, committed Communists could be persuaded to sign
for the sake of the Revolution – your Party demands it! Are you
defying your Party? Stool pigeons urged fellow prisoners to
confess – it's the only way to save your life, your family's lives!
Solzhenitsyn recounts how convinced Communists would
whisper to their fellows, 'It's our duty to support Soviet
interrogation. It's a combat situation. We ourselves are to
blame. We were too softhearted; now look at the rot which
has multiplied. There is a vicious secret war going on. Even
here we are surrounded by enemies.'

Lied to, tortured, living in a world of pain and confusion,
Bibikov the Party man for once refused to obey the Party's
orders and clung on to his innocence for as long as he could
bear. But, like almost all of them, he broke in the end.

Nineteen days after his arrest he signed his first confession. It
was a surprisingly long time to have held out. But nevertheless
Bibikov confessed abjectly, in writing, to crimes against the
Soviet Union. To the sabotage of the factory he helped to build.
To the recruitment of Trotskyite agents. To propaganda against
the state. He admitted that he had betrayed the Party to which
he had devoted his life. His closest colleagues implicated him,
and he, in turn, implicated them. None of the twenty-five
supposed members of his circle refused to confess.

The first confession is dated 14 August 1937. It is the first time Bibikov speaks in the file – the first hint of a human voice among the dry officialese. The crimes to which he confesses are so bizarre, so startlingly improbable, that I felt physically nauseous at the lurch from banal legalisms into the grotesque language of nightmare.

'Transcript of Interrogation. Accused Bibikov, Boris Lvovich, born 1903. Former Party member. Question: In the statement you have made today in your own hand you admit your participation in a counter-revolutionary terrorist organization. By whom, when and under what circumstances were you inducted into this organization?

'Answer: I was recruited into the counter-revolutionary terrorist organization by the former second Party Secretary of Kharkov, ILYIN, in February 1934 . . . We met often in the course of our Party work. During our meetings in 1934 I expressed my doubts about the correctness of Party policy towards agriculture, workers' pay and so on. In February 1934, after a committee meeting, ILYIN invited me into his study and said he wanted to talk frankly. That is when he proposed that I become a member of the Trotskyite organization.'

The transcript was typed, and Bibikov signed at the bottom. The writing holds no clue as to what was going through his mind as he scribbled his signature.

But one simple confession was not enough. The bureaucracy demanded more detail, more names to fulfil the quota of enemies of the people to be found in every district and region in the country. Like scriptwriters concocting a soap opera of grotesque complexity, the investigators required their vast cast to corroborate each others' stories, to add new layers to the plot. Bibikov's first confession brought no respite. The interrogations continued. But at some point something within him must have rebelled at the perversity and the horror, and he tried to claw his way back into the world of the sane. Those moments of defiance ring through the thin, laconic pages of the file like a silent shout.

'Question to Fedayev,' reads the stark text of the transcript of his first 'confrontation' with a fellow 'conspirator', the former head of the Kharkov Regional Committee. 'Tell us what you know about Bibikov.'

'Fedayev's reply: ". . . In the course of two conversations with Bibikov I confirmed that he was ready to take part in the organization of Trotskyite work. In our last conversation we agreed to set up a Trotskyite group at the KhTZ . . ."

'Question to Bibikov: "Do you confirm the suspect Fedayev's statement?"

'Bibikov's reply: "No. That is a lie. We never had such a conversation."

'This statement has been read to us and is accurate. (Signed) Fedayev. The accused Bibikov refused to sign.'

But in the end his defiance was useless, witnessed only by NKVD Lieutenants Slavin and Chalkov, who conducted the confrontation, and Fedayev himself, who was probably too terrified to think Bibikov's stand was anything other than masochistic stupidity. Bibikov eventually broke completely.

'At the Kharkov Tractor Factory we decided to sabotage an expensive, complicated machine which was crucial to the production of wheeled tractors . . .' he wrote in blotted, tiny writing in his third and last detailed confession. 'We persuaded engineer KOZLOV to leave a tool in the machine so that it would be broken for a long period. The machine alone cost 40,000 in gold and is one of only two in the whole country . . . At the KhTZ we plotted to throw an artillery round from the war into a blast furnace to put it out of action for two or three months . . . I also recruited my own deputy, Ivan KAVITSKY, into our organization . . . We attempted to undermine the work of the KhTZ by delaying the fulfilment of orders for the Hammer and Sickle Tractor station, and delayed the payment of wages to the workers.'

In the margin are inexplicable notes in his own writing,

apparently written under dictation, saying, 'Who, What, When?', 'More precise', 'Which organization?'

'Our evil counter-revolutionary act was averted only by the vigilance of senior engineer GINZBURG,' the last confession concludes. 'This is how I betrayed my Party. Bibikov.'

The manuscript had been carefully torn across halfway down the page. Above the tear are signs of some kind of scribble, as though the writer had tried, in despair, to erase the death sentence he had just written for himself.

Then his voice disappears. There are excerpts from the transcripts of other accused in which Bibikov's name is mentioned – sixteen interlinking confessions, all meticulously typed with angry, almost punched-through commas between the capitalized names, 'ZELENSKY, BUTSENKO, SAPOV, BRANDT, GENKIN, BIBIKOV. . .'

He was brought to trial before a closed session of the Military Collegium in Kiev on 13 October 1937, the so-called *troika* courts of three judges who heard *in camera* the cases of those accused under Article 58 of the Soviet Criminal Code, which covered 'any act designed to overthrow, undermine or weaken the authority of the workers' and peasants' Soviets'. The court's conclusion is long and detailed, mostly repeating word for word the accounts of acts of sabotage included in the confessions. But for good measure, the final draft upped the charges and concluded that 'Bibikov was a member of the *k.r.* [the term *kontrarevolustionnaya* is used so often that the typist begins to abbreviate it] Trotskyite-Zinovievite terrorist organization which carried out the wicked assassination of Comrade Kirov on 1 December 1934 and in following years planned and carried out terrorist acts against other Party and government leaders . . . We sentence the accused to the highest form of criminal punishment: to be shot and his property confiscated. Signed, A.M. ORLOV, S.N. ZHDANA, F.A. BATNER.'

Bibikov signed a form confirming that he had read the

court's ruling and sentence. They were the last recorded words he wrote. Signing off, with bureaucratic neatness, on the file which contained the state's version of his life's story. It was the final act of a life devoted to serving the Party.

The last form of the seventy-nine pages in the so-called 'living' file, the flimsiest of all, was a mimeographed quarter-sheet strip of paper roughly cut off at the bottom with scissors, which confirms that the sentence of the court has been carried out. There is no hint of where or how, though the usual method was 'nine grams', the weight of a pistol round, to the back of the head. The signature of the commanding officer is illegible; the date is 14 October 1937.

For the two days that I sat in Kiev examining the file, Alexander Panamaryev, a young officer of the Ukrainian Security Service, sat with me, reading out passages of barely legible cursive script and explaining legal terms. He was pale and intelligent, about my age, the kind of quiet young man who looked as though he lived with his mother. He seemed, underneath an affected professional brusqueness, almost as moved as I was by what we read.

'Those were terrible times,' he said quietly as we took a cigarette break in the gathering dusk of Volodimirskaya Street, the granite bulk of the old NKVD building looming above us. 'Your grandfather believed, but do you not think that his accusers believed also? Or the men who shot him? He knew that people had been shot before he was arrested, but did he speak out? How do we know what we would have done in that situation? May God forbid that we ever face the same test.'

Solzhenitsyn once posed the same, terrible question. 'If my life had turned out differently, might I myself not have become just such an executioner? If only it was so simple! If only there were evil people somewhere insidiously committing evil deeds, and it were necessary only to separate them from the rest of us and destroy them. But the line dividing good from evil cuts through the heart of every human being. And who is willing to destroy a piece of their own heart?'

Bibikov himself would have perfectly understood, with his rational mind, as he stood in a cellar or faced a prison wall in his last moments, the logic of his executioners. And perhaps – why not? – he might, if he had met different people in his early days in the Party, found different patrons, have become an executioner himself. Did he not explain away the famine which his Party had brought to the Ukraine as a necessary purging of enemy elements? Did he not consider himself one of the Revolution's chosen, ruled by a higher morality? Bibikov was no innocent, caught by an evil and alien force beyond his comprehension. On the contrary, he was a propagandist, a fanatic of the new morality – the morality which now de- manded his life, however pointlessly, for the greater good.

'No, it was not for show nor out of hypocrisy that they argued in the cells in defence of all the government's actions,' writes Solzhenitsyn. 'They needed ideological arguments in order to hold on to a sense of their own rightness – otherwise insanity was not far off.'

When people become the building blocks of history, in- telligent men can abdicate moral responsibility. Indeed the Purge – in Russian *chistka*, or 'cleaning' – was to those who made it something heroic, just as the building of the great factory was heroic to Bibikov. The difference was that Bibikov made his personal revolution in physical bricks and concrete, whereas the NKVD's bricks were class enemies, every one sent to the execution chamber another piece of the great edifice of Socialism. When one condones a death for the sake of a cause, one condones them all.

In some ways, perhaps, Bibikov was more guilty than most. He was a senior Party member. Men like him gave the orders and compiled the lists. The rank-and-file investigators fol- lowed them. Were these men evil, then, given that they had

no choice but to do what they were told? Was Lieutenant
Chavin, a man who tortured confessions from Party men like
Bibikov, not less guilty than the Party men themselves, who
taught their juniors that ends justify means? The men drawn
to serve in the NKVD, in the famous phrase of its founder
Felix Dzerzhinsky, could be either saints or scoundrels – and
clearly the service attracted more than its fair share of sadists
and psychopaths. But they were not aliens, not foreigners, but
men, Russian men, made of the same tissue and fed by the
same blood as their victims. 'Where did this wolf-tribe appear
from among our own people?' asked Solzhenitsyn. 'Does it
really stem from our own roots? Our own blood? It is ours.'

This was the true, dark genius behind the Purge. Not simply
to put two strangers into a room, one a victim, one an
executioner, and convince one to kill the other, but to convince both that this murder served some higher purpose. It is
easier to imagine that such acts are committed by monsters,
men whose minds had been brutalized by the horrors of war
and collectivization. But the fact is that ordinary, decent men
and women, full of humanistic ideals and worthy principles,
were ready to justify and even participate in the massacre of
their fellows. 'To do evil a human being must first of all
believe that what he's doing is good,' writes Solzhenitsyn. 'Or
else that it's a well-considered act in conformity with natural
law.' This can happen only when a man becomes a political
commodity, a unit in a cold calculation, his life and death to
be planned and disposed of just like a ton of steel or a
truckload of bricks. This, without doubt, was Bibikov's belief.
He lived by it, and died by it.

There was one part of the file that was closed to me. About
thirty pages of the 'rehabilitation investigation', instigated by
Khrushchev in 1955 as part of a wholesale review of the
victims of the Purge, had been carefully taped together. After
some persuasion, Panamaryev, as curious as I was, furtively

un-taped them and we began quickly to leaf through the closed part of the file.

The forbidden pages concerned the NKVD men who had participated in the interrogation of Bibikov. Even half a century later, the Ukrainian Security Service was trying to protect its own. Their files had been ordered up by the investigators who prepared Bibikov's rehabilitation. But the NKVD officers themselves could not be questioned, because by the end of 1938 they had themselves all been shot.

'Former workers of the Ukrainian NKVD TEITEL, KOR-NEV and GEPLER . . . were tried for falsification of evidence and anti-Soviet activity,' says one of the documents. 'Investigators SAMOVSKI, TRUSHKIN and GRIGORENKO . . . faced criminal proceedings for counter-revolutionary activity,' notes another.

Almost every person whose name appears in the file, from the accused and their NKVD interrogators to local Party Secretary Markitan, who signed the order to expel Bibikov from the Party two days after his arrest, were themselves killed within a year. The Purge had consumed its makers, and all that we are left of their lives are a few muffled echoes in a vast silence of paper.

The last document in the file, stamped and numbered, was a letter I had written to the Ukrainian Security Service that summer requesting to see my grandfather's file, invoking a Ukrainian law which allows close relatives access to otherwise classified NKVD archives. The file had been carefully un-bound by skilful hands and my letter stitched in and num-bered with the rest, at the very back of the dossier. So the last signature in the fatal file, scrawled across the bottom of the letter, turned out to be my own.

4

Arrest

Thank you, Comrade Stalin, for our Happy Childhood.
Slogan from a 1936 propaganda poster

E ven after years in Moscow, I could never quite shake the
feeling of being in a weird cat's cradle of conflicting ages.
There were quaintly historic touches: soldiers in jackboots
and breeches; babushkas in headscarves; ragged, bearded
beggars straight out of Dostoyevsky; obligatory coat checks
and rotary phones; fur hats; drivers and maids; bread with
lard; abacuses instead of cash registers; inky newspapers; the
smell of wood smoke and outdoor toilets in the suburbs;
meat sold from trucks piled with beef carcasses manned by a
muzhik with a bloody axe. Some rhythms of life seemed
absolutely unchanged from my father's day, my grandfather's day even.

There were a few moments when I think I caught glimpses
of the nightmare world my grandfather entered in July 1937.
For a few hours, I saw and smelt and touched it. It was
enough, perhaps, to give a sense of what it was like, at least
physically. What it was like in his head and heart is a place I
never wish to visit.

One night in early January 1996, a month after I had visited
Kiev to view my grandfather's file, I was walking through a

light snowfall towards the Metropole Hotel. I was trying to catch a taxi, and didn't notice that three men were following me. The first I knew of their approach was the sleeve of a yellow sheepskin coat coming up at my face, followed by a powerful blow to the jaw. I felt no pain, just percussion, like a jolting train. For two or three minutes of strangely balletic time, I stood, I fell again, I scrambled up, as the men continued to beat me. I smelled the wet fur of my hat as I pressed it to my face to protect my nose.

Then I saw, as I lay on the street, the caked front wheels and dirty headlights of a red Lada crunching through the snow towards us. Improbably enough, a man with his left leg in a huge plaster cast levered himself out of the passenger door. He shouted something, and the three men looked suddenly embarrassed and began wandering away with looks of feigned innocence. The men in the car helped me up, then drove off.

At that moment, a police jeep rounded the corner. I flagged it down, opened the door, mumbled what had happened, and got in. At the moment we picked up speed down Neglinnaya Street in pursuit of the assailants, I suddenly felt my brain clear, and time suddenly shifted gears in tandem with the police driver from very slow to very fast. We pulled out on to Okhotny Ryad and I saw my assailants playing in the snow by the Lubyanka Metro. The jeep pulled a stylish power slide across eight lanes of traffic and skidded to a halt.

The three men were reaching for their passports, looking calm and happily drunk, smiling, thinking it was a routine document check. Two had the Asiatic features of Tatars, the third was a Russian. When they saw me clamber out of the jeep they froze and seemed to shrink a size.

'Those are the men,' I said, theatrically, pointing at them. The two Tatars were bundled into a tiny cage in the back of the jeep. No more than a dozen minutes had passed since they had begun beating me.

The police station was impregnated with the eternal Russian prison odour of sweat, piss and despair. The walls were pale institutional beige at the top and dark brown at the bottom. My two assailants sat in a cage in the corner of the reception room, their heads in their hands, muttering to each other and occasionally looking up at me.

The desk sergeant sat behind a Perspex screen, his little office raised a foot above the rest of the room. In front of him were several large, Victorian-looking ledgers, a set of stamps, a pile of forms, and an ashtray made out of a Fanta can. He took my details impassively, then picked up his telephone and dialled his superiors. From that moment, I think, the men's fate was sealed. I was a foreigner, and that meant trouble for the police if the case wasn't handled properly – consular complaints to the Foreign Ministry, paperwork flying.

The investigator appointed to the case was Svetlana Timo-feyevna, a Lieutenant-Colonel of the Moscow Criminal In-vestigation Department. She was a confident and matronly woman who sized me up with a shameless, penetrating stare, well used to separating men into wimps and loudmouths. She was one of those portly, invincible, middle-aged Russian women, whose kind lurked like Dobermanns in the front offices of all Russia's great men; they ruled ticket offices and lorded it over hotel reception desks.

With great reverence, after we had been through the details several times verbally, Svetlana Timofeyevna pulled out a blank statement sheet headed *Protokol*, or official statement, and began to take down the official record of my testimony. I signed the bottom of each page and initialled each correction. Finally she reached for a blank folder headed *Delo*, or criminal case, and carefully filled in the accused's details on its brown cardboard cover. The file had begun. From that moment on, I, my assailants, the investigators, were all its creatures.

For the next three days I staggered over to the police station at Svetlana Timofeyevna's summons, groggy with mild concussion. The station was even more depressing in daylight, a low, two-storey concrete building in a courtyard full of dirty slush, litter bins and stray dogs. I met the policemen who had been with me on the night of the assault, and one of them assured me, in a confiding whisper, that 'we made sure those guys are having an interesting time'. I felt a guilty thrill of revenge.

Between long, fitful sleeps in my sunless third-floor apartment and long afternoons in the station, it seemed that I had somehow slipped into a pungent underworld, where I endlessly watched the investigator's pen crawling across reams of paper, my head throbbing, willing it to finish. I dreamt of it at night, a feverish frustration dream, obsessively focused on the crawling pen, the way it dented the cheap official paper, held by a disembodied hand and lit by harsh, institutional lamplight.

On the third day – but somehow it seemed like so much longer than three days, this waking-sleeping bureaucratic nightmare – I felt like an old-timer, trudging up the police station's worn stairs, past the stinking officers' toilet from which the seat had been stolen. I found Svetlana Timofeyevna in uniform for the first time since I'd met her.

'We're going to have the *ochnaya stavka* now,' she said. The *ochnaya stavka*, or confrontation, was a standard Russian investigative procedure in which the accused meets his accusers and their statements are read to each other. She scooped up the swelling file and led me downstairs to what looked like a large schoolroom, full of rows of benches facing a raised dais, where we took our seats in silence. I stared at the grain of the desk.

The men came in so quietly I didn't hear them until the policeman shut the door. They were both manacled, shuffling stiffly with heads bowed. They sat down heavily in the front benches, looking up at us sheepishly like guilty schoolboys. They were brothers, Svetlana Timofeyevna had told me,

Tatars from Kazan. Both were married, with children, and lived in Moscow. They looked younger than I had imagined them, and smaller.

'Matthews, please forgive us if we hurt you, please, if there's anything we can do . . .' the smaller man, the older brother, began. But Svetlana Timofeyevna cut him off. She read my clumsy statement, in the longest of its four versions, then a medical report. They listened in silence; the younger one had his head in his hands. Their own testimony was just five sentences, stating that they had been too drunk to remember what happened and that they freely admitted their guilt and contrition. At the end of each statement there was an awkward moment as she passed the accused papers to sign. Helpfully, I pushed the papers further forward on the desk so that they could sign in their clanking handcuffs. They nodded in polite acknowledgement each time.

'Do you have anything to say?'

The elder brother, still in his yellow coat, began talking. He was calm at first, a forced chumminess in his voice. He held my eye, and as he spoke I stopped hearing what he was saying and just felt its tone, and read the look. He was begging me to spare them. My face was frozen in a kind of horrified smile. He leaned further forward, a note of panic creeping into his voice. Then he fell on his knees and wept. He wept loudly, and his brother wept silently.

Then they were gone. Svetlana Timofeyevna was saying something, but I didn't hear. She had to repeat herself, and touch my shoulder. She was saying we should go. I mumbled something about dropping the charges. She sighed heavily, and told me, wearily, as though she was trying to explain life's hard facts to a child, that it wouldn't be possible. She was not a hard-hearted woman, even after years of busting stupid little people for stupid little crimes. Yet even though she had seen the men's weeping wives and knew the case was trivial, unworthy of the terrible retribution which she was about to unleash, she knew that that afternoon she would type up a full report recommending that the two men be remanded in custody pending trial.

We were all caught up in it now, the momentum, the grinding wheels. My foreignness meant all this was to be done by the book. The file, the all-important file. We were all forced to follow its course now, step by step, because what had been written could not be unwritten.

The two men spent eleven and a half months in the Butirskaya Prison, one of the most notorious jails in Russia, waiting for a trial date. I eventually got a summons to the trial, but was too scared to go. A friend went instead, to present my excuses. He heard that both brothers had come down with tuberculosis in jail. Even in the absence of the victim, they were convicted, and given a sentence matching the time they'd already served on remand. They had lost their jobs and their families had gone back to Tatarstan. By the time I heard the news the shock and even the memory of the night our lives collided so disastrously had faded. The story was lost, I tried to convince myself, in the Babel of horror stories which swirled in the newsroom where I worked. It was perverse, I told myself, to mourn the fate of guilty men when every day the papers which piled on my desk in drifts were full of terrifying stories of the suffering of innocents.

But the memory of the horror and the guilt I felt as those two men grovelled before me was buried deep, and it festered. Many Russians, I believe, carry a similar black slime inside themselves made of trauma and guilt and wilful forgetting. It makes a rich compost in which all their hedonism, their treachery, their every pleasure and betrayal, takes root. It's not the same for the cosseted Europeans among whom I grew up, though many of them were convinced they had suffered parental indifference, spousal cruelty or personal failure. No, the average Russian seventeen-year-old, I concluded from my years of wandering the nastier side of the new Russia, had already seen more real abuse and hopelessness and corruption and injustice than most of my English friends had seen in a lifetime. And to survive and be happy, Russians have so much to bury, to wilfully ignore. Small wonder that the intensity of their pleasures and indulgences is so sharp; it has to match the quality of their suffering.

For days after the Bibikovs' Chernigov apartment was searched there was no news. Boris did not return from his holiday. The NKVD kept telling Martha that she would be informed as soon as there were any developments. Varya was sent away to her relatives in the country, and Martha and her two daughters lived in the apartment's bathroom and the kitchen because all the other rooms were locked and sealed. Martha bought food with the money she had left in her purse, and accepted the charity of their remaining neighbours.

Bibikov's colleagues knew nothing – in fact many had themselves disappeared, and the rest were either terrified or naïvely confident that the NKVD would soon correct its error.

There was a moment of panic when Martha left the children alone to eat their cherry soup, a Ukrainian summer treat, while she went once again to the NKVD office for news. Lenina was reading a book her father had given her, and didn't notice that her little sister Lyudmila had stuffed all the cherry stones up her nose so far that they could not be extracted.

'I'm a money box,' Lyudmila told her sister as she pushed up another stone. There was uproar when their mother returned. Lyudmila was rushed to hospital to have the stones extracted by a stern nurse with long forceps apparently kept for the purpose. Lenina was given a hard smacking for her negligence, and wept because she could not go to her father for comfort.

After nearly two weeks of worry, Martha decided the only

thing left to do was to send Lenina to Moscow to her husband's well-connected brothers. Surely they could pull some strings and find out something about what had happened? She had no money to buy a ticket, so she wrapped a pair of silver spoons from the kitchen in a napkin and went to the station to beg a seat from a conductress on one of the Kiev–Moscow expresses which passed through Chernigov late at night. The conductress stowed Lenina on a luggage rack and told her not to move. She also told Martha to keep the spoons. Martha ran down the platform as the train pulled out, keeping pace as it gathered speed until she couldn't keep up any more.

Ten years before, Martha's father had sent her away from the home where she'd grown up. On a station platform in Simferopol, she had abandoned her dying sister to her fate. Now, as she stood watching the lights of the train bearing her elder daughter to Moscow recede into the night, Martha realized that the new family she had made was falling apart. She went to the telegraph office and sent a short telegram to her husband's relatives in Moscow telling them that Lenina was on her way. Then she walked home. She found Lyudmila asleep on a blanket on the kitchen floor, picked her up in her arms and, she told Lenina later, 'howled like a wounded animal'.

At Kursky Station in Moscow Lenina was met by her uncle Isaac, Boris's younger brother. Their other brother, Yakov, an Air Force officer, was serving on the Far Eastern Staff in Khabarovsk, near Vladivostok, and was still unaware of Boris's arrest. Isaac was twenty-three, a promising engineer at the Dynamo aircraft engine factory. He embraced his young niece and told her to save her story till after they'd ridden home on the tram to the small apartment he shared with his and Boris's mother, Sophia. In the kitchen they listened to Lenina's story in silence. Lenina began crying, sobbing that she didn't know what her father had done wrong. Isaac tried to reassure her. It was all a misunderstanding, he told her, he knew people who could sort it out.

The next day Isaac spoke to a friend of his at the Dynamo factory, one of the resident NKVD political officers. The man had until recently been one of the personal bodyguards of a senior NKVD general. The political officer said he'd ask his old colleagues and see if he could arrange an interview to sort out what he was tactful enough to call a 'terrible mistake'.

Two days later, Isaac came home early, told Lenina to put on her best summer dress and took her by the hand to the tram stop. They travelled to the NKVD's headquarters on Lubyanka Square in silence. The Lubyanka itself was a huge and bourgeois building which had once housed a pre-revolutionary insurance company. By 1937 it had been extended, its cellars converted to a sizeable prison and interrogation centre which was by then bursting with the Purge's nightly crop of new victims. Isaac and his niece went in to the main entrance, presented Isaac's passport to the desk sergeant and were shown upstairs to a waiting room. A man in a dark green NKVD uniform, with breeches and leather boots, came to speak briefly to Isaac – evidently the friend who had arranged the meeting.

When they were finally shown in to the office Lenina first thought it was empty. There was a huge dark wooden desk, with a bright lamp on it. The heavy curtains were half drawn, despite the summer sunshine outside. There were tall windows and a thick carpet. And then she noticed, behind the desk, a small, balding, bespectacled head. The general, Lenina thought, 'looked like a gnome'.

The gnome looked up at Isaac and the little girl, and asked why they were there. Isaac, faltering, began to explain that his brother, a good and loyal Communist, had been arrested due to some mistake, some oversight, perhaps excessive zeal on the part of his men in rooting out the enemies of the state. The general picked up a flimsy file from his desk as he listened, flipped through it as Isaac talked, and said one word: '*Razber-emsya*' – 'We'll sort it out.' That was the end of the meeting. Isaac, shaken, took Lenina home and the next day put her on a train back to Chernigov. A few days later, Martha sold whatever kitchenware she could and bought train tickets for herself and her children to the Crimea, to stay with her elder sister Feodosia. But before she left she dutifully filed her whereabouts with the Chernigov NKVD, so that her husband wouldn't worry when he returned to an empty apartment after the misunderstanding was rectified.

Winter closed in, and there was still no news. Martha and the children lived in the kitchen of Feodosia's small wooden house on the outskirts of Simferopol. It was a rude fall from grace after their life as members of the pampered Party élite in Chernigov. Martha got a job as a nurse in a children's hospital for infectious diseases, and would bring leftover food from the hospital home for the children.

The climate of the Crimea is milder than European Russia, but the winter brings a cold sea wind off the Bay of Sevastopol. Feodosia's draughty house was heated with a small metal stove known as a *burzhuika* – a 'bourgeois' stove which burned hot and quickly, but was cold by morning. The children weren't allowed to light it during the day while Martha was at the hospital, and they sat by the window, huddled in sweaters, watching the rain fall on the small orchard which surrounded their house.

Life was elsewhere, Lenina thought, during those slow months. She missed the bustle of their life in Chernigov, their neighbours and her school friends and the endless stream of officials and friends who would sit late into the night in their kitchen. But most of all she missed her father, who had been her refuge and her best friend. She never stopped believing that he was alive and well, somewhere, missing her as she missed him.

Lyudmila had always been a quiet child, but now she seemed to withdraw into herself. She played with her dolls in a corner of the floor of Feodosia's kitchen, next to the trunk on which Lenina slept, trying to stay out of the way of her scolding mother and aunt. Martha came home late and exhausted, her hair a straggling mess. Since her husband's arrest she had given up on her appearance.

In early December Lyudmila fell ill with measles. It seems she had caught it from the food, or maybe from her mother's hospital clothes. As the child's fever climbed Martha stayed at home to look after her. She would send Lenina to the chemist for mustard plasters to ease her sister's coughing, and eye drops for her swollen eyes.

On the third or fourth night of Lyudmila's fever there was a sharp knock on the door. Feodosia went to open it. Several men in dark uniforms with pistols on their belts pushed inside the house. They demanded to see 'Citizen Bibikova'. Martha, Lyudmila in her arms, scrambled to her feet as they opened the kitchen door.

'Get up!' one of the men ordered Lenina, and threw open the trunk she had been sleeping on, spilling her and the blankets on to the floor. Martha began to scream in protest, grabbing the officer by the arm. He pushed her backwards, toppling her into the open trunk with her three-year-old daughter in her arms. Lenina remembers the screaming, everyone screaming, her mother struggling to get up from the trunk, a moment of grotesque farce within the unfolding nightmare. The NKVD men pulled Martha out, held her arms behind her back and bundled her out of the house and into the garden, still in her nightdress. On the street they pushed her into one of two police cars – 'Black Crows' – waiting for them. Another officer followed with the two children, Lyudmila under his arm and leading Lenina by the hand. As they reached the street, Lenina struggled free from the grip of the man who held her and tried to run to her mother; she was caught and bundled with her sister into the second car. As they drove away Lenina clutched her feverish little sister, who was crying hysterically. At the end of the street the two cars turned in different directions. The girls were not to see their mother again for eleven years.

My own son, Nikita, is, as I write this, exactly Lyudmila's age when Martha was arrested – two months shy of four years old. He has a round face and a mop of dark hair, and his grand-mother Lyudmila's striking blue eyes. Lenina, when we went to visit a few weeks ago, hugged him so tight that he cried; she said he looked so like Lyudmila she couldn't bear it. 'I became a mother at twelve, when they took Mother away,' she said. 'Lyudmila was my first child. He's a little Lyudmila.'

Sometimes, as I watch Nikita play, I feel – like most parents, I suppose – a flash of obscure, irrational fear. As he potters in the flowerbeds rooting for snails or digging up bulbs, absorbed in his own thoughts, I fear that my child could die, or be somehow taken from me. At other times, usually when it's late at night and I'm drunk and far from home, on assignment in Baghdad or another of the Godforsaken hell-holes where I've spent much of my life since leaving Moscow, I imagine what will happen to him if I die. I wonder if he'll manage, what he'll remember of me, if he'll understand, if he'll cry. The thought of losing him is so horrifying it makes me giddy. I often think of Martha on that night and try to imagine how I would feel if it were Nikita snatched away from my arms by strangers. But I cannot picture it.

The NKVD men drove Lenina and Lyudmila to the Simfer-opol Prison for Underage Offenders, where they were to remain until the state determined their fate. By the grim logic of the Purge, the family members of an 'enemy of the people' were deemed to have been contaminated by his or her heresy, as if it were a disease. As the old Russian saying goes, 'the apple does not fall far from the apple tree'. Therefore these two children, aged twelve and three, were doomed to suffer for their father's sin. Like him, they were ordained by the Party to become the dross of history.

The prison was badly lit, and stank of urine, carbolic soap and coal-tar ointment. Lenina remembers the faces of the men who took down their details, the acrid smell of the crowded cell to which they were taken and told to find a space for themselves on the straw-covered floor, and the barking of the guard dogs in the corridor. Holding her moaning little sister, she cried herself to sleep.

Mila also remembers the night of her mother's arrest. It is her earliest clear memory. She is standing in her nightshirt holding a doll, a soldier pushes her, and everyone screams. Of her brief three years and ten months of normal family life she has no recollection, except for a ghost of a memory of being carried on her father's shoulders. From that moment on, Lenina became her little sister's surrogate mother. Two frightened children alone in a world that had suddenly become dark and incomprehensible.

5

Prison

We, the children of Russia's terrible years,
Don't have the strength to forget.
Georgy Ivanov

On a warm, foggy morning on Novoslobodskaya Street in the summer of 1995, I showed up at the gate of Butirskaya Prison, my reporter's notebook in my back pocket. The entrance was squeezed between a hairdresser's salon and a shop; I thought I had come to the wrong place. But through a dingy corridor between the drab Soviet buildings which lined the street, there lay a strange, closed world. Butirskaya was a vast fortress – literally a fortress, with towers, crenellations and a flock of crows wheeling around the rooftops, built by Catherine the Great for her adopted country's numerous criminals, including the peasant rebel Emeliyan Pugachev.

Outside on the street, the dusty heat of a Moscow summer was already building. But as we were led through a small, arched gateway the June heat immediately soured into a clammy pall which settled on my skin and clothes like someone else's sweat. Even in the administrative wing, the metallic smell of sour cabbage, cheap detergent and damp clothes was all-pervasive.

The cell I visited was about sixty feet by fifteen. A wave of male stink, rancid sweat mixed with urine, welled out as the guard opened the door. At first I thought that the prisoners were crowding towards the door to see who had come. Then, as I peered down the room, I saw that they were packed that tightly from the door to the heavy, shuttered window just visible at the far end. The cell was like a crowded Metro carriage. Two rows of wooden shelves covered in bedding and bodies ran along each wall. Rows of bunioned feet protruded from both tiers. In the space left in the middle stood a throng of men, naked except for their underwear, leaning against the bunks or perching on the ends of the beds. Some were playing cards, most of the reclining men slept, and the rest just stood, unable to move. Wet washing hung from makeshift clothes lines strung across the ceiling. A tiny, overflowing toilet and a single tap stood in the corner. The heat and humidity were so intense that it was hard to inhale, and the overpowering smell of concentrated human beings made me retch.

I pushed my way down the cell, as the guard watched from the door. It was an unwritten rule, he said later, that warders never went into the cells unless someone went berzerk, or there was a stabbing.

There were 142 men in the cell. They had empty, sunken eyes. Their legs and bodies were covered in flea bites and sores. About half had hacking, tubercular coughs, and spat copiously on the greasy floor. There was no natural light, the window was shuttered, with only two tiny sections opened to let in fresh air. The place was lit with four dim bulbs which shone sixteen hours a day.

I tried to talk to a couple of them, briefly, but it was so uncomfortable speaking to a stranger in such unnatural proximity, chest to chest, I found I had nothing to say. Neither then, nor later, could I humanize the prisoners or relate to them as people. They had passed into another reality; they had been transformed into something less than human, closer to a herd of animals. Even when they got out, I imagined, it would forever be a part of them. Whereas I, even as I squeezed among them, was merely on the outside, looking in. I could no more identify with them than I could with the mangy animals at Moscow's sad old Zoo. Never, before or since as a reporter in Russia, did I feel more intensely that I was Just Visiting.

Their faces were the faces of men whose whole lives had imploded into the space of a few feet of the fetid room they inhabited. They stared at me as I pushed past from a distance of six inches, but when I looked into their eyes I knew they were looking at me from a distance I could never, ever cross.

There is a photograph of Lyudmila and Lenina taken some time in early 1938. Lenina is wearing a headscarf to cover her shaven head, Lyudmila is clutching a homemade rag doll with pigtails and a white cotton dress and hat. Lenina is a beautiful girl, with big eyes, a broad forehead, a delicate mouth. Lyudmila, also shaven-headed and wearing a knitted waist-coat and white collarless shirt, looks like a round-faced boy as she leans her head against her sister's breast. Lenina's half-smile is wistful, and disconcertingly adult. Both sisters look haunted and serious. Their eyes are not children's eyes. The photograph stands on my desk. Despite its familiarity, I cannot look at that image without a pang of emotion.

At dawn on their first day in prison Lenina and Lyudmila's cellmates questioned Lenina on why they were in jail. They were all young girls, mostly thieves and prostitutes. On hearing that the newcomers weren't criminals, just 'politicals', as the children of enemies of the people were called, they pinched Lenina viciously and laughed at her sobbing. Two guards, one holding a barking Alsatian, opened the cell door and ordered silence. The girls were herded into a refectory, where they lined up at a small window for a bowl of soup. One of the older girls slapped the underside of Lenina's bowl as she came away from the window, spilling her soup on the floor, an initiation rite for the new kids. Lenina went back to the cell hungry. A few hours later a prison doctor came, diagnosed Lyudmila with measles and sent her immediately to the prison hospital, leaving Lenina alone with her tormentors.

After a few days Lenina was allowed to visit her sister during the daily exercise hour. She would save whatever scraps of meat or sugar lumps she could after the older girls had picked through her food, hide them in her underpants and give them to Lyudmila to keep up her strength. Sometimes their aunt Feodosia would come by with little packets of food, which Lenina would pull up on a string through the barred hospital window overlooking the street. Mila remembers the string and the little parcels of food. She also remembers being scolded for wetting the bed at night, and her sister Lenina crying all the time.

In late December, three weeks after they had been imprisoned, Lenina awoke in the middle of the night to find the cell filling with smoke. The cell door opened, and a panicking warder ordered the children out into the yard. The building had been set on fire by some older children to cover an escape attempt. The guards had let the dogs loose and they snapped at the children as they were ushered into the exercise yard. Ever since that night, Lenina has been terrified of dogs. The children shivered in the cold as the fire engines arrived. Lyudmila had also been brought out, lying on a stretcher, with other children evacuated from the prison hospital.

The prison burned all night. By dawn it was gutted and useless, and the children were frozen half to death in the yard, still under guard. A convoy of open trucks arrived to take them away in groups of twenty. Lenina and Lyudmila were on one of the last, bound for one of the more distant orphanages in the region. Their truck rode them north for most of the day, hungry and freezing cold, through driving sleet. Finally, they were unloaded at an 'allocation centre' for parentless children in Dnepropetrovsk. Lenina and Lyudmila were blue with cold and shivering so uncontrollably that Lenina remembers that she couldn't speak. They were herded into a large hall, already filled with the children of Spanish Republicans, evacuated to the Soviet Union to save them from the civil war. The Spanish children, far from home, were bawling and terrified as they waited to be assigned to local orphanages.

A harassed desk officer took the list of names and ages from the new arrivals' escort. He told Lyudmila to go with the other little children, and Lenina to stand aside and wait her turn. Lenina fell on her knees, pleading for the men not to take her sister away, embracing the pigskin boots of the guards. As she pleaded, a man in civilian clothes listened, leaning on the doorframe; as she told the story sixty-five years later in the kitchen of her apartment in Moscow, Lenina lumbered up and leaned by the kitchen door, arms crossed, to demonstrate. The man stepped forward, put his hand gently on the shoulder of the guard, said, 'I'll take her,' leaned down and helped Lenina up off the floor.

The man was Yakov Abramovich Michnik, the director of a giant newly built children's home at Verkhne-Dneprovsk, created to rehabilitate 1,600 street children, criminals and orphans and make then into new Soviet men and women. That evening Lyudmila and the youngest children, plus twelve-year-old Lenina, were driven to his orphanage in a bus. When they arrived, the children were showered and de-loused, and their heads were shaved. They were assigned to dormitories according to age. Lenina was given a cot beside her sister's bed in the hospital dormitory, down the corridor from the others. The nurses and supervisors confiscated the Spanish children's shoes and dolls and took them for their own children. Lenina still dreams about the way the Spanish kids cried without their beloved toys, their last physical reminder of home. All night, they cried out 'Mamá'.

As the shock of their arrest and imprisonment faded, Verkhne-Dneprovsk turned out to be a relatively happy place.

They had food, and the teachers were kind. In her first days at the orphanage, Lyudmila tried to cool her burning fever by burying her legs in damp sand in a sandpit. Within weeks, her measles were cured, but it was discovered that she had caught tuberculosis of the bones, which spread rapidly due to her weakened immune system.

Lenina came to see her little sister at the local hospital's infection ward every day after school. Lyudmila would stand on a chair and lean out of the window and wave and talk. One day when Lenina came to visit, she found Lyudmila red-eyed and silent. Her little Spanish friend Juan, 'Juanchik', who slept in the bed next to her had been taken away in the night, and no one would tell her where he had gone. The nurse told Lenina that Juan had died of tuberculosis. One by one, every one of the eighteen children who had been in the ward when Lyudmila was admitted died. My mother was the only child to survive.

Lenina couldn't write to her relatives in Moscow because she couldn't remember their address; even if she had, there was little chance that they would risk saving the children of an enemy of the people. She did write to their aunt Feodosia in Simferopol, but she didn't come for them. Feodosia did, however, send news of her sister Martha. She had been sent to a place called Kazakhstan, Feodosia explained to her young niece, to a prison camp called KarLag. Her address was a post box number. Lenina would walk three miles each day from the orphanage to the local school, and in her free time scrubbed floors for her teachers in exchange for onions, small pieces of smoked pig-fat, sugar and apples. She would take the sugar and apples to Lyudmila in the hospital, but she saved the onions. When Lenina had collected ten onions, she made them into a small parcel. She addressed the brown paper package carefully to the numbered post box in Kazakhstan, did more chores to pay for the stamps, and posted it from the orphanage. Months later, she got a letter back from Martha. She thanked her daughter for the parcel, but told her she was a 'fool' not to have wrapped the onions individually in paper. As it was, they had arrived frozen and spoiled, Martha complained. Nevertheless, she asked after Lyudmila and wished her daughters well. She promised to be back to collect them soon. It was the last Lenina was to hear from her mother until after the war.

My mother doesn't remember having any toys as a child, apart from a teddy bear she'd brought from Chernigov, which she lost in the children's prison. The doll in the photograph taken at Verkhne-Dneprovsk was a photographer's prop. Lenina remembers Lyudmila crying when she was told she couldn't keep it after the picture was taken.

Lyudmila had a passion for drawing, but never, as she put it, 'had any talent'. Despite her illness, she learned to read very early and soon was passing the long, lonely days in hospital reading books from the orphanage library. Books, and the wonderful worlds the words contained, took the place of friends. It was during the many months of enforced idleness in hospital which punctuated her childhood that she learned to live a fantasy life, constructed in her own lively mind. The mysterious, brooding forests of Pushkin's stories, the magic carpet rides above the sleeping houses of Baghdad in the Arabian Nights, the fabulous monsters encountered by Sinbad the Sailor, and the high-stepping horsemen and witches of ancient Russia illustrated by Ivan Bilibin – these were the places to which she would escape in her childhood imagination. The harsh, antiseptic, loveless world around her became more tolerable in the knowledge that somewhere, far away, was a better place to which she would eventually travel. Even when she grew into a woman and her crippled legs had finally healed, this

powerful vision of another, magical life – and the sense that
that life could be won by endurance and pure force of will –
was never to leave her.

At the orphanage Lenina had a dream. She was wearing her
white blouse and red Young Pioneer tie. Some children called
out to her, 'Your father! They're bringing out your father!'
She ran outside and saw her father from behind, being led by
three men with rifles. They took him to the steep bank of the
great Dniepr River, at the edge of the orphanage's grounds.
He stood on the edge for a long time, as Lenina looked on,
frozen in the paralysis of the dream. Then the three men fired
their rifles into her father, silently. He fell, bouncing down the
bank. It was the only time Lenina ever dreamt of her father.

By the end of 1938 Lyudmila had recovered sufficiently to
go to kindergarten, but was in and out of hospital for a series of
crude operations to cut away more and more tissue. The
bones of her right leg had been rotted by the tuberculosis and
she walked with a heavy limp. Nevertheless she was a cheerful
and intelligent child, devoted to her sister. The orphanage was
the only world she could remember, and she attained a kind of
happiness there.

It was harder for Lenina, for her former life began to haunt
her. She had been told by her teachers that her parents were
'enemies of the people', and were being punished. She should
try to forget them. Uncle Stalin, whose portrait hung in the
classroom, was looking after them now. Lenina chanted along
with the other children, 'Thank you, Comrade Stalin, for our
happy childhood.' But she still never doubted that she would
see her beloved father again. When the teachers talked about
the 'bright future', Lenina pictured being reunited with her
father.

The steppes of the eastern Ukraine were flat and feature-
less, a land of giant skies as big as the whole world. In summer,
Lenina would often go down to the Dniepr with the other

children to bathe in the wide, slow-moving river, sliding on its muddy banks as they scrambled into the water. The stern rhythms of orphanage life left Lenina little room for reflection. And among hundreds of parentless children like themselves, the Bibikov sisters were more fortunate than most. They at least had each other.

But the peace the sisters found at Verkhne-Dneprovsk was soon shattered in its turn.

In the summer of 1941, Lenina was sixteen and Lyudmila seven. Lyudmila was looking forward to starting her first year of school, and Lenina was a senior member of the Young Pioneers, proud to wear the smart, starched uniform. Most mornings there was a parade, the various school classes dragooned into neat rows, with two older children acting as honour guards as the Soviet flag was run up the flagpole to a scratchy recording of the Soviet national anthem. Lenina and the older children sometimes sat reverently in front of a large Bakelite radio, listening to improving speeches and homilies on the children's programme of Soviet State Radio. Later, in private, the adults listened to the evening news of the war that Germany had unleashed on France and Britain. But the conflict seemed a distant thing, the death throes of the decadent capitalist world as it turned in upon itself. The Soviet Union and Germany had signed a non-aggression pact two years before. The war concerned other people, far from the Dniepr plains.

It was a scorching summer. The steppe wind blew in clouds of dust from the dry fields, covering the orphanage buildings and the trees in the playground with a fine brown pall. For the children, life continued as normal during those baking days, as the German Army massed on the Soviet–Polish border.

Then, on 22 June 1941, Hitler launched the *blitzkrieg* assault codenamed Operation Barbarossa, which quickly crushed Soviet resistance. Unbeknown to the sisters, their uncle Isaac, the engineer now turned pilot, was shot down and killed over Belarus in the first days of the war at the controls of his Polikarpov fighter, outmanoeuvred and outgunned by the swarms of Messerschmitt fighters who cleared the skies ahead of the advancing Wehrmacht. His family never found out where, or even if, he was buried.

Lenina and Lyudmila only heard the news of the attack days later from their solemn teachers, who had in turn heard it on the radio, which announced that the Red Army was heroically repulsing the invaders. It wasn't true. Within ten days, Minsk had fallen. By 27 June, two German armies had advanced 200 miles into Soviet territory, a third of the way to Moscow. By 21 August the Werhmacht had cut the Moscow–Leningrad railway line and German Panzer divisions were advancing fast across the wheat fields of the Ukraine, pushing towards Stalingrad and the Caucasus oilfields.

Kiev fell on 26 September. Days later, the sound of distant guns could be heard at Verkhne-Dneprovsk, carried eastwards on the wind. Lenina was at school when the trucks came to mobilize the older orphanage children to dig trenches. They were told to leave their books and load up as quickly as they could. Lenina thought that they would be back soon, even in time for supper. Her sister, at school with the junior class, didn't see her leave.

Lenina never returned to Verkhne-Dneprovsk. Her detachment of child trench-diggers was driven to the outskirts of the city, where they spent days shovelling the black earth on to the four-handled trays Russians use in place of wheelbarrows. Within days they began to fall back eastwards as the Germans advanced. They slept when they could, on sacks on the floors of hastily evacuated factories, or on the soft freshly dug earth. They would dig during the day and walk at night, moving back daily before the German offensive. There was no way to return to the orphanage, or to find news of Lyudmila or the other children they had left behind.

Lyudmila herself remembers very little of what happened next. Her recollection of that time seems as opaque as Lenina's is clear. Lenina only heard the story after the war from one of her classmates who had stayed behind to do chores the day the older children were taken to dig, and again from Yakov Michnik, the director of the children's home, who came to be a friend and benefactor.

As the front line approached Verkhne-Dneprovsk in the first days of October, the children left at the orphanage and at the hospital were stranded. All available transport had been mobilized, and as the bombing grew closer the last remaining staff decided to evacuate the infants by the only route still open to them – via the great steppe river which ran by the end of the orphanage's territory. The orphanage director commandeered two large river rafts, designed to be hauled up river by horses, from a local collective farm. He loaded the forty remaining children on board. Then, as dusk fell and an artillery barrage flashed in the sky, the six remaining staff pushed the barges full of children out into the stream, propelling the rafts with poles until the current caught them and carried them away into the darkness.

6

War

Die, but do not retreat.
Iosif Stalin

The barges drifted in the Dniepr's slow stream all night. At dawn they ran aground near a village on the eastern bank of the river. The local peasants still had carts and horses, and the orphanage director arranged for the children to be loaded up and transported to the nearest railhead at Zaporozhiye. There, amid the tumult of a city preparing to be overrun by the Germans, Michnik passed his children into the care of the local authorities. He saw no more of them – except for a few who survived the war and came, as Lenina did, to visit, in curiosity and gratitude, as adults. At Zaporozhiye, the children joined a giant, chaotic stream of human flotsam fleeing before the German advance.

Lyudmila's own memory of her evacuation through the chaos of the Red Army's retreat in the autumn and winter of 1941 is a disjointed series of images. She remembers standing at a high window, looking out over a flat landscape, watching bombs falling in the distance with great white flashes, feeling the percussion through the floorboards. She remembers standing with the other orphanage children in a line by the side of a muddy road one rainy autumn day, holding out mugs of water for an endless stream of soldiers trudging by on their way to the front. She recalls spending nights in the forest, shivering under thin blankets and listening to the eerie woodland silence.

They were constantly on the move. Some nights there were searchlights and explosions. One day, Lyudmila remembers, she and other children travelled in a heavy peasant cart, with each child holding a branch to camouflage them from the aeroplanes which buzzed overhead. The horse was a huge lumbering thing, and its harness was also covered in branches. This is the image which has lodged, for some reason, most vividly in my mind's eye – my mother, sitting in the bed of the cart among other children, hopefully clutching a branch like a talisman against the German planes, a small crippled child alone and frightened, trundling eastwards into the emptiness of the Volga steppes.

The children were evacuated in stages, deeper and deeper into the hinterland of Russia, spending a few days or weeks wherever their transport ran out, waiting for someone to take charge of them, to pass them to safety. Somewhere to the west of Stalingrad they got stuck, washed up by the stream of men and machines which filled the steppes. Lyudmila spent the harshest winter months billeted in a snowbound village, chewing dry ears of corn filched from the barns and fighting with the local children for food. In the early spring of 1942, someone remembered the beleaguered little party and moved them to a collective farm closer to the Volga. Mila remembers scavenging for berries in the quiet, cold woods and helping peasant women scrub floors in exchange for crusts of bread.

Somehow, in a small miracle of war, just as the German Sixth Army began its advance on Stalingrad, somebody managed to find the children places on a big American Studebaker truck, the luxury of luxuries. It drove them to the city, reaching the Volga just days ahead of the Germans. The date must have been shortly after 23 August 1942, the day Red Army sappers blew the bridges, because Lyudmila remembers crossing the Volga with the other orphanage children on a steel barge, packed to the gunwales with refugees. She saw the girders of the blown-up bridges dipping into the river at a crazy angle. The windows of all the schools and public buildings in the city were filled with wounded soldiers swathed in bandages. That image became one of Lyudmila's most vivid memories of that time – 'They stood there, all wrapped in bandages, so many of them, by every window.'

On the other side of the river, Lyudmila and the other children found themselves stranded once again. In the scramble to reinforce the city before the arrival of the Germans, and during the first, chaotic weeks of the battle, every available form of transport was needed to ferry men and supplies to the stricken city, and to bring back casualties.

The orphans were billeted in villages near the river. Lyudmila remembers crowds of refugees passing through her village on foot, sleeping in the fields when their strength failed, packing into barns and peasant huts so tightly that they couldn't close the door. Their snoring made an eerie rumbling noise in the darkness, as though the earth itself was trembling. There were air raids at night, and Mila remembers running for safety into the tall grass of the steppe as the black bombs tumbled slowly out of the sky.

Day and night, horse carts trundled through the village full of horribly injured soldiers, covered in blood, some missing limbs. At night the river glowed red from the burning city, and when the wind blew eastwards it carried the heat and smoke of the great battle. She saw bodies and parts of bodies floating past in the water.

Food was the only thing Mila thought about. The children ran wild, fending for themselves, begging for scraps from the streams of refugees, hunting in packs for wheat and barley stalks. Mila and the other children would gather up dry leaves and crumble them with the tobacco of cigarette butts they would find by the roadside. They would sell the mixture as *makhorka*, rough soldiers' tobacco, to the lines of troops who passed every day, exchanging it for sugar cubes or lumps of bread. Many of the soldiers had flat, Mongolian faces. They had come all the way from Siberia, marching days from the nearest railhead and sleeping on the roadsides before moving in inexorable human waves into the city.

Half a century later, I witnessed the Russian Army in action myself. I stood on the Russian front lines in the northern outskirts of Grozny, Chechnya, as a mighty firestorm of artillery roared overhead and the rebel city burned around us. The city centre was obscured by a drifting pall of bitter-tasting gun smoke. All around were the jagged husks of buildings, nibbled by gunfire and then shelled and shelled again. Sukhoi fighter bombers screamed in fast and low every minute to deliver half-ton bombs, which fell with terrible grace towards their targets before exploding with a boom which seemed powerful enough to fell the whole city. The bombardment was so overwhelming it felt like a physical presence; it thundered under my feet like giant doors slamming deep in the earth.

I spent days with Russian soldiers in trenches dug out of the sandy soil, and slept side by side with snoring conscripts in bivouacs they'd made in the ruined houses. Their faces were filthy with smoke and dirt, and they swore and spat and laughed uproariously at the slightest joke. One evening as we ate bully beef from tins one young sergeant tossed a grenade to me across the room by the light of a hissing kerosene pressure lamp. The pin was out and the safety handle gone – for a moment I stared at the little steel egg in incomprehension before the room cracked up. It was a dummy.

They were just kids, delirious from danger and war. But

when we went out on patrols, crunching house to house through broken glass and piles of bricks, they went silent and tense, as all infantrymen do in battle. Their technique was to move forward until they came under fire, then locate the shooter and call in artillery before scrambling back to their forward base as fast as they could move, praying that the Russian gunners weren't drunk or ranged their rounds short. It was a tactic little changed since the street fighting of Stalingrad. As we settled in for the night the young soldiers would kick off their high pigskin boots and unwind the foot cloths which Russian soldiers wear instead of socks before plumping their fur hats into makeshift pillows. Outside, some other unit was coming under fire, and we could feel the roaring rip-rip-rip of multiple rocket launchers resonating through the concrete floor. The scene, down to the candle stubs and wooden matchboxes the kids carried in their top pockets and used to light their cardboard-filtered *papiros* cigarettes, could have been from their grandfathers' war.

Today, the steppe country around Stalingrad is empty and silent. The collective farm fields stretch as far as the eye can see, ploughed with crooked furrows and punctuated by half-ruined log cabins and long concrete barns. The far bank of the huge river is lost in the mist, and the slow grey water swells and falls as it laps the banks. It seems as though the giant fields and swaying trees are brooding on the strange convulsion which brought so many humans here, half a century ago, to spill their blood on the sandy soil.

I visited Volgograd, as Stalingrad has become, in the winter of 1999. A heavy, soul-sapping blandness covered the city like a dirty snowfall, oppressive as the winter sky which hung low over the landscape. It was depressingly similar to other provincial backwaters, a place where the bitter concentrate of reality withered the spirit like a pickle in a jar of brine.

On Mamayev Kurgan, a low, partly man-made hill in west

Stalingrad, scene of some of the bitterest fighting, stands a monument to Mother Russia. It is a concrete statue 279 feet high depicting a woman brandishing a giant sword aloft, calling for vengeance, or victory. She is a young woman with strong arms and thighs, and she half-turns to call over her shoulder for her children to follow. She is Russia as a vengeful goddess, Russia as a consuming force of nature, demanding impossible sacrifices from her children as her right.

As the winter of 1942 closed in and the momentum of the German advance stalled in the ruins of Stalingrad, the authorities began rounding up the lost children and packing them into trucks heading north for Kuybishev, now Samara, on the Upper Volga. Mila was caught like the rest. She remembers a cold and crowded train, heading further north still, which delivered her and several thousand other lost children to a giant camp for orphans in Solikamsk, near Perm, in the foothills of the Urals.

Solikamsk was a world of human beings cast adrift by the war. The whole town, it seemed, had been swamped by orphaned children with the stroke of a bureaucrat's pen. The place was governed by what Lyudmila called 'wolves' laws', the children fighting each other for survival. The older children would try to make the younger ones hide ten-gram pieces of meat from their lunchtime soup in their long knickers, and hand them over on the way out of the kitchens. If the younger children refused they'd 'put you in the dark' – throw a blanket over you and beat you up. There were three shifts for lunch, the youngest children going first, with teachers patrolling to make sure the children ate their meat and didn't hide it for the older ones. Lyudmila and the other children collected steppe grass, mixed it with salt and ate it. It helped their bodies' craving for vitamins, and to stave off rickets. Mila's stomach became distended from hunger, her legs thin as sticks.

There were moments of kindness. At the village school, the teacher would tell the village children not to eat their tiny fifty-gram pieces of lunchtime bread and to leave it for the orphans instead – even though the villagers were near starving too, living off bitter black radishes and tiny potatoes, the only crop the villagers could cultivate in the short Urals growing season.

When the summer of 1943 came, the children of Solikamsk were sent in their hundreds into the wild *taiga*, the marshes and forests around the town, to collect berries for wounded soldiers. Their quota was to collect half a bucketful each. Mila was terrified of falling into the deep, marshy water-holes concealed in the thick moss of the *taiga*. On one such expedition the children had to walk sixteen miles into the forests to find berrying areas which hadn't been picked clean by the villagers. On the way back Mila, though only nine, led the huge crowd of children, hobbling in front despite her crippled leg and singing Young Pioneer songs. When they arrived back at the orphanage with their load of berries Mila's eyes were deep red and filled with blood as a result of the physical stress. The wolves' laws of Solikamsk had taught her one thing – that the only way for the physically weak to survive was to find a way of leading the rest by sheer force of character.

Dnepropetrovsk had fallen after a week's battle. Lenina and the older orphanage children, just like her sister and millions of other refugees, made their way east by foot, in carts and trucks. Everywhere her work detachment stopped they dug fresh trenches and tank traps.

By early September of 1942, Lenina found herself in the Stavropol region, just beyond the furthest line of the German advance. Hitler had ordered that the push towards the Caucasus and the oilfields of Baku be suspended while all available forces were mobilized to the battle for Stalingrad, 300 miles to

The Party man. Official photograph from Boris Bibikov's Party card, taken in 1936. He had recently been appointed to head the Party's Regional Committee in Chernigov; he was thirty-three years old.

'Not men, but giants.' Bibikov (*front row, second from right*) with young factory colleagues at the Kharkov Tractor Factory, around 1932.

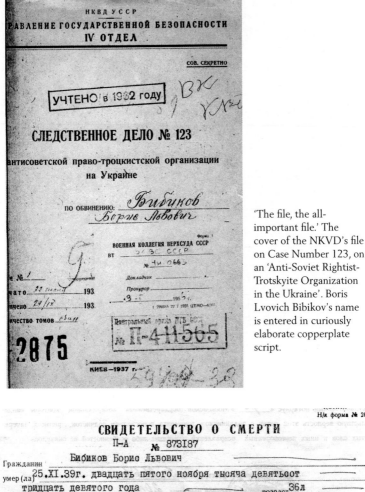

'The file, the all-important file.' The cover of the NKVD's file on Case Number 123, on an 'Anti-Soviet Rightist-Trotskyite Organization in the Ukraine'. Boris Lvovich Bibikov's name is entered in curiously elaborate copperplate script.

Boris Bibikov's first death certificate. The cause and place of death were left blank. The authorities only finally acknowledged the truth in 1988 – that Boris Bibikov had been shot somewhere near Kiev on 14 October 1937 and buried in a communal grave.

Lyudmila and Lenina Bibikov, aged four and twelve, at the Verkhne-Dneprovsk children's home, some time in early 1938. Both their heads had been shaved as a precaution against lice; the doll was a photographer's prop.

'Remember the good people.' Verkhne-Dneprovsk orphanage director Yakov Abramovich Michnik with Lenina's elder daughter, Nadia, in 1950. Michnik saved Lenina and Lyudmila from being separated when they first arrived at Dnepropetrovsk in November 1937; in 1941, as the Germans advanced, he rescued the remaining orphanage children, including Lyudmila, by putting them on a barge and setting them adrift on the Dniepr.

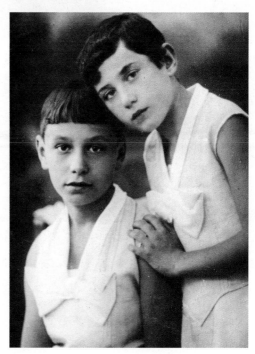

'Thank you, Comrade Stalin, for our Happy Childhood.' Lenina (*right*) and an unidentified friend at Verkhne-Dneprovsk in 1938.

Captain Alexander Vasin, 1942. Soon after proposing to Lenina his car ran over a mine near Smolensk and his leg had to be amputated using a wood-saw.

Boris's brother Yakov Bibikov in his Air Force Lieutenant-General's uniform, 1970s.

Lenina (*left*) and an unidentified friend, Moscow, late 1940s.

A rare photograph of
Lyudmila at the orphanage
of Saltykovka, near Moscow,
in 1949, in between
operations at the Botkin
hospital in Moscow to
repair her crippled leg.

'I grew wings.' Lyudmila (*far right*) with her Moscow theatrical friends,
waiting at Moscow's Vnukovo airport for the French actor Gerard Philipe
to arrive from Peking, autumn 1957. He inscribed a copy of *Le Rouge et le
Noir*: 'Pour Lyudmila, en souvenir du soleil de Moscou.'

Lyudmila on holiday
in the Russian
North, 1965.

Karl Marx's great grandson Charles Languet visits the Institute of Marxism and Leninism; Lyudmila (*middle*) interprets.

Lyudmila (*right*) with her friend Galina Golovitser in Lyudmila's room on Starokonushenny Pereulok, 1962. The photo was taken by the East German husband of a ballet-dancer friend.

The British embassy staff, autumn 1958. Mervyn Matthews is in the back row (*middle*), in grey Astrakhan fur hat. Note ambassador Sir Patrick Reilly's black Labrador, in pride of place.

'Adventures can be wonderful things.' Mervyn in the diplomatic apartment on Sadovaya-Samotechnaya in Moscow, 1958.

the north. Lenina was abandoned with a dozen other older children in a village and its neighbouring collective farm.

Lenina wasn't much help on the farm because her hands were covered in sores, rubbed raw from digging and now painful and infected. One of the farm workers showed her how to drive a horse and cart full of produce from the fields to the barns, which was her job for the harvest season. One of the village women, an Armenian, offered Lenina extra food if she would scrub the wooden floors of her cottage clean with a brick of carbolic soap and a knife, and do odd jobs around the house. Lenina, as she told the story, cramped her fingers on her kitchen table to the length of the short, blunt knife the woman had given her to scrape the floor, and motioned rinsing her bandaged hands in the hot, soapy water.

As Lenina scrubbed and the woman cooked for her family, they talked. The woman told Lenina that she had been evacuated from Moscow. Lenina in turn told the woman her story, and how she too had relatives in Moscow. The house-wife made Lenina an offer. If Lenina would go with her younger daughter to Moscow with some dried fruit for the market, she would buy the train tickets, which because of the war were only on sale to people with a Moscow registration stamp in their passports. Lenina, desperate to find her family now that she had been parted from Lyud-mila, agreed. A week later, she and the woman's daughter, loaded with eight bulging suitcases tied together in pairs with strips of cloth and stuffed to bursting with dried apricots, found space on a Moscow train and made their way, taking a detour far to the east of the Volga basin to avoid the fighting, to the capital.

At Kursky Station the girl's Armenian cousins came to meet her and took the suitcases away from Lenina. They waved goodbye and disappeared into the Metro. Lenina walked the six miles to Krasnaya Presnya Street and found her grand-mother's old apartment from memory. It was empty. But some neighbours, who remembered Lenina from her last trip four years before, told her that her grandmother and cousins had been evacuated. They dug out the telephone number for where Lenina's uncle Yakov was living and went to the public telephone in the street to call him. An hour later he arrived in his Air Force staff car and took Lenina to his apartment near Taganskaya Square.

Yakov was Boris's elder brother. He shared Boris's intense stare, his charisma, and his love of womanizing. In old age he became heavy set and jowly, but Yakov's official retirement photograph, taken in 1969, shows a proud man, the chest of his Lieutenant-General's uniform covered with medals. He looks a proud servant of the Motherland.

Like Boris, Yakov had excelled at school, been inspired by the Revolution and all that it stood for, and had become a committed Bolshevik. While his brother made a career in the Party, Yakov went into the fledgling Soviet Air Force. By the time of Boris's arrest in 1937, Yakov was a Major-General, serving on the staff of Marshal Vasiliy Blucher, an old Civil War hero, commander of Russia's Far East military district headquartered in Khabarovsk, near Russia's Pacific coast. By October 1938 the Purge was spreading to the military. Blucher, an old comrade-in-arms of Trotsky's, had a keen sense of how the political wind was blowing. He summoned his three deputies to his office and ordered them to go to Moscow at once, giving no explanation. Yakov went home immediately and, without stopping to pack, ordered his heavily pregnant wife Varvara on to the next train west.

Blucher was arrested a few days later, and died at the hands of the NKVD interrogators in the Lubyanka. Varvara gave birth on the train, but by leaving for Moscow the family successfully lost itself in the convoluted bureaucracy of the Purge. It was Stalin's strange logic that millions of innocent family members of enemies of the people were arrested, while some of the Party's top cadres survived the imprisonment of their closest relatives. The wife of Stalin's Foreign Minister, Vyacheslav Molotov, was sent to the camps, and the wife of the dictator's personal secretary Alexander Poskrebyshev was shot. 'We will find you a new wife,' Stalin told his secretary nonchalantly.

So Yakov survived, and by 1942 had been made a Lieutenant-General. He lived in a large apartment in a handsome building for senior military officers. Varvara and her young child were hostile to the new arrival. Their reaction was perhaps a rational one. Harbouring the daughter of an executed and disgraced Party member put them in terrible danger. Nevertheless, Yakov insisted that his niece stay, and Varvara was grudgingly grateful for extra help with household chores. Lenina became a kind of unpaid servant, but she was at least comfortable and with her family. Yakov told Lenina about her uncle Isaac's death. He also told her he'd had no news of Boris or Martha, and sternly warned her not to talk to anyone about what had happened to them. As the brother of a traitor, only good luck, and the war, had saved Yakov himself from a similar fate.

Lenina told the family how she had lost touch with her sister Lyudmila in the chaos of retreat. Varvara told Lenina, meanly, that she should not give herself any false hopes of ever finding her sister again.

Yakov secured Lenina a job as a radio operator at the Khodinskoye airfield in the suburbs of northern Moscow, where test pilots would fly the new Yak fighters rolling off the production lines of the Dynamo factory, where Isaac had once worked, as well as from the Lavochkin Construction Bureau, where Yakov was in charge of military procurement. She was good at the job, and the pilots liked her. They would sing duets with her over the radio waves as they flew their test flights. To the end of her life, she remembered her call sign – 223305 – and got indignant if anyone suggested she'd forgotten it. 'I'll forget my own name before I forget my call sign,' she joked. In the evenings, with her uncle's help, Lenina wrote requests for information about Lyudmila and delivered them by hand to the Ministry of Popular Enlightenment, responsible for the Soviet Union's orphanages. But there was no news.

Lenina spent the next two years with Yakov's family. Like the years in Verkhne-Dneprovsk, it was a sort of peace. The tide of the war had turned after Hitler's Sixth Army was surrounded and destroyed at Stalingrad, and the Red Army was beginning to advance westwards.

In the summer of 1944, as the fighting crossed into Poland and the Allies landed in Normandy, Yakov told Lenina he had a job for her. A colleague of Yakov's, also a general, had heard that his son, with whom he had lost touch when the child was evacuated along with thousands of others from besieged Leningrad, was in a camp for displaced children in the Urals. Lenina was to fly to the camp with the necessary paperwork and bring the boy back to Moscow.

A week later Lenina was on a military flight to Molotov, now Perm, with the Russian crew of a Lend-Lease American Douglas transport plane. She wore her Air Force uniform, with her fore-and-aft *pilotka* cap jauntily perched on the back of her head. It was the first time she had ever flown.

In Perm the director of the local aircraft factory, a personal friend of Yakov's, had arranged for an old two-seater Polikarpov fighter to take her to the displaced children's camp to pick up the general's son. The camp's name was Solikamsk.

The battered little Polikarpov bounced to a halt on a makeshift airfield on the outskirts of the town, and Lenina and the young pilot walked together through the muddy streets to the main orphanage, an ornate pre-revolutionary red-brick building surrounded by a low wall. In the playground hundreds of ragged children were running around. As

Lenina walked through the gates and up to the front door of the building she noticed a lame child lopsidedly running towards her.

'*Tak tse moya sestra Lina!*' shouted the child, in Ukrainian. 'That's my sister Lina!'

Lyudmila was toothless, her belly distended by hunger. As Lenina fell to her knees to embrace her sister, Lyudmila started crying and asking for food.

'*Yisti khoche! Yisti khoche!*' – 'I want food!'

Lenina couldn't speak. The pilot looked on in amazement, not understanding what had happened. Unable to separate the two sobbing sisters, he hustled them both inside and into the director's office.

The director, a woman, broke down in tears when Lenina told her she had found her sister. She released the four-year-old boy Lenina had come for, but they had to wait agonizing hours as the pilot put a call through to his boss in Perm to ask him to call Moscow for permission to take Lyudmila back to Moscow. Someone reached Yakov by phone – no mean feat in wartime Russia – and he pulled strings. Permission was granted. Lenina flew back to Perm with two vomiting children squeezed on her lap in the gunner's seat of the plane.

They stayed the night with a colleague of the aircraft factory director, who lived in one room of a communal apartment. Lenina noticed that the children kept getting up in the night to go to the toilet. In the morning she was woken by sounds of outrage from the communal kitchen. The children had eaten everything from the neighbours' food cupboards, including a huge pot full of chicken and rice. Even as they left for the airport to catch a transport plane back to Moscow, Lyudmila and the boy began a massive bout of diarrhoea. Their malnourished bodies couldn't cope with so much rich food.

Back in Moscow there was no room in Yakov's apartment for the sick child, but he made sure that Lyudmila was sent to

a centre for displaced Party members' children in the Danilovsky Monastery. All the food was Lend-Lease aid from
America, an unimaginable luxury. There was tinned Campbell's tomato soup, corned beef, tuna and condensed milk.
Most impressive of all were giant cans of Hershey's chocolate
powder, which Mila found so beautiful that she still remembers them fondly. Inside the tin lid was a seal of gold foil,
which she would watch the hospital cooks reverently cut
open. Nestling in the dark brown chocolate was a Bakelite
spoon for measuring out the portions. Lyudmila felt deep
wonder at seeing packaging so perfectly designed – and the
idea of a disposable spoon was simply incomprehensible. To
her it seemed that such a tin of chocolate could only come
from the magic other world of her dreams.

7

Mila

We were born to make a fairytale become real,
To overcome space and time,
Stalin gave us steel wings in place of arms,
And instead of hearts, a fiery engine.
'The Aviator's March', popular 1930s song

Mila quickly put on weight, though her body was still deformed by tuberculosis. She spent six months at the Danilovsky Monastery, avidly reading big coloured American children's comic books. She was ten years old. She had survived.

In the spring of 1945 she was transferred to a special home for sick children at Malakhovka, a short ride on the *electrichka* suburban railway from Moscow, where she began her recovery in earnest. Her belly was still distended from starvation – 'it stuck out further than her nose,' Lenina remembers – and her left leg was withered. But she was unfailingly cheerful, singing songs in the yard and playing hopscotch with the other children. Mila would volunteer for the food checking rota, in which children stood in the kitchens and watched the cooks open up the big tins of American corned beef to make sure that every gram of it went into their soup. Despite the wonderful American food, she was never to lose the psychological scars of starvation. 'Childhood hunger stays with you your whole life,' she told me. 'You can never ever feel truly full again.'

All in all, among a generation which had survived the famines, the Purges and the war, Lenina and Lyudmila could count themselves among the lucky. They had their lives, and each other. All around them were those who had lost much more. Perhaps that is why the sisters were not torn apart by experiences so traumatic that it seems, to us, almost inconceivable to have survived. Mila had lived when the Spanish children with her had died; Lenina found her sister by pure chance when thousands of children never did. That was already plenty to be grateful for.

Also, undoubtedly, Lenina and Lyudmila's survival had something to do with the natural resilience of children, their ability to live in the moment. Blind to the wider world, they lived their lives in terms of the here and now, which is perhaps the most powerful weapon there is against despair. And, for Mila at least, there was the great, shielding ignorance of the past she had lost, buried in the hazy half-memories of childhood – which made the reality of prison and orphanage a given, something to be endured but at least not regretted, or understood. She had been scarred, physically and mentally, but not broken. The Hershey's chocolate and corned beef healed her body, and her spirit was intact, and ready to take on the world.

Soon after Lyudmila's return from Solikamsk, a young tank captain named Alexander Vasin paid a visit to the Bibikov apartment on Taganskaya Square. Yakov's wife Varvara was his aunt. Lenina was there, and shyly greeted her distant cousin. Alexander – Sasha – was healthy and handsome, with a winning smile and a loud laugh. He looked splendid in his olive-green uniform, with breeches and soft officers' boots, epaulettes and crew-cut blond hair.

Lenina and Sasha had met briefly in 1937 during Lenina's first visit to Moscow, just after her father's arrest. Sasha joked how pretty his young cousin had become. Sasha offered to see her to the Metro as she left for work. Half jokingly, he flirted and tickled her on the Metro escalator, saying that he would like to marry her. They met again a few days later, on their first date, in Krasnopresnensky Park, near the Zoo. He took her to a café in the park, the first time in her life Lenina had ever been to a restaurant of any sort. Thirty-six years later, after Sasha's death of a heart attack, his colleagues arranged his wake, by coincidence, in the same restaurant.

After two weeks of courtship, Sasha had to go back to his unit. He proposed marriage to Lenina before he left, and she accepted.

Three days after he had left Moscow, as Sasha's car neared the front line west of Smolensk, it hit an anti-tank mine. His leg was shredded and had to be amputated at the knee with a wood saw. He was flown to one of the giant military hospitals in Ivanovo to recover. From there, Sasha wrote Lenina a strange letter. He told his fiancée that he had been in a fire and was burned and disfigured, and that she should find someone else to marry. When she got the letter Lenina ran to her uncle. Yakov, pulling strings, arranged a seat for Lenina on an American Douglas transport plane to Ivanovo, and instructed the crew to prepare to bring a wounded man back with them to Moscow. Lenina found the hospital and as she ran up the steps she saw Sasha standing in his underwear on crutches in the hospital yard, not burned but missing a leg. Lenina brought him back to Moscow and they were married three months later. She was nineteen, he was twenty-six. Strangely, after a marriage that lasted nearly four decades, Lenina cannot now remember which leg he had lost.

I remember Sasha as an overwhelmingly masculine presence, strong-jawed and decisive, with an explosive laugh and a manner which brooked no nonsense. He was in many ways a perfect Soviet man, bluff and cheerful, always seeing the good even when confronted, as every Soviet citizen constantly was, with incompetence and ugliness.

In many ways, I think, he was the opposite of his young sister-in-law Lyudmila. She was ambitious and uncompromising, always seeking to shape the world around her. He was content with simple pleasures: the respect of his friends and colleagues, his small apartment, the dacha which he built with his own hands from scrounged planks and bricks. He also knew the power of his good looks. It was as though Sasha felt that his virility was a gift which it was his duty to share among a generation of women where men were in short supply. But he never gave Lenina, who was terribly jealous, any reason to suspect infidelity. 'Maybe he was unfaithful,' she used to say of him in approval. 'But he made sure I never, ever, knew a thing.'

Moscow in the closing months of the 'Great Patriotic War' was a city close to exhaustion. Far to the west, the Red Army fought through eastern Prussia to beat the Western Allies to Berlin. But back home, the women and children waged a more banal war against hunger and cold among the ruins of a country wrecked by the war effort. They worried about their men at the front, their fear of terrible news made all the more poignant by the imminent certainty of victory.

The streets were filled with men in uniform, the evenings were dark because street lighting was, like everything else, rationed. Life was suspended pending the war's end, everyone concentrating on survival, not daring to think of the future. Daily existence revolved around little cardboard ration cards and rumours. Varvara and her daughter stood for hours in queues at street corners on the promise of an imminent delivery of food; Lenina scrounged milk from maternity hospitals to take to her always-ravenous little sister Lyudmila. In the evenings Lenina and Sasha sat by their big radio listening to the announcer reeling off strings of Soviet victories in places with German-sounding names, and felt righteous and pleased.

Lenina was selfishly happy that her Sasha was alive, unlike the sweethearts of so many of her girlfriends at the Khodinskoye airfield. The young couple were allocated a tiny apartment in the basement of a pre-revolutionary mansion on Herzen Street. It was cramped and the small windows were high in the wall, but it was Lenina's first home since childhood, and she was determined to make it comfortable for her new little family.

The kitchen became Lenina's kingdom, and food was the currency of her love. A lifetime after she began to cook for herself in the tiny stove on Herzen Street, I would sit in my aunt's kitchen on Frunzenskaya Embankment, and she would feed me the same dishes she'd first learned to cook for Sasha – sour cabbage soup, pea soup, beef cutlets and fried potatoes. As I ate, she'd watch me closely for signs of appreciation. For both Lenina and my mother, food and happiness were to be closely intertwined.

In January 1945, shortly before her eleventh birthday, Lyudmila was deemed to have recovered sufficiently to be discharged from the children's home at Malakhovka. But there wasn't space for her in Lenina's one-room Herzen Street apartment. Lenina was already pregnant with her first child, and Sasha's sister Tamara was sleeping on a folding bed in the kitchen. Lenina called her aunt Varvara, but she also refused to take in Lyudmila – 'Another scrounger on the phone,' she told her husband when he asked who was calling. So Sasha helped find Lyudmila a place in an orphanage at Saltykovka, twenty-five miles outside Moscow. Lyudmila took with her a single cardboard suitcase filled with American Red Cross clothes, some children's books, and a doll.

Saltykovka is a pleasant, sleepy little place. My mother and I went to visit on a dusty summer afternoon in 1988. We took the *elektrichka*, as my mother had often done as a child, from Kursky Station. The platform at Saltykovka was a single strip of concrete, and after the train had clanked away down its narrow canyon cut through the birch forest the only sounds were of birds and the distant revving of an engine.

'It hasn't changed at all,' my mother announced as we walked, arm in arm, along the single unpaved street which ran through the village. The wooden houses were ramshackle, painted green or dull yellow, and at the end of the street stood the grand orphanage gates. Picket fences, leaning at drunken angles, framed tiny allotments and the houses were half-hidden by outsize sunflowers and jasmine bushes running wild.

The old buildings of the orphanage where my mother had spent most of her childhood stood on the edge of the forest. The current generation of orphans was away at summer camp; the place was deserted. It had the melancholy feel of children's institutions when the children are away, an air of regimented jollity, and the poignancy of children's loneliness.

Yet Mila was happy at Saltykovka, as happy as anywhere else she could remember. She went to her first normal school, and loved it. Her years of enforced idleness in hospital beds had taught her to love books, and Lenina would bring her novels from Yakov's library, which she read voraciously. The schoolmistresses were strict and dedicated, pedagogues of the old school, drilling their pupils in correct Russian grammar and the works of Pushkin. On Sundays, soldiers would come and take the children to a nearby cinema in big army trucks.

Mila remembers sitting for hours on the lap of the elderly peasant woman who stoked the bath-house furnace as she combed out the lice from the children's hair. One of the teachers, Maria Nikolaevna Kharlamova, spent hours of her own time coaching my mother in Russian literature and history.

When my mother and I knocked on Maria Nikolaevna's door she recognized my mother immediately, and burst into tears.

'Milochka! Can it be you?' she kept repeating as they embraced.

Maria Nikolaevna fussed over tea and home-made jam for us both, then as we sat at her kitchen table she hunted through piles of old papers to retrieve a little envelope of local newspaper clippings she had kept on Lyudmila – news of her admission to Moscow University, news of her prize-winning 'Red Diploma' on graduation.

'I was so proud of you!' Maria Nikolaevna whispered, staring across the rickety table at her star pupil with all the satisfaction of an elderly mother. 'I was proud of all of you.'

Mila also spent months at a time away from Saltykovka, enduring painful operations on her leg and hip in the Botkin Hospital in central Moscow. The deformities wreaked by her childhood tuberculosis had left one leg sixteen centimetres shorter than the other, and when she was fifteen the Botkin surgeons had to break the bone and put weights on Lyudmila's leg to make it grow longer.

When she was allowed back from the oppressive silence of the hospital wards to the clamour of Saltykovka, Mila threw herself into games and group activities. She was always a leader, a Young Pioneer 'Activist', a leader of the Communist version of the Scouts or Guides, with a special badge on her white shirt to show her status. 'In place of arms, we have steel wings; In place of a heart, a fiery engine,' went a stirring song of the time, and Mila, despite her disability, tried hard to live up to the ideal.

Mila was outspoken, too, and thoughtful. Both were dangerous habits, even in school. One day shortly after the end of the war, during an obligatory classroom reading of the editorial page of *Pionerskaya Pravda* (the children's version of the great Party newspaper), the teacher recited the new anti-

American rhetoric. Mila put up her hand in the approved Pioneer fashion – fingers pointing straight up to the ceiling, elbow on the desk – to ask a question.

'But the Americans helped us a lot during the war, didn't they?' she asked.

The teacher was horrified and sent Mila immediately to the headmaster, who hastily convened a session of the *druzina*, a supposedly informal children's court which was the junior equivalent of a Party meeting. Dutifully assembled, Mila's classroom colleagues pronounced that she must be more attentive to political education, and formally censured her. It was not the only time she would face such a hypocrites' court.

There was a burning will in that crippled little body, even then. Later, she wrote to her future husband, my father, of her refusal to compromise, to accept the realities of Soviet life. 'I want life to show me in practice the strength of my principles,' she wrote. 'I want it, I want it, I want it.' In a world where the most her contemporaries aspired to was to get by, to do the best they could with what they had, Mila believed that her will could conquer the world. The poet Yevgeny Yevtushenko called the anti-hero of his and Mila's generation 'Comrade Kompromis Kompromisovich' in sardonic tribute to the men and women who negotiated their way through the hypocrisy and disappointments of Soviet life by a million small compromises. Mila was not one of them.

Despite her crippled leg, Mila became skipping champion of her class. At Saltykovka she organized class lice checks and hikes, singing sessions and games of hopscotch. When she visited her sister on Herzen Street she'd throw herself into the street's hopscotch championships, chalking the boxes on the asphalt with the neighbours' children. Lyudmila almost always emerged as the winner, even on one occasion when she had to compete with a broken arm in a plaster cast.

*   *   *

News of victory came sonorously over the radio on 9 May 1945. Lenina heard the radio announcement at the Dynamo factory. She remembers feeling infinite relief, and an overwhelming weariness. A few days later there was a parade of German prisoners down the Garden Ring road, and Lenina went to the top of Herzen Street to see the enemy at first hand. The crowds watched in silence. She noticed the strong smell of the leather of the German prisoners' boots and webbing. They walked in good order, expressionless. The prisoners were followed ostentatiously by trucks spraying the street to wash away the contagion of the Fascist presence. Fewer than one in ten of the prisoners would ever return to their homeland.

Yakov moved his family into a larger, more stylish apartment. He had acquired a trophy Mercedes looted from Germany on a trip otherwise devoted to dismantling German rocketry laboratories and shipping them back wholesale to the Lavochkin Construction Bureau in Moscow. The Mercedes was a huge black shining beast, the mark of giddying rank. Yakov would drive around Moscow giving lifts to young girls in his car, a pastime which Varvara eventually discovered and which threw her into violent frenzies of jealousy. Yakov's new job as head of the Soviet Union's fledgling rocket programme, staffed by captured German scientists, opened a world of privilege to his family, which they were in no hurry to share with their poor relatives. For Lenina and Lyudmila, the drabness of wartime austerity continued for years after the end of the war. But there were plenty of bright parades full of gaudy paper slogans and banners, and a great sense of pride and achievement. Whenever Lenina and Sasha, medals arrayed on his chest, would walk with their new baby Nadia it seemed that she had, at last, escaped the wreckage of her childhood.

*   *   *

Boris Bibikov was due to be released from prison in June 1947, according to his official sentence of 'ten years without the right of correspondence'. Despite the slim chance that he could have survived the camps and the war, Lenina continued to hope that he would return.

Even after what they had been through, the Bibikov family retained a naïve faith in the essential probity and rightness of the Soviet system. Like tens of millions of other relatives of the victims of the Purges, they believed that their loved one had suffered an injustice which was exceptional. Boris's mother Sophia wrote letters to the Interior Ministry asking for news of her son in the unshakeable belief that justice would eventually prevail. For years she received no answer, yet the faith remained. But Boris's release date came and went with no news.

In the winter of 1948, Lenina, pregnant with her second child, went to stay for a few months with Sasha's mother Praskovia in a village twenty miles from Kaluga, in central Russia where fresh milk was plentiful and where the village women could look after young Nadia as Lenina waited for the new arrival. Sasha was studying law in Moscow; every Saturday night he'd take the train to Kaluga with a battered bicycle he'd repaired himself, cycle (with one leg) to the village, spend the day with his family, and cycle back in the evening to catch the Moscow train.

One day Sasha brought a letter postmarked KarLag. It had no envelope; instead it was folded into a triangle and tucked into itself, in the manner of the time. It was from Martha. She wrote that she had been released from prison the previous spring and was living close to the camp under 'administrative detention'. She had a newborn baby boy called Viktor. The child's father was a priest, she said, whose life she'd saved in the camp. But he'd been released and gone back to his own family in the Siberian region of the Altai.

Now, Martha said, she expected to receive permission to

leave Kazakhstan soon, but wondered where she could go since she had no passport. Though she didn't spell it out, Lenina knew what her mother meant – her travel documents marked her as a political prisoner, she was not allowed to live closer than 101 kilometres to a major city. There was precious little room for her in Lenina's tiny apartment in Moscow, but Sasha's mother Praskovia insisted: Lenina must do everything she could to get Martha to Moscow. Lenina wrote a letter telling her mother to disregard the 101 kilometres and come to live with them in the capital as soon as she was able. Sasha posted the letter from Moscow the next day.

The locomotive pulled slowly into Kursky Station belching soot and steam. Because of a shortage of rolling stock the train was made up of cattle wagons instead of carriages. Martha hadn't been allowed to buy a ticket on the normal train from Semipalatinsk because of her lack of papers, so she came on an unscheduled train full of passport-less human driftwood like herself, sending a brief telegram to her daughter as she embarked warning of her arrival. The train disgorged streams of bedraggled travellers, most of them ex-convicts, exhausted and stinking after their five-day journey.

Lenina's abiding memory of her mother was as a fashionable Party housewife. Now, as she staggered down the platform, Martha looked like a beggar woman. She was filthy and lousy and wore a convict's black padded jacket. She had no luggage except for a dirty bundle of clothes. She was alone.

Martha barely smiled as she saw her daughter, heavily pregnant with her second child, waddling towards her. They embraced, and wept. Lenina asked what had happened to her mother's new baby. 'Eh, it died,' Martha said, dismissively, and pushed off into the crowd heading towards the exit. They rode the Metro in silence to Barrikadnaya Street, where Lenina took her mother straight to a public bathhouse near the Zoo to get her cleaned up and de-loused.

At home that evening in the basement apartment on Herzen Street with Lenina, Sasha and their daughter Nadia, Martha seemed to recede into a kind of stupefied shock. She complained that the bed they had made for her was too soft and that her granddaughter was crying too loudly. By the end of the evening, Lenina was in tears, being comforted by Sasha as his mother-in-law paced, sleepless, in the kitchen.

The next day Lenina took the *elektrichka* to Saltykovka to fetch Lyudmila. When the two girls arrived at Herzen Street, Martha was waiting impatiently by the apartment door. The apartment was at the end of a long corridor, and the first glimpse Martha had of her younger daughter was a crippled silhouette at the end of the hall. Martha called out Lyudmila's name, and howled as the little girl ran lopsidedly towards her. Lyudmila remembered that awful wail all her life – the wail of a woman who had last seen her daughter as a plump, happy toddler and then lost her for eleven years, only to find her again as a hobbling, emaciated fourteen-year-old.

Martha held her for a long time, weeping. Mila, when she recalls the meeting now, shakes her head as she searches for any trace of the emotions she felt at the time. But she felt nothing. 'I probably hugged her. I probably said "mother". But I can't remember.'

For Mila, the word 'mother' had become little more than an abstraction. It had no place in the world of orphans in which she had spent her childhood. She had no memory at all of her parents, except for the one image of the night of her mother's arrest and the ghost of a memory of her father. She had written a dutiful letter to her mother in Karlager as soon as Lenina had told her that their mother was alive and well. But the assurances of devotion in the letter were, in truth, just an invention. Mila really had no idea, except from books, what a real mother was like, or how one should feel about her.

When she left in the late afternoon to return to Saltykovka,

Lyudmila's overwhelming emotion was gratitude for the large meal Martha had cooked for them. Years later, she wrote to her fiancé that she had wept when she first heard that her mother was alive, but had ruthlessly suppressed her tears as a sign of weakness.

Martha never became a real mother to Lyudmila. The bond broken in December 1937 would not be re-formed. Mila often came to Lenina's apartment, but quickly found she couldn't bear Martha's brooding manner and flashes of anger. Within months of Martha's return to Moscow, they slipped into a dutiful rhythm. Most weekends, Martha and Lenina would come out to Saltykovka. Lenina would collect her sister from the orphanage for a walk; Martha, still officially a non-person, would wait by the village pond for her daughters. They'd walk and talk, and Martha would hand over the sweets and biscuits she'd bought or made, which Mila would share with the other children.

Lyudmila loved her mother 'like a dog loves the person who feeds it,' she told me on a hot summer night at my home in Istanbul. 'I understood the Party, Stalin, the People. But I never knew what the word "mother" meant.'

Though her mother was alive, Mila remained, in her heart, an orphan. But long before Lyudmila became a mother herself, she was obsessed with the idea of motherhood, and what kind of mother she would be herself. She would often write to my future father about their unborn children, and the awful fear she had of losing her children as Martha had lost hers.

'All night I dreamt I was carrying a small boy in my arms, our son,' Mila wrote to my father in 1964. 'He was very gentle and affectionate. But the road was very difficult and long, it went up and down and into underground labyrinths. Carrying him was very hard but I couldn't leave behind such a wonderful being in whom everything was yours, even his voice, nose, hair, fingers. For some reason we came to the old Moscow State University building on Mokhovaya Street and an old man was choosing the best children out of a crowd and my boy was one of them. Everyone was happy that their children were being chosen, but I was crying bitterly because I didn't believe they would return him to me.'

Mila was filled with the need to protect her own children, even before we were born. But her mother Martha seemed, at times, consumed with an irrational hatred of hers. There were moments when, irritated by something Mila had done or said, Martha snapped at her that she was an 'orphanage cripple'. Hysterical, she would call her elder daughter 'Jew-spawn' and swear in the most filthy prison language she could summon. At other times she lapsed into hysterical displays of self-pity and affection, clutching at her children in a torrent of tears.

Martha had gone mad in the camps. That much seems obvious from her behaviour after her return from Kazakhstan. But such was the general fear and ignorance of psychiatry then that no one thought that she needed treatment, and the family suffered her self-hating craziness in silence. 'Psychiatrists were worse than the NKVD to us,' Lenina says. Martha always had a vicious streak. Life in the camps had turned her rage at the world into an uncontrollable force.

Martha, who had been rejected by her father and abandoned her sister, in her turn rejected her own daughters. It was as though she believed that by meting out hatred and extinguishing love and hope in those around her she could somehow revenge herself on the world which had treated her so cruelly. She seemed to be driven by some inner perversity to create a world of spite around herself.

Yet at the same time she was capable of acts of great generosity, her old, better self fighting through all the bitterness. When I was born, in 1971, Martha wrote to congratulate Mila, and told her that she'd opened a bank account for me, and was earning money by cooking lunches for her local parish priest which she'd faithfully deposit in the account. When she came to visit us in 1976, she brought the deposit book to show Lyudmila. It was a kind of peace offering, a way of atoning for her daughter's own loveless childhood. When Martha died Lenina couldn't find the deposit book. She suspected Martha's Ukrainian relatives of stealing it. But I think of Martha standing, day after day, by a stove cooking cutlets and soup, thinking of the child in London she had met for only a few weeks, and then lumbering down to the post office to deposit her kopecks for her grandson.

Lyudmila was spared the worst of her mother's demons, seeing her only at weekends. Lenina was less lucky. She earned a few extra rubles by donating her copious breast milk to a hospital for abandoned infants on the other side of Herzen Street, and she managed to get Martha a job as a cook at the hospital, which kept her out of the house for most of the day. But at night she would sit in the kitchen and mutter evilly at her daughter. Martha would ask Lenina sarcastically why she had married 'a cripple instead of a general' and try to persuade Sasha and Lenina to leave each other. She flirted openly with Sasha, provoking furious fights with her daughter. Several times Martha attacked Lenina with a knife; once, Lenina broke her mother's finger trying to restrain her after a hysterical battle which left half of Lenina's prized crockery smashed. At night Martha would weep and curse Boris as a 'treacherous fool' for having brought down such misery on her, saying she never wanted to see him again and hoped he was dead.

'We tolerated it all,' remembers Lenina. 'But how much blood she drank! She lived off our suffering.'

It took months for the story of how Martha had spent the previous decade to emerge, and even then the stories were spat out, accompanied by cynical comments. Martha had been convicted within weeks of her arrest. She seems to have had some kind of nervous breakdown under interrogation, and confessed to whatever she was told, including to her husband's guilt. She was given ten years' hard labour for being an 'accessory to anti-Soviet activity'. Martha and several hundred other women prisoners were put on cattle trucks and sent to a remote railhead in Kazakhstan. There, they were marched across the steppe to Semipalatinsk, a primitive camp of tents, and put to work building their own prison from rough timber and barbed wire.

A friend of my wife's family, the son of a Gulag prisoner, once told me about how his father had survived in the camps. Forget your past life as though it was a dream, the old man had said, give up hope about getting back, empty your mind of anger and regret and dissolve in the present, appreciate the joys of camp life, a hot stove, soap at the *banya*, the watery Siberian winter dawns and the silence of the forest, the discovery of a clump of cranberries in the *taiga*, a small kindness of one's cellmate. But it took a strong personality, maybe even superhuman strength, to actually live like that, and most men and women who faced the test were destroyed by it.

Martha almost never spoke of her life in the camp. She told Lenina only one story, one so cruel and grotesque that she had little desire to hear any more. One autumn, before the war, the camp's cows were calving. After every calf was born, Martha had to gather up the steaming placenta and caul in a bucket and throw them in a barrel outside, and cover them with carbolic acid to prevent the rats from eating them. Martha went inside to attend another calving, and when she came out she found two men, little more than skeletons, writhing in agony by the refuse barrel. They were newly arrived convicts from another camp, all former priests, now more dead than alive. They had crawled to the cowshed to eat the raw placentas. Martha pulled one of the men into the shed and fed him fresh milk to counteract the carbolic acid. He survived. The other died where he lay. Later, after they were both released, Martha lived with the man she had saved; he was the father of the child who died before Martha returned to Moscow.

After the final calving that night Martha had to help collect the bodies of the convicts who had died on arrival. She and another woman loaded them on to a cart, which Martha then drove alone into the steppe to the camp's remote burial ground. Martha told Lenina that steppe jackals got wind of the dead meat in the wagon and chased her. To save herself, Martha told her daughter, she had thrown one of the bodies to the wild dogs.

Martha finished her sentence in early 1948, but was not allowed to return home. First she was released into 'administrative detention', which meant that she was forced to stay in a village of ex-convicts not far from the camp. She and the priest, whose name she never told Lenina, created a new life for themselves in a log cabin on the outskirts of KarLag, tending a tiny vegetable plot and doing odd jobs for the camp's personnel.

She almost never spoke of her camp 'husband' or of their child Viktor, who Martha said had died just before her return to Moscow. But Lenina always suspected that Martha had given the child away after her priest had left her to return to his own family, handing over the infant to local doctors or an orphanage. Lenina never cited any evidence for this belief; she just suspects that it is so, for no other reason than 'I see it with my heart.' In Moscow in 2007 she encountered a local prosecutor called Viktor Shcherbakov; but after close examination by my aunt the man turned out to be not her long-lost half-brother but a stranger who shared her mother's surname. After a few days' reflection Lenina decided, at the age of eighty-two, not to pursue Viktor, the little boy lost in 1948. 'What if I find him and he's just a bum?' she asked. 'He doesn't have Boris's blood, which made us all great. He has Martha's blood, and we don't need any more of that.'

Instead of a normal passport, Martha was given a piece of

paper confirming her release and a special passport restricting her from living in or near a major city for life. The Soviet Union of the 1940s abounded with such people, whose freedom of residence was limited – they were condemned to a life as a non-person because of the fatal stamp in their passport.

Luckily for Martha, her son-in-law Sasha was already working as a junior lawyer in the Ministry of Justice. He saved her by a loophole in the paperwork. Martha's family name appeared in the prison paperwork as 'Shcherbakova', the Russianized, female version of her surname. But on her birth certificate she was 'Shcherbak', the neuter Ukrainian spelling. Sasha convinced his local police office to issue a passport to Martha Shcherbak, an innocent person with no police record and no official 'limit' on her existence. On paper, then, she was an upstanding Soviet citizen. Inside, it seemed to those around her, her soul had been shredded.

Most of the children of Lyudmila's orphanage finished their schooling at fourteen, and after a year's technical training in the sewing room at Saltykovka were sent to the textile mills of Ivanovo, 120 miles north of Moscow, to work as seamstresses, or to noxious chemical factories in central Asia. Lyudmila's teachers petitioned the local authorities to have her sent to another local school where she could study three more years and have a chance of applying to university. Permission came through, though Lyudmila had to earn her keep at the orphanage by teaching some of the younger classes and organizing amateur dramatics. This is where she first practised the emphatic pedagogical manner she has today, singing out instructions syllable by syllable as she drills classes of slightly terrified English students in the arcana of the Russian verb, brooking no nonsense or error during the class, but then gushing with unexpected emotion for years afterwards at her pupils' successes.

If Stalin had not died on 5 March 1953 of a brain

haemorrhage, my mother's life would have been very different. The news of the dictator's death was broken to the children at Saltykovka by the head teacher, near-hysterical with grief, and all the children burst into tears at the news. For many of the orphans, the avuncular, mustachioed great leader was the closest thing they had ever known to a real father. In Moscow, Lenina stood in the two-million-strong crowds at Stalin's funeral. She, too, wept genuine tears for the passing of Stalin, without ever thinking that this kindly, smiling man was responsible for taking her parents away from her.

With Stalin gone, Lyudmila's world tilted on its axis. She graduated from the Saltykovka school top of her class, with a near-perfect grade (she still remembers the mistake that cost her a perfect score: mistakenly putting a comma in the sentence 'hippopotamuses, and elephants'). Under Stalin, a place at a prestigious university would have been unthinkable for a child of an enemy of the people. Mila would probably have gone to a provincial teachers' training college, and spent her life as a schoolmistress.

But now Lenina dared to hope that the stain on her sister's record could be overlooked. She was now working as a copy editor of doctoral theses at the Institute of Jurisprudence, a job wangled for her by Sasha. Lenina found an acquaintance who knew the Rector of the History faculty of Moscow State University, and arranged a meeting to lobby for Lyudmila's admission. She was lucky. The man was either simply kindhearted, or bore secret scars of his own from life under Stalin. As Lenina explained what had happened to her and her sister since their parents' arrest, the man broke down in tears. In September 1953 Lyudmila was admitted to read history at the Soviet Union's most prestigious university, housed in a vast, newly constructed Stalinist skyscraper on the Lenin Hills – a palace of Socialist learning with all of Moscow spread at its feet. When she heard the news, she says, 'I grew wings.'

*   *   *

Stalin's death also brought the hope that their father might be released from the Gulag. In 1954 the MVD, the latest incarnation of the NKVD, broke their seventeen-year silence on the fate of Boris Bibikov. In response to yet another letter from his mother they replied, in terse officialese, that Bibikov, B.L., had died of cancer in 1944 in a prison camp. The next year Sophia wrote a personal plea to Stalin's successor, the new Party General Secretary Nikita Khrushchev, that at least his name be cleared. The letter was duly entered into her late son's file.

'Respected Nikita Sergeyevich,' she wrote. 'I am turning to you as an old woman, a mother who had three sons, three Communists. Only one is left [Yakov], who serves in the ranks of our glorious Soviet Army. One [Isaac] died on the front in the Great Patriotic War, defending our Motherland. The other, Bibikov, Boris Lvovich, was arrested in 1937 as an enemy of the people and sentenced to ten years. His term should have expired in 1947.

'Nikita Sergeyevich, my son . . . I feel, I am sure that Boris was innocent, that there was a mistake. Is it not possible after eighteen years to sort the matter out, and rehabilitate him? I still cannot find the truth, to know, in the end, what happened. I am not a Party member, I am eighty years old, but I honestly raised my children to love their Motherland and to serve her faithfully. They gave her their knowledge, their health, their lives, for the joy of Communism, for peace on earth, so that their great Motherland would prosper . . . Dear Nikita Sergeyevich, I ask you to look into this matter as a Communist, and if my son is innocent, to rehabilitate him. Respectfully yours, Bibikova.'

Boris Bibikov's case was re-opened in 1955, one of the very first wave of the so-called rehabilitation investigations, judicial reviews of the victims of the Purges ordered by Khrushchev in the wake of his 'Secret Speech' denouncing Stalin at the Twentieth All-Union Party Congress. The task of reviewing Bibikov's case, and thousands like it, was a colossal bureaucratic undertaking. Detailed depositions were taken from dozens of witnesses who knew Boris Bibikov and the files of everyone involved in his case were closely studied. Ironically, the part of the file covering the rehabilitation investigation was almost three times longer than the spare seventy-nine documents it took to arrest, convict and kill him.

All those who were questioned about Boris's supposed counter-revolutionary activities pronounced him a sincere and dedicated Communist.

'I can only describe him positively; he gave himself wholly to the Party and to the life of the factory and had tremendous authority among the workers,' Ivan Kavitsky, Boris's deputy at the KhTZ, told the investigators. 'I know nothing of his anti-Soviet activities – on the contrary, he was a devoted Communist.'

'I never heard of any political deviation on [Bibikov's] part. People said he had been arrested as an enemy of the people but no one knew why,' said Lev Veselov, a factory accountant.

'I remember that my comrades in the management expressed surprise when he was arrested,' said the typist Olga Irzhavskaya.

On 22 February 1956, a closed session of the Supreme Court of the USSR produced a lengthy report, marked 'Secret', formally overturning the decision of the Military Collegium reached on 13 October 1937. A short note was sent to Boris's family announcing his rehabilitation, along with a death certificate. The 'cause of death' clause was left blank.

University was heaven for Lyudmila. She moved into a hall of residence at Stromynka Street in Sokolniki in north Moscow, where she shared a dormitory with fifteen other girls. In time she moved to her own room in the main university building itself, in its spreading grounds in the Lenin Hills. Her whole childhood had been spent in Soviet institutions, and the crowded social life of the university was a decent substitute for a family. She immediately made lifelong friends among the brightest of her generation. One was Yury Afanasiyev, a stocky, outspoken fellow historian who was to become one of the intellectual leading lights of Perestroika. Another contemporary was a former farm boy from Stavropol with a thick country accent and a total lack of cosmopolitan irony about Soviet life which Mila and her friends were quickly developing. He tried doggedly to court Lenina's friend, Nadia Mikhailova, who found him insufferably provincial and repeatedly turned him down. His name was Mikhail Sergeyevich Gorbachev. 'How can a descendent of a prosperous Moscow merchant marry a Stavropol truck driver?' Nadia used to joke.

Lyudmila learned good French and some basic Latin and German, and the art of outward conformity and hard work. Her essays, written in a perfect copperplate hand, are models of thoroughness and diligence. She was a creature of the Soviet system which had brought her up, with its emphasis on hearty communal activity and its complete lack of physical or mental privacy. The student life of the 1950s was filled with semi-voluntary after-class readings of Molière, nature rambles and amateur dramatics. But despite the constraints of ideology and communal life, Mila felt exhilaratingly free, at last, to explore the foreign and limitless world of literature. She read Dumas and Hugo, Zola and Dostoyevsky, the sentimental outpourings of Alexander Grin and the pastorals of Ivan Bunin. There, in books, music and theatre, she finally found her own private window on to a world big enough for her huge energies.

Lyudmila was popular. Her passion – or one of her many passions – was ballet. Lenina had introduced her to the Bolshoi theatre after Sasha had insisted that his young sister-in-law be given 'a start in life', and they would go as often as they could.

Lyudmila's love affair with the great nineteenth-century

theatre on Okhotny Ryad burgeoned during her student days. She and her friends would go several times a week to the Bolshoi, applauding wildly from the cheap seats at the end of every act and then keeping a cold vigil on the street outside Door 17 to greet the dancers as they came out with huge bunches of flowers. Valery Golovister, a thin and sensitive young man, the brother of Lyudmila's best girlfriend, Galya, was her closest male friend. They were both fervent balleto-manes. He seemed to have no interest in girls, despite his good looks, but those were innocent times and no one, at least not Lyudmila and her not-very-worldly girlfriends, thought to suspect him of the homosexuality he carefully concealed.

For Lyudmila and her friends, it was not enough just to see – they had to throw themselves into the performance, to adore the actors and dancers and weep over the libretto. They stood in shifts for tickets to the touring Comédie Française, the first foreign company to play in Moscow since before the war, and went to almost every one of the forty performances of the repertoire, which ranged from Molière's *Tartuffe* to Corneille's *Le Cid*. They whooped '*Vive la France!*' from the gallery, and threw flowers every night. Outside the theatre on the last night of the season, they were in the cheering crowd which followed the actors from Theatre Square to the National Hotel. KGB men in the crowd kicked Lyudmila viciously from behind with heavy boots, trying to subdue the girls' unseemly adulation of the visiting foreigners.

When Gérard Philippe, the greatest French actor of his generation, came to Moscow the next year for a film festival, Lyudmila's gang mobbed him. He chatted politely to his Russian fans and promised to return. After Philippe had returned to France, Mila and her friends had a whip-round and collected money for a present for their hero. One of the girls took the train to Palekh, a village famous for its minia-tures on lacquer boxes, and commissioned a portrait of Philippe as Julien Sorel in the film *Le Rouge et le Noir*. When the French Communists Elsa Triolet and Louis Aragon visited Moscow a few months later Lyudmila and four of her friends marched into the Hotel Moskva – a bold move, since the place housed foreigners and was crawling with KGB officers – and called Triolet from the lobby, explaining that they had a present they wanted her to take to Gérard Philippe in Paris. Mystified but impressed, Triolet came down to collect it and duly delivered the gift to Philippe when she returned. Madness, unthinkable madness to do such a thing just five years before. But the Khrushchev thaw had changed the rules, and Lyudmila and her friends tested the limits of the new world as far as they dared.

In *L'Humanité*, the French-language Communist daily which was the only French paper available to the Soviet public, a friend of Lyudmila's read that Gérard Philippe was in Peking on a cultural trip. For a lark – a dangerous lark – the girls went to the Central Telegraph on Gorky Street and booked an international phone call to China. They had no idea which hotel he was staying at, so the operator, a young woman who appreciated the audacity of the thing, told her Chinese counterpart to put them through to the biggest hotel in town. Half an hour later, Lyudmila's friend Olga was talking to Gérard Philippe, who told her he would be stopping over in Moscow on his way back to Paris.

At Vnukovo Airport the police tried to stop them, but the twenty girls rushed past on to the tarmac and crowded round the steps. Philippe was by then terminally ill with hepatitis picked up in South America. He was ashen and looked far older than his thirty-seven years. He recognized Lyudmila and greeted her warmly. She asked him to sign her copy of Stendhal's *Le Rouge et le Noir*.

'*Pour Lyudmila, en souvenir du soleil de Moscou,*' Philippe wrote. It is still on a shelf in my mother's bedroom.

Mila graduated from Moscow State University with a Gold Medal, one of the ablest students of her year. On leaving,

Lyudmila took the risky option of turning down a university-assigned position and instead looked for a job on her own. She rented a room from a middle-aged couple near Lermontovskaya Metro, where she slept on a camp bed. Her landlord was an aviation engineer, and Lyudmila tutored their son in return for board and lodging. The engineer didn't have any official work, except for odd jobs among his neighbours, and Lyudmila suspected he was in disgrace of some sort and lying low. The family eked out a living in the cracks of the Soviet system, where a man without a job was a non-person with no money, no access to school for his children, to work canteens or holidays. The family lived on carrot and bone soup; Lyudmila would bring sausages when she found them and had time to wait in line.

Yekaterina Ivanovna Markitan, the wife of an old Party colleague of Boris Bibikov from the Kharkov Tractor Factory days, came from South Russia on a shopping trip and stayed at Lenina's. She told Luydmila that an old friend was now director of the Institute of Marxism and Leninism, dedicated to the study and preservation of the legacy of Communism's founders. Her name was Yevgeniya Stepanova, and when Mila contacted her she immediately offered Mila a job as a junior researcher. Lyudmila had no great personal enthusiasm for Marxism or Leninism, but the job was in Moscow, and it was intellectual, so she jumped at it. Her work was to help in the giant task of collating and copy-editing the collected works of Karl Marx and his friend and sponsor, Friedrich Engels. She found the voluminous outpourings of the two men tedious. But the Institute had an outstanding library, her job gave her ample opportunity to practise her French, and she found her colleagues intelligent and lively. Foreign Communists and senior academic practitioners of the almost theological science of Communist doctrine would visit often, with Lyudmila being called upon to translate and accompany them. And then there was the excellently stocked staff canteen, on the ground floor of the small neoclassical palace which housed the

Institute, which had formerly belonged to the Princess Dolgoruky and served as the headquarters of the Nobles' Assembly before being put to a more egalitarian use.

In 1995 I stumbled on the old Institute of Marxism and Leninism by chance. With the demise of the Institute and indeed of Marxism and Leninism in general, the old palace had come down in the world. A group of descendants of Russia's nobility had somehow managed to reclaim the building, but had no funds to restore it. So it sat mouldering in its overgrown garden, lonely and irrelevant.

The newly re-formed Nobles' Assembly threw a fundraising ball in a disused gym which occupied one wing. I went in my father's old dinner suit, which he had worn when he met Nikita Khrushchev as a young diplomat in 1959. The vestiges of Russia's noble houses, those who had not emigrated and yet managed to escape the Revolution, the Civil War and the Purges, were out in force, inexpertly dancing as a Russian army band played mazurkas and Viennese waltzes. But the organizers were groping for a past no one remembered, and striving to revive traditions which lived on only in their imaginations. Prince Golitsyn, in grey plastic shoes, chatted to Count Lopukhin, in a worn polyester suit, as their heavily made-up wives fluttered plastic Souvenir of Venice fans.

The palace had once been magnificent, but decades of aggressive Soviet philistinism had reduced it to a soulless warren of cheap chipboard partitions and corridors lined with curling linoleum. The high, heavy windows overlooking the courtyard had long ago been painted shut. Everything which could be stolen had been, including the door handles and light switches.

I tried to imagine my mother, young and full of enthusiasm, limping down these corridors for her first job interview with the Institute's director. Or my mother, defiant and voluble, facing the viciousness of her colleagues at the Party meeting convened to censure her for her romance with a foreigner. But she wasn't there; I couldn't feel any ghosts in the place as it reverberated to the oompah music of the dance band.

By the spring of 1960 Lyudmila had been made a full staff member of the Institute of Marxism and Leninism, yet the creaking wheels of the housing bureaucracy turned slowly. She was eligible for her own apartment or, as an unmarried woman, more likely a room in a communal apartment. In March her colleague Klava Konnova, her two children and ageing father, were finally allocated an apartment of their own, and they moved out of a tiny, seven-metre-square room in a *kommunalka* on Starokonushenny Pereulok, near the Old Arbat. Lyudmila put her name down for it, and moved in. It was tiny, but it was a home. She was twenty-six years old, and for the first time in her life she had a space entirely to call her own.

8

Mervyn

In the eyes: dream . . .
And all the rest so curtained within itself
and effaced, as though we could not understand it
and clouded deep out of its own depths.
You swiftly fading daguerreotype,
In my more slowly fading hands.
Rainer Maria Rilke

I was always fascinated by my father's study, on the first floor of the narrow Victorian house in Pimlico where I grew up. It smelled of French cigarettes and Darjeeling tea, and it was filled with the sound of Bach cantatas and Handel operas. Now it seems a small room, but in my mind's eye it is always enormous, seen from the height of a seven-year-old hovering by my father's venerable armchair and gazing up at the towering walls of books. The cavalry sword hanging over the mantelpiece and the collection of model steam engines spoke of an unknowable but overpowering masculinity, while the drawers full of telescopes, compasses, family photographs and knick-knacks were a forbidden treasure trove. Even in my mid-teens, as my father and I grew apart, I remained fascinated by his past, which he refused to discuss and the key to which seemed to be inextricably linked to the mystery which was his study.

Once, when I was about sixteen, I found a packet of photographs of my father while illegally rooting though his desk drawers. The images were not of the father I knew, but a surprisingly cool-looking young man in a sharp sixties suit and Malcolm X-style sunglasses. In one photograph he was strolling along a sunlit seaside promenade. Other photos showed him in a heavy overcoat, standing on the ice of a giant lake; browsing among watermelon stalls in a picturesque marketplace in Central Asia; looking relaxed and confident in a seaside restaurant, surrounded by pretty girls. The photos all had when and where they were taken neatly marked on the back in pencil in his careful hand.

I asked my father later that day, perhaps seeking to provoke him with a confession of my brazen invasion of his hallowed desk, what he had been doing in Bukhara and Lake Baikal in 1961. He looked away, smiling thinly – his favourite mannerism – and settled into his chair.

'Oh,' he said noncommittally, as he poured himself tea through a strainer. 'Baikal? The KGB took me there.'

My father was born in July 1932 in a tiny terraced house on Lamb Street in Swansea. He grew up in a world of coal grates and tiny, unheated bedrooms, unused front parlours packed with heavy furniture, strident women and hard-drinking men. I visited the street where he grew up a couple of times as a child, always on blowy days when a grey sky spat drizzle and the streets were empty. Swansea, in my mind's eye, is always suffused with a dirty yellow light, somehow poisoned and gravity laden. The sea wind from the great sweep of Swansea Bay brought the smell of salt and oil. The streets were monochrome, as was the human flesh: heavy, sagging complexions the colour of suet.

South Wales seems a washed-up place now, ugly and unsure of itself, filthy and emphysemic after many lifetimes of toil and smoke. But in my father's childhood it was very different. Swansea was one of Britain's busiest coaling ports, and the giant ships which docked there were the arteries of an empire which was still the greatest in the world. My father grew up during the twilight years of a great Victorian port city. Belching steam engines still hauled the colliery cages up and down, and a few handsome old sailing schooners still moored among the great liners and freighters at the docks.

I imagine that I have, at various moments in my life, experienced a few echoes of that vanished world of my father's childhood. Driving on a foggy evening through a miserable mining town in Slovakia in 1993, when I breathed damp night air suffused with the smell of coal smoke and frying onions. Standing among the endless rusty cranes and cargo ships at the port of Leningrad, leaning into a biting sea wind which came off the Gulf of Finland, bringing the tang of rusting steel and the clang of metal on metal. And there was a week in Chelyabinsk, an industrial city in the southern Urals, in the company of miners, hard-muscled men with moustaches and grimy faces who drank with grim determination, and said little. Their women looked drained, struggling to keep up appearances with a smear of lipstick and a fading perm. These are the images which populate my picture of South Wales during the Depression. A place, I imagine, where everyone's share of happiness was tiny and precious, to be paid for by a lifetime's drudgery.

Mervyn's immediate family were poor but respectable, clinging desperately to the bottom rung of petit-bourgeois life, keeping up appearances. Some time around 1904, my great-grandfather Alfred took his family to the photographer's for a formal portrait which exactly reflected the family's strained circumstances. In the daguerreotype, Alfred is every inch the Edwardian paterfamilias, in his stern black suit and gold watch chain; his son William and daughter Ethel are prim, he in an outsize jam-jar collar, she in a high-necked black dress and black stockings. But his wife, Lillian, looks pale and unhealthy, and the heavy chairs and potted aspidistra which frame the stiff group are photographer's props, grander than anything they had at home. The giant photograph, expensively hand-tinted and framed, presided over Mervyn's modest young life in the tiny house he shared with his mother and grandmother in the Hafod area of Swansea, like a reminder of the family's inexorable fall from respectability.

My father's father, William Alfred Matthews, organized the loading of coal into the holds of ships so that it didn't shift as the ship rolled. It was called 'trimming' the ships, and was, in its modest way, a skilled job. It was filthy work, but at least not quite at the bottom of the working-class social ladder. That place was reserved for the navvies who actually shovelled the coal, stripped to the waist and knee deep in the coal dust.

William Matthews seems to have been a man of no ambition at all. His major interest in life was drinking his wages away at the Working Men's Club with his old comrades from the trenches. He had been wounded five times in the Great War. But like many of his generation he had nothing to show for it but a strong head for drink, a collection of medals and the respect of his fellows in the Comrades' Sick Club, a kind of co-operative health-insurance society, from whom in 1932 he received a cheap mantel clock which still ticks in my father's study, in recognition of his services as Secretary. German mustard gas on the Somme had also fatally weakened his lungs, which he further abused by chain smoking Players' Navy Cut.

My grandfather was a handsome man. He always wore sharp three-piece suits with his father's heavy gold watch chain, adorned with a sovereign in a gaudy gold holder. When he died in 1964, one of the few things he left his son were his pocket diaries, in which he'd marked off the days when he'd met his fancy women in Swansea parks.

He neglected his son Mervyn and couldn't bear to live with

his wife Lillian. He took little interest in his son's schooling and never read a book in his life. Mervyn was always deeply repelled by his father's philistinism; one reason, perhaps, that he himself became so bookish and studious. From time to time William would assert his paternal authority arbitrarily over a son he certainly sensed was cleverer than himself, refusing to lend Mervyn his precious tools or scoffing at his lack of physical toughness.

The humiliations inflicted by his father echoed through Mervyn's whole life. In the letters he was to write to his Russian fiancée, Mervyn comes back time and again to his father's cruelty and selfishness. Their shared experience of neglect in childhood became a powerful bond between Mervyn and Mila.

'Your joyless, nasty, humiliated childhood, the constant lack of warmth and affection, kindness, respect, all your humiliations, illnesses, tears, I understand them all, to the point of pain,' wrote Mila to Mervyn in 1965. 'How I hated your father because he refused to give you his wood plane when you wanted to make yourself something out of wood. What horrible cruelty, what a lack of respect for a person – I suffered the same a thousand times! I so wanted to return those for ever lost minutes and buy you a whole workshop, to give you everything you wanted, to make your life rich and happy.'

Mervyn grew up a rather lonely boy, I think. He liked to spend hours wandering alone through the shunting yards of the great docks and the machine houses of the collieries which ringed the grimy city, admiring the steam engines. On Sundays he would walk to the tops of the vast colliery slag heaps and look down on the ships in the channel, and the Irish Sea beyond, and he would dream, in the manner ascribed to young boys who end up following unusual destinies, of travelling to distant lands.

He spent much of his childhood with his mother Lillian and

his crippled grandmother. The family's life was punctuated by screaming rows between his parents, which either ended in one of his father's regular walk-outs, or by his mother taking little Mervyn and running away to stay with her mother. Mervyn's mother was an emotional woman, prone to hysterics. Her son was the focus of her hopes, and she lived entirely for him – and Mervyn was to devote much energy to getting as far away from his mother's intense, controlling love as possible. In later years, Mervyn frequently complained to Mila that his mother, addicted to hyperbole, would accuse him of 'killing your old mother with your thoughtlessness'.

Lillian's emotional volatility is hardly surprising. Her life had been permanently scarred at the age of nineteen when she became pregnant by a married man, a local solicitor who refused to recognize the child. In the stern, Methodist world of South Wales, a child born out of wedlock was a stain for life. When William Matthews married her she was a fallen woman, a fact which coloured their relationship for ever. My father was brought up believing that his half-brother Jack was his uncle, and only learned the truth in his late teens.

The coming of the Second World War provided a deeply thrilling interlude in Mervyn's boyhood. His stories of the war filled my own childhood – the drone of bombers on moonless nights, the sight of the docks and railway lines bombed. At the war's outbreak, along with his schoolmates, Mervyn was hastily evacuated to the flower-filled meadows of Gwendraeth on the Gower Peninsula, clutching a small cardboard suitcase with his name and address carefully pencilled on to it. But most of the children soon returned from evacuation after their mothers decided the dangers had been exaggerated.

They were wrong. Mervyn was in Swansea during the heaviest bombing raids of 1941. He remembers the great thundering of the bombs slamming into the town, and the excitement of scurrying to the air raid shelter at the bottom of the garden with candles and an old brass miner's lamp.

Just before one of the worst air raids, Mervyn's mother took the boy to spend the night at his grandparents' house. There was no particular reason for her decision; she had simply been seized by a powerful desire to get out of her house. As Mervyn and his mother crested the hill to Lamb Street the next morning, walking hand in hand, they found that their house had been completely demolished by a direct hit from a German bomb. Half the street had disintegrated into a pile of smoking bricks, and many of their neighbours had been buried alive in their Anderson shelters. Mervyn was horrified, and, as any little boy would be, profoundly impressed.

Every father, I think, re-visits his own boyhood when he plays with his son. And by the same token, every small boy shares his father's passions, until puberty interposes the desire to break free. The landscape of my own childhood in London was populated by mementoes of my father's youth. More so, I think, than my schoolfellows, I had a very 1930s childhood. One of the first books I remember reading was my father's copy of *Snow White and the Seven Dwarves*, produced for the 1937 Disney film and illustrated with three-dimensional pictures you viewed through a pair of cardboard spectacles with red and green celluloid lenses. Later I loved his old *Boys' Own* annuals and thick adventure books filled with biplanes and menacing fuzzy-wuzzies. On the morning of my eighth Christmas I discovered a great hessian-covered suitcase standing in my bedroom. It contained a wonderful 0-gauge Hornby electric train set, with a magnificent green locomotive called the *Caerphilly Castle*. It had been one of the few gifts my grandfather had given to my father, for the Christmas of 1939. Another year my father gave me his boyhood Meccano set, in a special wooden box with drawers and compartments for the bolts and girders and accompanied by wonderfully illustrated instruction books featuring boys in shorts and long socks. I would spend hours, alone, sitting on the floor of my attic bedroom constructing elaborate gantry cranes, armoured trains and suspension bridges for the *Caerphilly Castle* to cross over.

Sometimes my father would set his collection of model steam engines spluttering into life, powered by a little boiler fired with a methylated spirit lamp. I loved the smell of hot engine oil and steam. At weekends we'd drive to the East End to see the Thames barges at St Katharine's dock, or we'd go scavenging for bits of clay pipes and old bottles on the mud flats of the Thames at low tide. When I grew a little older, we'd go for long walks every evening through Pimlico. We'd ignore the neat white Thomas Cubitt façades of the main streets and turn instead down Turpentine Lane, a short cut which led us down to the great, sluggish Thames opposite Battersea Power Station. Of all the streets I've seen in London, Turpentine Lane, with its smoke-blackened brickwork and tiny backyards, looks the most like a South Wales backstreet.

We made model sailing boats together, not from kits but carved out of giant blocks of wood we'd scavenge from skips. We made the spars, sails and tackle with a little vice, a Stanley knife and an old pair of pliers. With special pride, he gave me a lovely wood plane with which I fashioned a large and beautiful Thames barge.

The turning point of my father's boyhood came when he broke his pelvis falling off a bicycle, aged fifteen. The break revealed that Mervyn had been suffering from a rare, wasting bone condition. To heal the pelvis and his brittle right hip, doctors prescribed a course of traction. Mervyn was strapped into a special bed and his legs were encased in plaster and weights attached to them. For hours at a time he couldn't move, or see anything but the hospital ceiling.

In all, Mervyn was hospitalized for over a year, most of it in agonizing traction. Like his future wife Lyudmila, also in hospital with a crippled right leg at exactly the same time,

Mervyn had no choice but to devour books, and to think. It seems that the intense boredom of forced immobility at a formative age sowed a lifetime's restlessness in both of them. Their bodies were immobilized, but their young minds wandered far. My father's deep need to travel and appetite for quixotic adventures, his contempt for authority and his penchant for taking risks was born, I believe, at this time – along with a certain talent for self-pity and unhappiness.

'It seems to me that my childhood mirrored your childhood, my universities were the same as your universities, my thoughts, your thoughts, your doubts and fears matched my doubts and fears,' Mila wrote to him in 1964. 'A certain physical defect and a mental superiority over your peers (remember how you wanted to excel at sport but were the first in your class instead?) – everything was similar in our lives, identical, even our illnesses.'

It was soon after his time in hospital that Mervyn developed an interest in Russian. For a young boy from the Valleys who had never travelled further than Bristol, the enthusiasm was eccentric, to say the least. Now, when I ask him to talk about the decision which was to shape his life, he can think of no other reason than that Russian was the 'most exotic possible thing I could think of'. Russian was the language of a universe utterly unrelated to the reality of his life in the Hafod.

It is hard, now, to strip away the Cold War associations and envisage just what Russia meant for an impressionable schoolboy in 1948. In the United States, the House Un-American Activities Committee had just launched its investigation into Communist infiltration in Hollywood, searching for metaphorical Reds under the beds. But in Britain, attitudes were more equivocal, especially in a working-class city like Swansea where Trade Unionism and Socialism went hand in hand. Just a few miles away from Swansea in the collieries of the Rhondda Valley, Harry Pollitt, General Secretary of the

Communist Party of Great Britain, had recently narrowly failed to get elected to parliament. There were plenty of Communists in William Matthews' Comrade's Sick Club who had yet to get the message that Uncle Joe Stalin, an ally just a few years before, was now on the other side.

But, as the ousted Prime Minister Winston Churchill had recently observed in a speech at Fulton, Missouri, an 'iron curtain' had descended across Europe. The Soviet Union was rapidly transforming, in the eyes of its former allies, into a dark and threatening place. And when the atomic scientist Igor Kurchatov detonated Russia's first atomic bomb on 29 August 1949 at Semipalatinsk – the Godforsaken piece of Kazakh steppe where Martha Bibikova had been imprisoned in 1938 – the Soviet Union became a very real and immediate enemy. The culture and country with which young Mervyn was becoming fascinated was, in every sense, alien.

By the time I was growing up, Communism and Russia were synonymous with menace. The only voice of dissent was a lumbering elderly neighbour called Vicky, who was the first person outside my family whom I had ever heard speak well of Russia. She lived round the corner in a council flat, had a beard and didn't wash very often (though I noticed her bitter smell was quite different from the hormonal, foody smells of Russian old ladies). Vicky would sometimes walk me to school and back, and on the way tell me riveting tales about 'milk bottle bombs' – incendiary bombs shaped like old-fashioned broad-necked milk bottles – which fell on London during the war. She'd also tell me how her father was in an Allied convoy taking American supplies to Murmansk which was torpedoed by a U-boat. He had been a stoker, and I was fascinated to learn that he was first scalded by the boiling water from the bursting boilers, then frozen as he drifted in the sea. I was convinced the two would cancel each other out, leaving warm bathwater.

'Them Reds,' said Vicky in her high-pitched cockney voice, 'was very good to me Daddy. I won't hear a word against them.'

My own school contemporaries had other ideas. The realization that Russians were enemies, Reds, Communists, dawned on some of my fellows, and spread through that strange psychic osmosis by which childhood cruelties multiply. When I was about seven, someone at school accused me of being a 'Red', and demanded to know when we would pull all tanks out of Afghanistan. When I protested that I wasn't, I was called a liar and, worse, a sneaky liar because of the vehemence of my denials. The crowd of boys, canny as a pack of bloodhounds, caught the scent of my desperation, and sensed something was amiss – did I really have something to hide? If I was so upset, I must be a Red, and that must be very bad. A fight ensued, and I ran home with a black eye. For nearly three years afterwards, I refused to speak Russian at home.

In 1950, after passing his Russian A-level, Mervyn was accepted by the fledgling Russian faculty of Manchester University. He was overjoyed finally to get away from the Hafod, and away from his mother. Among the thick fogs and flat vowels of Manchester he applied himself to the study of Russian, of which he achieved an impressive mastery. By the end of his Finals he had struggled through all 1,200 pages of *War and Peace* in the original, a spectacular feat of masochism which he would often mention in relation to my own, more faltering efforts to master written Russian.

My father graduated from Manchester with a solid First and his tutors recommended that he go to Oxford for a postgraduate degree. St Catherine's, the university's newest college, would be the place for a bright young chap from South Wales who had intellectual spark but not much social polish, they thought, entirely correctly. St Catherine's was an energetic institution, though not yet installed in its current modernist campus, which Mervyn, a conservative in architecture as in so much else, strongly disliked. When he turned up to his first out-of-college tutorial at New College, his new tutor asked politely if English was the young Welshman's first language.

Despite such hitches, Mervyn thrived, worked hard and avoided the beer-drinking social life of the college. After two years at Catz he was offered a junior research fellowship at St Antony's, a far more prestigious college which was home to the best British experts on the Soviet Union. It was the crucial first step to becoming a tenured don. To all intents and purposes, Mervyn, purely by dint of hard work, was on the verge of becoming a made man in the fast-growing profession of sovie-tology, one of the many bright young fellows then speculating on the strange machinations of the Red empire rising in the east.

But peering at the strange land from a distance was not enough. In 1957, the opportunity to visit Russia, unimagin-able for anyone but accredited diplomats or the occasional journalist for the previous two decades, suddenly arose. Khrushchev had ordained a great Festival of Students and Youth in Moscow, with young guests from all over the great community of socialist nations (which Battista-controlled Cuba had yet to join) and also, stunningly, from among the 'progressive elements' of degenerate capitalist countries too. Mervyn signed up. Much to his surprise, he was granted that rarest of official favours, a Soviet visa.

The festival was a carefully scripted and tightly controlled affair, but to Mervyn and the six hundred Western students who attended it was an intoxicating immersion in the world they had studied for so long. Mervyn was so thrilled he barely slept, even though he found himself instinctively disliking the communal sing-songs and flag-brandishing parades through stadiums full of cheering young Communists. Muscovites were no less intoxicated. Young Westerners were as exotic as mythical beasts, all the more so because for the past two decades any contact with foreigners had been easy grounds for a spell in the Gulag. Some of the African comrades present took fuller advantage of the opportunities for fraternization than the authorities had anticipated, fathering a whole generation of mixed-race babies for ever known as Children of the Festival.

Mervyn fell in with a couple of bold spirits who had taken advantage of the atmosphere of licence the festival had created to chat to foreigners. One was a devilishly handsome young Jewish theatre student called Valery Shein, who wore jaunty caps and striped shirts, and his quieter cousin Valery Golovitser, an intense balletomane a couple of years Shein's junior. The three young men walked down Gogolevsky Boulevard, locked in intense and earnest conversation about their respective lives. When Mervyn's all-too-brief week in Moscow ended, they swapped addresses. It seemed unlikely, to all concerned, that the miracle of the festival would ever repeat itself, or that Mervyn would ever be allowed back. The prospect of the two Valerys ever having the opportunity to visit Britain was so remote as to be laughable. In a sense, they were right. Moscow was not open to a mass influx of foreigners again until the 1980 Olympics.

But the following year, 1958, Mervyn heard of a job opportunity in Moscow. True, it was in the British embassy, and he would have to live the hermetic life of a diplomat, sealed off from the real Russian life that he had tasted during the festival. But the job, a humble one in the research department, would at least get him to Russia.

The post was applied for, arrangements were made for a sabbatical from St Antony's, and in due course a formal letter of acceptance on Foreign Office notepaper arrived in Mervyn's college pigeon-hole. He bought an extremely heavy dark blue overcoat in the Oxford Co-op in anticipation of the hard Moscow winters, which I still wear to this day. And some time in late summer Mervyn took a can of black oil paint and sat down to mark his handsome new steamer trunk with the

neatly printed words 'W.H.M. Matthews, St Antony's College, Oxford, АНГЛИЯ,' the last word in bold Cyrillic
letters, leaving no doubt as to the trunk's destination.

People, detached from their homes and set loose in the world,
drift till they find the places that fit them. By the end of my
first week in Moscow in April 1995, I knew that I had found
my place in the city's rampant, filthy raucousness. I thought:
either this is the real world, or there is no real world.

The Russia I knew had caught a viral dose of the century's
chaos. It was long in incubating, but suddenly, almost without
warning, the whole rotten edifice collapsed under the weight
of its own hypocrisy and dysfunction. For Russians the shock
of the implosion of the system which had sustained their every
physical, spiritual and intellectual need was far more profound
than anything the Soviet system had ever thrown at them –
even the Purges, even the Second World War. Both those
horrors, at least, had easy-to-understand narratives. But now
they were hit by something entirely inexplicable – not an
enemy, but a vacuum. They had nothing but their Russianness
to fall back on, the intense experience of being Russian which
pulled them together like straggling soldiers in a blizzard.

People reacted in different ways. Blinking like earthquake
survivors, some quickly found their new God in money, sex,
drugs, nationalist fantasies, mysticism, charismatic religious
sects. Others rediscovered the stern and ancient Orthodox
God of All the Russias. Some, possessed by aimless frenzy,
thrived on looting trinkets and scraps from the ruins. Others,
who would soon become the country's new masters, ignored
the scraps and went for the treasures.

And yet, with so many jeopardies inwardly stalking them,
most Russians still lived their outward lives on spec, on
spiritual credit. In other countries a trauma of this magnitude
has ripped society apart and plunged it into decades of soul-
searching. But in Russia the twin forces of fatalism and apathy

meant that the country reacted with little more than a collective, resigned shrug and slogged on with the painful business of staying alive.

I came to Moscow desperate. After graduating from Oxford, I had spent two years of hapless wandering in the generation expat hinterlands of Prague and Budapest, drinking strong coffee by day and cadging pints of beer from American girls by night. I was trying, though not very hard, to write, which brought me eventually to besieged Sarajevo on a freelance reporting trip with a borrowed flak jacket and a rucksack full of blank notebooks. I found the thrill I had been seeking by riding UN armoured personnel carriers past piles of shattered concrete and the beautiful, boyish debris of my first war. I walked down unlit streets filled with people strolling on a summer's night like the damned in a Gustave Doré engraving. I read *The Brothers Karamazov* during a bout of shelling, imagining myself in communion with the darkest forces of the world. But then I saw a child shot dead by a sniper as he ran across a road, picked up off his feet by the impact of the bullet and thrown down lifeless like laundry tossed from a basket, and felt a surge of revulsion at my own voyeurism. On my return to Budapest I decided I could no longer face the Bohemian folly of café society, and began to seek something bleaker and more hard-bitten.

A few months later I found myself standing on the rain-washed pavement outside a McDonald's in downtown Belgrade counting change for a hamburger and chips. I was unsuccessfully stalking a man called Željko Ražnjatović, aka Arkan, one of the most notorious warlords of the Bosnian war, who had retired from his career of marauding into a soap-star lifestyle of unrestrained kitsch, football fanaticism and mafia violence which I thought would make a good magazine piece. I stalked him at the Red Star Belgrade football matches, I stalked him at his home and his office, I visited his former pet tiger cub mascot, now grown huge and morose in a cage in Belgrade Zoo. Good material it may have been, but I was finally out of money, and there was no sign that Arkan was willing to talk to me.

I called my mother in London from the Belgrade Press Club (whence I discovered one could make international calls for free). She told me that a local English-language paper in Moscow, to which she had encouraged me to apply during one of my periodic bouts of jobless idling in London, had offered me a post as a staff reporter. It was time to get a job. Time to go to Russia.

I had visited Moscow several times before: as a small child with my mother, and later as a teenager with my father when he was allowed back into the Soviet Union in the mid-1980s. I'd never liked it much. I always hated the lack of privacy in my aunt Lenina's two-room apartment and I was constantly irritated by the stream of self-righteous advice and correction which Russian old women consider their right to mete out to youngsters. I found the hospitality overwhelming, and the effusiveness of everyone I met embarrassing. Elderly friends of my aunt's were recruited to troop me round museums and theatres, and their teenage grandchildren tasked with taking me to dilapidated Soviet amusement parks and to listen to street singers on the Arbat. I was shy and fogeyish, and found my young companions' open adoration for all things Western uncomfortable – all the more so because I hated pop music and discos, which seemed to be their idea of nirvana. Above all I found the place impossibly claustrophobic, not least because my Western clothes made me the object of una-bashed stares wherever I went – or so it seemed to my self-conscious sixteen-year-old self.

In the summer of 1990, after finishing school, I was finally allowed to go to Moscow alone. I found a summer job as a translator at the British embassy thanks to former students of my mother's who worked there. Like my father four decades before, I found myself employed in an office in the former stable block behind the old Kharitonenko mansion, ferrying piles of visa application forms and occasionally being trotted out to pose as the vice-consul whenever angry visa applicants demanded to speak to a real, live Englishman. I was eighteen years old. I learned croquet from the sons of the chargé d'affaires on the immaculate lawn of their residence just off the old Arbat, and hired an official black Volga sedan to pick me up at my aunt's apartment and transport me to work in the mornings.

Moscow had changed almost unrecognizably since I had last visited; there was a palpable sense that the old order, which had once seemed so permanent, was disintegrating. Traffic police seemed powerless to stop motorists from executing illegal U-turns; everyone roundly ignored the official prohibition on using private cars as taxis. The black-market exchange rate was ten times the official one, making me rich overnight. True, there wasn't much to buy, but I did clean out the Melodiya record shop on the new Arbat of every classical disc they had for a total of twenty pounds, and staggered home with parcels of art books bought for pennies at the Tretyakov gallery shop. The newly opened McDonald's on Pushkin Square, the first in the Soviet Union, had sent the embassy some vouchers for free Big Macs, so one lunchtime some British colleagues and I commandeered the ambassador's Rolls-Royce and trundled over to get some lunch. The line of Russians waiting patiently for their first taste of the West snaked down the street. Stepping out of the Rolls we marched straight in, waving our vouchers and our foreignness as self-evident marks of privilege. I'm not proud of it now, but Moscow made me feel, for the first time in my life, flushed with cash, cool and ineffably superior.

Everything about Moscow still seemed dilapidated and terminally shoddy: people's clothes and shoes were shoddy; so were the cars and the electrical goods and the bus tickets and the buses. But there was a new hope for the future in anyone who was young and intelligent. Friends took me to a history lecture by Yury Afanasiyev, my mother's old classmate, who spoke about Stalinism for two hours to a huge hall packed to bursting. The fact that he was addressing a taboo subject so openly seemed intoxicating. The audience wrote questions on slips of paper and passed them to the speaker in a constant stream after the lecture, in approved Soviet style, and the meeting broke up only when someone came to warn them that it was nearly time for the last bus. There was a hunger for truth among these people which impressed me profoundly – supported by a powerful faith that somehow the truth would make them free. I found my new Soviet friends sentimental and naïve, but there was no mistaking their earnestness, and their conviction that, as Solzhenitsyn had exhorted, they should not live by lies any longer.

Five years later I passed once again through the mirror into Russia via the infinitely depressing half-gloom of Sheremetyevo Airport – this time not as a visitor but to start a new life. The old smell of Soviet detergent and mouldy heating was still there, remembered from childhood trips. But much else had changed. Instead of empty, echoing corridors and stern-faced border guards, I found myself in the middle of a throng of hustling taxi-drivers. Garish hoardings advertised imported beer and More cigarettes. Beefy female shuttle traders pushed past me, hauling massive bags full of coats and boots bought on shopping sprees in Dubai and Istanbul. I was picked out from the scrum by Viktor, a *Moscow Times* driver, who bundled me into his ageing Lada and steered it through the weaving traffic of Leningradsky Prospekt.

The overcast sky was the colour of smoke, and the watery late-winter light washed the city in pale grey. On either side of the road lines of apartment blocks marched out towards a horizon of billowing chimneys and haze. Heavy-set buses trundled along, cowlings flapping, belching black exhaust.

At the edges of the road huddles of pedestrians waited to cross the Prospekt's forbidding sixteen lanes. Even as we approached the centre of the city, there was still something of the steppe in these great windblown spaces.

It must have been very different when my father first arrived in Russia. The city's soul was swelling with victory and pride, not deflating in exhaustion. The Moscow he knew was spick and span, the carefully planned capital of an expanding empire. It was a controlled, oppressive place, not the teeming mayhem into which it was to descend after the Soviet Union collapsed. And emotionally, for my father, the distance was greater. For a generation unused to travel, Russia might as well have been on a different planet. But Mervyn could not have been happier. He had finally loosed himself from his home and was drifting towards a place which would fit him.

The time and city were pregnant with pitfalls for a young man in love with Russia and blessed, or cursed, with a strong wayward streak. The Cold War was approaching its height. Soviet tanks had recently crushed the Hungarian Rising and there was no doubt in the minds of many in the West that it was the ambition of Socialism to conquer the earth. It was a time when the world was cleanly divided according to moral absolutes, when the opposing teams wore different coloured jerseys and the nuclear handicaps were listed on the programme.

It's hard, now, to imagine the thrill and the mystery of living in the secretive capital of a parallel, hostile world. The Moscow my father knew is separated from the Russia in which I lived not just by half a lifetime but by a seismic shift of history. My father's generation was defined by a bitter ideological divide which ran across the world, and he, for reasons that I only began to understand when I went to live in Russia myself thirty years later, did everything in his power to

live on the other side of that divide. To the embassy cold
warriors with whom he worked, if not to Mervyn himself,
Moscow was the heart of all the darkness in the world.

There is a photograph of my father I had never seen until he
handed me a copy of his memoirs, without comment, on the
stairs of our London house late in 1999, before turning away
with an embarrassed smile and retreating back into his study.
It is a photograph of a surprisingly handsome young man, his
tie and collar slightly askew, looking dreamily and slightly self-
consciously over the photographer's shoulder as he stands on
the balcony of the diplomatic block of flats on Sadovaya-
Samotechnaya Street – known to its inmates then, as now, as
'Sad-Sam' – some time in the early autumn of 1958. He is
staring into the middle distance over the Garden Ring – not
yet a choking artery of solid traffic – and he seems a serious
fellow, eager to please, a little unsure of himself. The photo
was taken shortly after he arrived in Moscow. He was twenty-
seven years old, had a promising academic career ahead of
him, and was delighted to be in the Soviet Union. The great
adventure of his life was beginning.

Mervyn's life was comfortable – or, by Soviet standards,
positively luxurious. He shared the three-room apartment at
Sad-Sam with another young embassy staffer, Robert Longmire. The power plugs and appliances were imported from
England, and the telephone was marked 'Speech on this line is
NOT SECURE'. They had a lackadaisical cleaning lady called
Lena and a Siberian cat called Shura, and stocked up on home
comforts like whisky and digestive biscuits at the embassy's
little commissariat shop. The dinner suit Mervyn had bought
when he went up to Oxford was in constant use for diplomatic
cocktail parties, which he found insufferably dreary.

My father may have been physically in Moscow, but he
quickly found that he and his fellow foreigners were forced to
live separate lives from the Russians who surrounded them.

His foreign accent and clothes would raise frank alarm and wonder among shop cashiers and tram passengers. Contacting his old friends from the festival was unthinkably dangerous, not for Mervyn but for them. His every move was monitored by gangs of KGB plain-clothes officers – dubbed 'goons' by the young diplomats, after the thugs of contemporary American gangster films – who trailed him on his nocturnal wanderings around the Boulevard ring. Mervyn invented games to play with his minders. One of his favourites was to break into a run on a crowded street, and glance backwards to see who also started running. On the Metro, Mervyn, in a flippant mood, once went up to a KGB watcher he recognized and said, 'How many summers, how many winters?', the standard greeting for those one has not seen for a long time. The man remained absolutely expressionless and said nothing. The KGB, to Mervyn, was no more than a slightly menacing prop in his young man's world of adventure.

Luckily for Mervyn's sanity, a saviour soon appeared in the diminutive form of Vadim Popov. Popov was a junior official from the Ministry of Education, who became my father's first real Russian friend. They met when Mervyn visited the ministry to begin his official duties, which consisted of compiling a paper on the Soviet university system. Vadim was slightly older than Mervyn, strong and squat with a square Slavic face. He was a drinker, and fancied himself as a ladies' man, and at times could be bluff and even abrasive. But Mervyn found himself warming quickly to his new comrade's rough charm.

Vadim appointed himself Mervyn's guide to what my father fondly imagined was the 'real' Russia – a Russia of smoky restaurants, animated conversations and body-odorous embraces. Over months, and in gradual degrees, Vadim drew Mervyn out of his shyness, and led him into a glamorous world of flirtatious women and sentimental, vodka-induced confidences.

Though Mervyn reported his first, official meeting with

Vadim to discuss Soviet higher education policy, he did not, as embassy regulations required, report the many drunken dinners which followed. He didn't dare. If some fool in Chancery found out they would probably have banned Mervyn from seeing his one Russian chum, his sole window on to a Moscow his embassy colleagues never saw.

By day, Mervyn toiled in the high-ceilinged, bourgeois splendour of the embassy, housed in the former Kharitonenko mansion, a hideous miniature stately home situated directly across the Moscow River from the Kremlin. By night he would spend hours chatting with his flatmate over cups of Ovaltine, or giving his KGB goons a good night-time exercise as he wandered up and down Tsvetnoi Boulevard and Petrovka Street. On the blessed evenings that Vadim invited him out, he would sneak away from Sad-Sam to a forbidden but fascinating night of bad food, terrible music and real, true-to-life Russians on raucous Gypsy restaurant-barges on the Moscow River. He was as happy as he'd ever been.

Winter in Moscow comes down like a hammer, crushing out light and colour, beating the life out of the city. It closes overhead like a pair of musty wings, enveloping Moscow in a cocoon, cutting it off from the world. The city begins to look like a black-and-white dreamscape, disorientating and subtly disquieting. On the streets streams of huddled figures hurry through pools of dirty yellow light before disappearing into doorways or the Metro. Everything becomes monochrome, the people in black leather and black fur, the city swathed in black shadows. In the underpasses or in shops, the only places one sees people in bright light, faces are pale and strained and everything is pervaded with the wet-dog smell of damp wool. The skies are dirty grey, low and oppressive.

Every winter I spent in Moscow I had a sense that the world was closing in on itself, shrinking into a state of siege behind double-glazed windows, taking shelter in the fug of state-provided steam heating, and that we were powerless in the face of this overwhelming force of nature, fragile, unable to do anything but accept our lot.

As the first frosts of December 1958 began to bite, Mervyn's dinners with Vadim were becoming more regular. They would arrange the date and time of meetings before they parted; both, for unspoken but obvious reasons, preferred not to call each other on the telephone.

One evening, Mervyn set out for Manezh Square by trolleybus, expecting to go to Aragvi, one of their favourite Georgian restaurants, or perhaps the National Hotel. But to his surprise, and slight alarm, he saw Vadim standing near the trolleybus stop next to a purring official ZiL limousine. Vadim greeted him warmly, and explained offhandedly that the car belonged to his uncle, who'd loaned it for the night to take them to his dacha, where dinner was waiting. Vadim held the door open expectantly. Mervyn wavered, turning over the possible consequences of breaking the rules imposed by the Soviet government banning foreigners from making unauthorized trips beyond the city limits. Then he climbed into the ZiL and drove with Vadim to the dacha, far beyond the city's edge and deep into the wintry countryside, and into a new stage of his life, strange and dangerous.

The dinner was excellent. Mervyn and Vadim ate caviar, herrings, vodka, smoked sturgeon and steaming boiled potatoes served by an elderly cook. They sat by the dacha's log fire discussing women, and drunkenly attempted to play billiards. The cutlery was of heavy Victorian silver, the fireside armchairs were overstuffed and of pre-revolutionary vintage. A friend of Vadim's was there, a fat and jovial gynaecologist who cracked jokes about his research work, which consisted of inflating the wombs of female rabbits. Vadim reminisced about his latest conquests. Politics were not mentioned. Mervyn relaxed, fuzzy with the vodka, for which he always had a weak head. When he praised the house, with its vast dark oil paintings and sweeping staircase, Vadim muttered casually that his uncle was quite the *bolshaya shishka*, literally, the 'big pine cone', slang for big boss.

At one in the morning the cook came up to tell them that their ZiL was waiting. They drove to Moscow in silence, sated, drunk and happy. Back on familiar territory as the huge car eased around the turn on to the Garden Ring at Mayakovsky Square, a rational thought struggled through the vodka haze. Mervyn ordered the driver to stop a couple of hundred yards short of Sad-Sam. He got out in a flurry of thanks and goodbyes, and walked the rest of the distance home. A young British diplomat arriving outside a foreigners' compound in a Soviet official limousine in the small hours of the morning might have been misunderstood if any of his cocoa-sipping colleagues had happened to notice. This would be my father's little secret, a secret life with the Russian friends he had discovered which no one at the embassy could take away from him.

My first Moscow apartment was a dingy little place just round the corner from Sad-Sam; from my windows I could see the same intersection, clad in a pall of grey exhaust. In the evenings I would walk down Tsvetnoi Boulevard, alone. No goons followed me.

My place of work in Moscow was on Ulitsa Pravdy, literally the Street of Truth. Every morning I would hail a passing car, briefly haggle with the driver over the two-dollar fare and be driven to work. Some days polished black government Audis with tinted windows would stop for me, sometimes ambulances and, on one occasion, an army truck full of soldiers. In any case, whatever the vehicle, I trundled or bounced past Sadovaya-Samotechnaya, turning north up Leningradsky Prospekt. The old *Pravda* building, where the *Moscow Times* leased half a floor, was a grimy constructivist hulk crouching among backstreets lined with sagging warehouses. I would be at work within fifteen minutes and would run up the stairs to the cavernous newsroom.

The paper was run by bright young expatriates, mostly Americans. It was owned by a diminutive Dutch former Maoist who also published the Russian editions of *Cosmopolitan* and *Playboy*. Most of my new colleagues were well-educated Russian majors, all bright, friendly and enthusiastic. My own brief at the paper was a simple one. While my more serious-minded colleagues toiled over Kremlin intrigues and the state of the economy, I was cut loose with an open brief to hunt and gather quirky feature stories in the human jungles of the city. It was, for someone of twenty-four, with exactly two years of rather diffident journalistic experience under his belt, a small, but remarkable, professional miracle. Quite unexpectedly, I found that I had the whole screaming, teeming, outrageous, lurid underside of Moscow more or less to myself.

Moscow in the mid-1990s was vulgar, venal and violent. It was manic, obscene, uproarious and Mammon-obsessed. But above all, I found almost everything about it hilariously, savagely funny. Everything, from the way thuggish New Russians would leave the 'UV Protected' stickers on their sunglasses to their habit of stealing oil companies from each other, the way they placed TNT under cars and staged shoot-outs in public places, was comic. By the time you had soaked up enough of the country's penetrating cynicism, even the tragedy was, on some level, darkly amusing. Soldiers blew themselves up hammering open the warheads of surface-to-air missiles, trying to steal gold circuit boards. Ambulance drivers spent their working day moonlighting as taxis. Policemen ran prostitution rackets and delivered the girls to their clients in squad cars.

Russia's president cavorted on a band stage in Berlin drunkenly conducting an orchestra. Russia's cosmonauts fixed their spacecraft with a monkey wrench and duct tape in between filming ads for Israeli milk and pretzels and drinking cans of vodka labelled 'Psychological Support Materials'. Girls who went home with you after fifteen minutes' drunken conversation in a nightclub would be mortally offended when you didn't bring flowers to a second date. Gogol captured Russia's sordid craziness best – the nightmarish mood of dislocation, the mad, scheming little people, the petty vanities, the swinish drunkenness, the slobbering sycophancy, the thieving, incompetent, churlish peasantry.

Like my father must have done, I found Russia not just another country, but a different reality. The outward trappings of the city were familiar enough – the white faces, the Western-style shop fronts, the neoclassical architecture. But this European crust only sharpened the sense of otherness. Instead of reassuring, the distortion of the familiar was even more disturbing. Moscow felt as surreal as a colonial outpost on which some distant master had tried to transplant grimly imperial architecture and European fashions. Underneath all the affectations the city's heart was wild and Asiatic.

One of my first assignments was to cover Moscow's First Annual Tattoo Convention. The convention was conservatively billed as a *kulturny festival* in the bemused Moscow press. It was, in fact, a clan gathering of the capital's alternative society, an exuberant, pagan orgy of nonconformity. A thick wall of body odour welled out of the dark entrance of the Hermitage club, propelled by high-decibel punk rock. Inside, the two main rooms were wreathed in the rancid smoke of cheap Soviet cigarettes and filled with the heaving forms of dimly lit, half-naked bodies, mostly male. Moscow's punks, skinheads, bikers and a few culturally confused hippies were milling in one giant, pungent, heaving mass, intensifying into a frenzied rhythmic pogoing in front of the stage, where four punks, their Mohican haircuts plastered to their heads with sweat, were pounding out bad Sex Pistols covers.

Another evening found me in Dolls, a flashy and fashionable strip bar where teenage acrobats danced naked on the tables. Paul Tatum, a prominent American businessman, was there, sitting alone at one of the luncheonette-style stools at the edge of the stage, nursing a drink. Tatum was something of a local celebrity for his prolonged business dispute with a group of Chechens over ownership of the business centre of the Radisson-Slavyanskaya Hotel. I greeted him as we came in, but he seemed distracted, his usual bullishness strained. We chatted for a while about the 'freedom bonds' he had issued to raise funds for his legal battle with the Chechens and sold to his friends.

We were joined by Joseph Glotser, the club's owner, who complained, half-joking, in a thick Brooklyn Russian accent about how hard it was to 'make honest living in zis town'. Tatum seemed keen to get back to his bird-watching, so I wished him luck and rejoined my friends.

A month later Tatum was dead. Someone put eleven AK47 rounds in his neck and upper back as he entered the pedestrian underpass outside the Radisson. Tatum hadn't been wearing his customary bulletproof vest that evening, but even if he had it wouldn't have done him any good because the assassin had fired from above, straight down through his clavicle and upper vertebrae. Tatum's two bodyguards were unharmed. It was a classic Moscow hit. The shooter dropped the Kalashnikov and walked calmly away, and a couple of hours later the police issued the standard statement, that they believed that 'the killing was connected with the professional activities of the victim'.

Soon the only person left alive who remembered our brief conversation that night at Dolls was me. Joseph Glotser bought it too, a couple of months after Tatum, a single sniper round to the side of the head from across the street as he emerged from Dolls. The marksman was so sure of his shot he didn't even bother with a follow-up.

Soon after, for a feature on Moscow's death industry, I interviewed a mortician who specialized in patching up the corpses of Mafia victims for presentation in open coffins. The man wore a Hawaiian shirt under his stained lab coat, and spoke of contract hits as a ballet connoisseur might talk of his favourite performances. The Glotser hit, he said, with deep appreciation, was one of the 'finest, cleanest assassinations' he'd ever seen. The cheery mortician was a true hero of the times, wearing his cynicism lightly, making a joke of the awfulness around him so that it wouldn't get inside. My *Moscow Times* colleagues and I, it occurred to me, were morticians too, with lab coats over our Hawaiian shirts, all feigning a detached connoisseurship of Moscow's gothic wickedness.

Spring began one night in late April, a few weeks after my arrival. The evening before a wintry chill had lurked in the night air, although the last, tenacious remnants of filthy snow had finally melted the previous week. The lawns were bare and scrubby and the earth smelt bitter and dead. But when I woke the next morning the sky was a vibrant blue, the tentative buds which had begun to emerge days before had all suddenly burst out and the boulevard exhaled an unmistakable tang of life. By that evening spring was firmly established across the city.

Like emerging butterflies, the girls in the streets shed their winter coats and emerged in high heels and miniskirts. On Sundays I would walk down the gravel paths of Tsvetnoi Boulevard to the Garden Ring. At Sad-Sam, I'd turn towards Mayakovsky Square, and head to the American Bar and Grill. There, a gaggle of *Moscow Times* staffers were usually hunched, gossiping, under a pall of cigarette smoke and half-hidden behind crumpled newspapers, trailing in the remains of eggs Benedict. Here it was at last, I told myself, the life of a foreign correspondent: the glamour, the girls, the hard-drinking, boots-on-the-brass-rail colleagues, the camaraderie of young men far from home in a strange and wonderful city. In truth, I was acutely aware, even at the time, that I was living the headiest and most adventurous days of my life. Though in the company of my new colleagues, of course, I was careful to conceal my joy under a cultivated veneer of world-weary flippancy.

9

Drinks with the KGB

It's not the ice, it's what's underneath that's frightening.
Alexei Suntsov to Mervyn, 1961

Producing tedious reports on Soviet higher education at the embassy was quickly losing its appeal. The new world Vadim had opened was the Russia Mervyn had come to experience, the exciting, romantic land he had dreamed of as he diligently taught himself Russian after school and ploughed painfully through *War and Peace*. Russia, its warmth and expansiveness, its unpredictability and excitement, was penetrating his blood. And with it came a recklessness, and with the recklessness a kind of liberation.

An Oxford friend wrote to ask Mervyn a small favour. The friend was editing a collection of the poetry of Boris Pasternak, author of *Doctor Zhivago*, and wanted some of the author's early work, available only in the Lenin Library in Moscow. He asked Mervyn to copy the poems and send them to Oxford. There was one small problem. A few months before, in October 1958, Pasternak had been awarded the Nobel Prize for Literature in recognition of *Zhivago*. Under pressure from the Writers' Union, who along with the Party considered the book a pernicious celebration of pre-Revolutionary Russia, Pasternak had been forced to turn down the prize. Indeed, only Pasternak's international fame had kept him out of the

Gulag. Getting the writer's unpublished material out of the Soviet Union was going to be dangerous, probably illegal, and certainly career-threatening. Mervyn immediately agreed.

My father spent the next two weeks snapping away with a small camera at the manuscripts in the professors' reading room of the Lenin Library, where they were available to anyone with a reader's ticket, as the other scholars hissed him to silence and the library attendant complained archly. He slipped two packages of the photographic prints into the embassy's diplomatic bags on consecutive weeks to avoid their being confiscated by Soviet customs.

A week later, a summons from the head of Chancery was solemnly passed down the embassy hierarchy to Mervyn. There was no doubt that a stiff dressing-down was in the offing. Hilary King was urbane and condescending as he received my father in his magnificent office on the ground floor of the embassy. But King had found out about Mervyn's unofficial packages from the Foreign Office in London, where the contents of diplomatic bags were scrutinized. The embassy was very vulnerable to complaints from the Soviet side, intoned King in tones of biting politeness. There would be terrible trouble if they found out about Mervyn's secreted photographs of the works of a banned author.

I can imagine the look on my father's face as he left the Chancery, fuming. I have seen it often, a suppressed aggression which comes out in flashes of fury, usually after simmering for a few hours or minutes under a façade of icy cordiality. Mervyn had prudently apologized to King. But the anger was there, inside, pent up, at the Foreign Office's pandering to the Soviets' petty administrative demands. He was being scolded for an action which to anyone outside the pygmy world of the diplomatic bureaucracy would have appeared eminently right, and that rankled, deeply. Mervyn walked away, seething, down the thickly carpeted corridor to his own tiny office in the stable block at the back of the building.

Shortly afterwards, in one of the infinitely subtle ways the embassy found to express disfavour, they moved a lowly radio operator into Mervyn's apartment and gave Robert Longmire his own apartment. Then they cut off Mervyn's servant allowance.

It was time to jump. An advertisement in an airmail copy of *The Times* seemed to be the lifeline, announcing a graduate exchange programme between the Soviet Union and Britain, the first ever. It was the opportunity Mervyn had been waiting for to swap cold smiles in Chancery for smelly student dorm corridors and freedom – perhaps – from the ever-present goons. But there was a problem. Mervyn was an accredited diplomat – albeit the very last name on the 1958 Moscow Diplomatic List – and it was unlikely that the Soviet Ministry of Foreign Affairs would believe his sudden change of status to that of a humble academic. Mervyn's first step was to take himself off the restricted list for sensitive documents and get rid of his security clearance. The embassy seemed only too happy to relieve him of both. The paperwork for Mervyn to apply for the graduate exchange was approved by the embassy and duly sent off to the Ministry of Foreign Affairs. And, duly, after proper consideration, refused.

Over kebabs and vodka in an Azerbaijani restaurant, Mervyn drowned his sorrows with Vadim. The Russian nodded his head in mute sympathy as he poured vodka, firmly and deliberately, into their glasses while Mervyn recalled his tale of the intransigence of the Ministry.

'Don't jump to conclusions, Mervyn,' Vadim assured his friend. 'I'll find out if my uncle can help.'

Mervyn was immensely cheered. Vadim, with his mysterious friends in high places with their ZiLs and dachas, would surely be able to persuade the Ministry to change its collective mind. Vadim mentioned nothing of what would be expected from Mervyn in return. They toasted

Mervyn's future as a Soviet student, and friend of the Soviet people.

'So, you're going to Moscow State University.' The ambassador, Sir Patrick Reilly, was friendly, despite the hitches in Mervyn's short embassy career, as his soon-to-be ex-employee came to say goodbye. 'Most unusual. I wonder why the Ministry allowed you to do it?'

There was a long silence. This was not the time or the place for Mervyn to reveal the story of Vadim and his uncle, their evenings on the town with his new friends, the Ministry's inexplicable last-minute change of heart. He said nothing. Receiving no answer, the ambassador held out his hand. 'Well. Good luck.'

To use up the remaining few days of holiday time he had outstanding from the embassy, Mervyn took a trip to Soviet Central Asia. A woman in the Chancery, whose job was to burn sensitive documents in an iron pot, advised him that Bukhara was worth a detour from Samarkand and Tashkent. Mervyn talked over his plans excitedly with Vadim, who was unimpressed with his English friend's enthusiasm for historical sites. Mervyn set off eastwards in a series of small but sturdy Aeroflot planes. Bukhara was to be his last stop.

The desert city turned out to be cold and uninviting, a stretch of mud-walled houses huddled along the airport road giving way to some new but already dilapidated-looking Soviet concrete blocks closer to the centre. The taxi driver, a Bukharan Jew, chatted all the way about the brand new Intourist hotel and, when they arrived, complained about the heaviness of Mervyn's suitcase and hiked the already exorbitant fare. The hotel was indeed new, but as he pushed through the doors Mervyn found that inside it was colder than out on the street. The receptionist had moved her desk closer to the door in order to keep warm.

Mervyn asked if the heating would be switched on soon. 'This is a new hotel,' said the receptionist, offended by the foreigner's prissiness. 'And the lifts don't work. You'll have to take the stairs.' She gave him a room on the top floor.

Dragging his suitcase up the stairs Mervyn noticed a pair of familiar legs descending. Vadim, it seemed, was in Bukhara on official business, quite by coincidence. Even better, Vadim happened to be free that day to take Mervyn round the sights of Bukhara, with an official car, and in the evening it turned out that a Russian friend of Vadim's had laid on a little welcoming party in his house on the outskirts. Vadim announced proudly that there would be some girls there.

After a day touring the sites, far too perfunctorily for Mervyn's liking, they made their way down some unpaved streets to the town's outskirts. Vadim's friend's house was in an old Russian quarter of traditional log houses quite different from the native brick-built Uzbek courtyards. Volodya, their host, greeted them warmly and plied them with vodka. They ate turkey, the largest Mervyn had ever seen in Russia, and danced to old American records. One of the three girls at the little party, Nina, turned out to be staying in the same hotel as Mervyn and Vadim. They walked home together in the moonlight, and said their goodnights in the foyer.

'You'll come to my room later?' Mervyn whispered as Vadim turned to go up the stairs. Nina squeezed his hand.

Mervyn tipsily wove his way down the corridor towards his room. The light was on, and someone was inside. Whoever it was had heard him coming upstairs and opened the door. Backlit from the room, Mervyn didn't see the man's face, but demanded to know what he was doing. 'Fixing the electricity,' the man said calmly. 'But we're done now.'

After the men had left, Mervyn sat down heavily on the bed. Even here in the middle of Central Asia, the KGB was tailing him. Mervyn noticed that on the table were two empty glasses. Secret policemen, apparently, liked to have a quick drink on the job.

He undressed quickly, shivering, and got into bed. There was a soft knock on the door. Thinking it was Vadim, Mervyn got up and opened it. It was Nina. She pushed him inside the room, frisky. He bundled her back out. A rape scandal was the last thing Mervyn needed; he pictured Nina's plump embrace turning into a wrestling hold, and help waiting just outside the door as she screamed for rescue. He climbed into his frigid bed alone.

Moscow State University was the largest of Stalin's grandiose highrises which punctuated the Moscow skyline like a ring of watchful vultures. It was also, at thirty-six storeys, the tallest building in Europe at that time. On the sweeping terrace in front of the building were gigantic statues of well-muscled male and female students looking up confidently from their hefty stone books and engineering instruments into the bright future. It was a long way from the haphazard sandstone quads of Oxford.

The university put Mervyn up in the 'hotel' wing, in fact identical to the rest of the university's five thousand-odd rooms except that, unlike ordinary students and professors, guests were provided with the luxury of a cleaning woman. The room was small, furnished with a sofa-bed, a deal desk and a built-in cupboard. The oversized window, dictated by the monumentalism of the façade, was completely out of proportion to the size of the room.

Nevertheless, Mervyn was delighted to be there. The university was the antithesis of his closeted diplomatic life; it was earthy and profoundly Soviet. Above all, Mervyn was significantly more free than when he was at the embassy. True, KGB radio cars stood outside, ready to put tails on foreigners as they left the building, but the surveillance was mercifully sporadic, and his fellow students, though still wary, were freer in associating with Mervyn than any Russians, apart from Vadim, had been before.

Mervyn had made a point, while at the embassy, of eating whenever he could at *stolovayas* – cheap public canteens – and riding on public transport wherever possible. Now at the university Mervyn ate in the canteen every day, with its papery meatballs, thin soup and watery potato puree. He had no choice but to pile on to trolleybuses, packed with the heavily padded *narod*, or people, and the smell of sweat and pickle-breath. He loved it.

Georges Nivat, a young Frenchman who was one of Mervyn's fellow students and a friend from St Anthony's and the festival, shared his love for immersing himself in Soviet life. Georges lived on a floor of the university which he shared with some Vietnamese graduates. The smell of their cooking, peppery chicken feet and garlicky cabbage soups, wafted down the corridors, much to Georges' distress. 'It is ruining my life!' he would complain with Gallic élan when he came to Mervyn's room for solace, tea and biscuits, gesticulating fatalistically. 'Ruining my life!'

Georges' fascination with Russian literature had brought him to Moscow. Soon after he arrived at the university he began frequenting one of Moscow's great literary salons, the apartment of Olga Vsevolodovna Ivinskaya on Potapovsky Pereulok. Ivinskaya had been the typist and collaborator of Boris Pasternak since 1946. She was also the beleaguered poet's mistress, and was the inspiration for Lara, the heroine of *Doctor Zhivago*. She had paid heavily for her association with Pasternak. In 1949, after refusing to denounce her lover as a British spy, Ivinskaya was imprisoned for five years. She was pregnant by Pasternak at the time but lost the child in prison. She returned to Potapovsky Pereulok only after Stalin's death in 1953, and they recommenced their affair. But all her life, Ivinskaya was tortured by Pasternak's refusal to abandon his wife and children. The two families lived in a curious ménage, with the poet lunching and spending the afternoons with Olga before bowing politely to his mistress's guests and leaving to join his wife for dinner.

Irina Ivinskaya was Olga's daughter by a previous marriage to a scientist who committed suicide rather than face arrest in the Purge of 1938. But despite the tragedy which dogged her mother's life, Irina was charming, happy and passionate about books and ballet. Georges fell utterly in love. Within months, he proposed. Pasternak toasted the young couple at a crowded tea party at his dacha in Peredelkino. Mervyn was invited to go and meet the author, but says he was too shy. 'I would have nothing to say to Pasternak,' he told me.

I have often thought about this strange refusal, because it sits so ill with my father's apparent love of risk and danger at that time in his life. Perhaps it was because he only felt at ease with his friends and social equals and couldn't stand formal functions – a dislike which continues to this day. He has always struck me as a very private man, cocooned in a protective world he weaves around himself to keep the outside world at bay. His study in London, the various austere academic apartments he occupied during visiting professorships, these were all fashioned into small masculine nests where he could escape into his piled papers, his pots of tea and his Bach. At social events he usually wears his frayed two-pound charity shop shirts and sagging tweed jackets, and hangs in a corner with a forced smile, waiting until it's time to leave. In a fit of shyness, he even left my wedding dinner early. I said goodbye to him on the steps of the old Splendid Hotel on the island of Buyukada, near Istanbul, as he stood in his antique dinner suit and a beige mackintosh. He thanked me warmly for a good party, as the music of a raucous band of young Gypsy delinquents belted from the dining room. 'I don't really like these big gatherings,' he explained, and turned to walk back alone to our house through the light evening drizzle.

*   *   *

Soon after Georges' engagement party, Vadim invited Mervyn to dinner at the Praga restaurant to celebrate Vadim's
newly won MA degree in oriental studies. The other guests
were mostly elderly academics, Vadim's supervisors and department heads. But opposite Mervyn sat an elegantly dressed
man, about five years his senior, with a distinctive grey streak
in his combed-back hair. Vadim whispered to Mervyn that the
man's name was Alexei, a 'research assistant' to his mysterious
uncle. But he didn't introduce them, and they did not speak.
Alexei made a long, witty toast. Mervyn made conversation
with his stony-faced neighbours and drank too much.

A few days later Vadim called to pass on a message from
Alexei: he wanted to invite Mervyn and Vadim to join him for
an evening at the Bolshoi ballet. Mervyn was surprised, and
flattered. Though they hadn't spoken at dinner, Alexei was
probably interested to meet a foreigner, Mervyn reasoned. He
accepted the invitation.

Alexei was poised and confident, a true member of the
post-war Moscow *nomenklatura*, or official élite. He wore
foreign-made clothes and had travelled; his wife, Inna Vadimovna, was tall and slim, and, Mervyn noticed when they met
at the Bolshoi, wore an expensive gold bracelet with a watch
set in it. Alexei remarked proudly that his wife was 'a typical
Soviet woman'. Mervyn thought of his cleaner, Anna Pav-
lovna, panting to the bus stop with her string bags full of eggs
from the university canteen. She seemed to Mervyn to be a
more typical Soviet woman.

The evening was a success. Alexei loved ballet, and he and
Mervyn had a friendly conversation during the interval, as the
more philistine Vadim hovered around the buffet, looking at
girls. Alexei began calling Mervyn regularly, inviting him out
to dinner at the Aragvi, at the Baku, the Metropole Hotel, the
National Hotel – the finest restaurants Moscow could offer.
Alexei had money, and he had some mysterious special
relationship with the maîtres d'hôtel of the city, booking at

short notice, always welcomed with an obsequious smile and shown to a good table or private room.

Alexei was more forward than Vadim in conversation, more overtly political, less chummy. He never spoke of women, and drank in moderation. Alexei expressed interest in Mervyn's childhood, his background, but Mervyn found from his trite responses that he could not conceive of poverty, or class, beyond Marxist-Leninist platitudes. An irony: Alexei, the Soviet champion of the international working class, himself from a privileged élite, and Mervyn, a naïve but sincere British patriot, profoundly anti-Communist, yet in Marxist terms a natural revolutionary.

Over one of their ever more frequent dinners, Mervyn and Alexei got on to the subject of the strict visa regime, surveillance and spies. They were at the National Hotel, a favourite watering hole of the capital's beau monde for the best part of the century. Alexei remarked that the Soviet Union had to be very careful of foreign spies. Mervyn, perhaps to prove that he wasn't one of 'them', to neutralize the implicit suspicion, jokingly told Alexei that it was a regular source of amusement at the embassy that there was a goons' booth under the Bolshoi Kamenny Bridge, just round the corner from the embassy, where KGB men would play dominoes while waiting to be called out.

Alexei listened with interest, suddenly even more serious, carefully questioning Mervyn on where the booth was. After dinner he insisted that they drive under the bridge to take a look. Perhaps sensing Mervyn's discomfort, Alexei made a disparaging remark about the work of MI5 and MI6, as though to suggest that if Mervyn were on the payroll he would know about it. Mervyn didn't argue with him.

When Mervyn drove past the bridge a few days later he noticed that the booth and the goons were gone.

Vadim arranged another evening at his uncle's dacha. As before, they went in a ZiL, but this time Vadim had brought along a ski instructor friend and three plump but lively girls. They went cross-country skiing at night among the pines, ungainly Mervyn falling frequently into snow banks as the girls giggled. They warmed up with vodka in front of the fireplace, and then retired upstairs with their respective girls. Mervyn's girl was large and, he thought, on the old side. But she seemed willing enough to play the role of his bed mate for the night, and it would have been rude to refuse.

Mervyn and Alexei sat in a private room at the Aragvi, well into the Tsinandali wine. On the table in front of them were the ruins of a gigantic meal of lamb kebabs, green bean *lobio* and *khatchapuri* cheese bread. Alexei was, for once, in an expansive mood, striking the avuncular tone he sometimes used with Mervyn. He had decided to take a more active interest in Mervyn's career, he announced. Would Mervyn like to do some travelling? If so, where? Mervyn, delighted, unthinkingly said Mongolia. Not possible, said Alexei. How about somewhere in the Soviet Union? Mervyn suggested Siberia. Alexei was enthusiastic. The great Bratsk Dam, perhaps? Lake Baikal? Mervyn was thrilled and agreed immediately. They drank a toast to seal the bargain.

At what point did Mervyn realize that he was getting in too deep? He may have been naïve, but surely not that naïve. Alexei's KGB connections were becoming increasingly obvious – the disparaging remarks about British intelligence, the mysterious and prompt disappearance of the domino-playing 'goons' under the bridge, the leading questions about Mervyn's politics. It was surely blindingly obvious to Mervyn that he was being recruited.

I think the truth is that they never really understood each other. Alexei's dogma prevented him from seeing the deep-rooted patriotism of Mervyn's class and generation, who considered it the height of bad taste to leave a cinema before 'God Save the King' was over. And Mervyn's vanity got in the way of ever seriously questioning why it was that Alexei was courting him, an obscure research student, so assiduously, spending so much money and time. I am quite sure that Mervyn knew he was flirting with the KGB. What he didn't know was just what a dangerous game that could prove to be. Even as he agreed to the Siberia trip, he must have strongly suspected that some time, sooner or later, he would be asked to pay the bill. But adventurousness – again, that now long-buried adventurousness – won out. Whatever happened, it would be exciting. And wasn't excitement exactly what he had come to Russia to find?

Flying over Siberia at night, in winter, there is an eerie sense of having flown off the edge of the world. The dreamscape of snow-covered forests below seems to stretch black and un-broken not just to the horizon but beyond, for ever. When I visited Baikal in 1995, en route to Mongolia – which my father never did get to see – I flew in a tiny Soviet aeroplane, a vintage An-24 which must have begun its long career in my father's day. It lurched in the slipstream, the roar of the propellers drowning out conversation as we flew on into the night, the light dying behind us in the west.

Solzhenitsyn named the network of prison camps which stretched across the Soviet Union the Gulag Archipelago. But in truth all of Russia is an archipelago, a string of isolated islands of warmth and light strung out in a hostile sea of emptiness. Somewhere in this very vastness of Russia lies one key to the Russian experience. The vague-ness and fatalism born of living in a land which once took half a year to cross; a chronic resignation before the whims of authority born of the historic impossibility of commu-nicating with the outposts of such an ungovernably huge empire. When I read of Peter the Great's famous *ukaz* (decree) angrily ordering his citizens to obey all previous *ukazy*, I pictured him as a mad radio operator sending indignant messages into space, and receiving only faint cosmic echoes in reply.

Phone lines, satellite TV and Aeroflot appear to have brought Russia closer together, but in some ways electronic communications only serve to deepen the sense of uncrossable distance. Russia remains the largest country in the world; even after the loss of 17 per cent of its territory after the fall of the Soviet Union, it still spans eleven time zones. A former State TV cameraman once told me that the television signal of *Vremya*, the Soviet nightly news programme, had to be repeatedly bounced off the stratosphere to compensate for the seventy-degree curvature of the earth between Moscow and the far-eastern extremity of the country at Chukotka. By the mid-1990s one could easily direct-dial the Pacific coastal regions of Kamchatka or Magadan, but the time difference was almost the same as to New York. The final section of highway linking European Russia to the Far East was completed only in 2002 – before that hundreds of miles of makeshift road ran upon the ice of the frozen Amur River, and were passable only in winter.

No wonder, then, that most of those born to life in these great, empty spaces grow up with an instinctive sense of helplessness in the face of the impossible physical realities which define their lives. These physical limitations seem to make the constraints of human making all the easier to accept. 'God is high up and the Tsar is far,' goes the old Russian saying, and it could be no coincidence that one of the central teachings of the Russian Orthodox Church was of *smireniye*, or submission to the burden the Lord has given believers to bear. The combined hostility of distance and climate seems to conspire to wither the spirit and humble the ambition of all but the strongest. Anton Chekhov caught this ennui in his *Three Sisters*, a study of three young women crushed by provincial isolation, their youthful hopes and spirit slowly but inexorably extinguished by Russia's infinite inertia. Even life in Moscow, where the sophisticated élite is cocooned from the isolation and medieval darkness of the village, seems defined in a powerful but intangible way by the greatness of the land that surrounds it, just as life on board ship is pervaded by a knowledge of the deep, cold sea all around.

Alexei and Mervyn flew to Siberia in April 1960, as Mervyn's first term at Moscow State University drew to an end. They travelled across the white vastness of Russia in a series of tiny An-24 planes. Their first stop was Novosibirsk, a new, grey industrial sprawl built around a low-rise Tsarist frontier town, all tumbledown log huts and sagging merchants' houses in the centre and wide boulevards lined with identical apartment blocks on the outskirts. Mervyn found it depressing and soulless, despite Alexei's apparently genuine enthusiasm.

They moved on to Bratsk, little more than a shanty town then. Beyond Bratsk lay a great frozen river, and a vast, half-melted lake. A great Socialist lake, Alexei explained, created by the will of the people and the labour of a million workers. In front of the lake stood a great concrete and steel hydroelectric dam, taming nature for the greater good of the workers' paradise.

They checked into a makeshift Intourist hotel, a jerry-built construction among the muddy streets, put up to accommodate visiting dignitaries who were brought to be impressed by the great hydroelectric wonder. They visited the dam the next morning. The spring floodwater roared through the turbines, the concrete curved balletically into the distance. Mervyn agreed with Alexei that it was marvellous, quite marvellous. Alexei nodded silently in approval. Young Mervyn was coming along nicely. 'Was there no end to the exciting surprises in the wonderland which was Russia?' my father wrote later in his memoirs – with irony, or in an echo of his young enthusiasm, I cannot decide.

The last leg of Alexei's grand Siberian tour, planned as a tourist expedition but which had become, unaccountably, a sort of official progress through the wonders of Socialism, was Irkutsk and Baikal. Forest, again endless forest, a horizon so vast it seemed to belong in the landscape of a dream. Lake Baikal, the biggest lake in the world, was flat and blinding white, a gigantic prairie of ice over an expanse of cold, black water 5,000 feet deep.

'In Baikal there are over 300 species of fish,' enthused the plump collective farm director who had mysteriously got wind of Alexei's arrival with his distinguished foreign visitor. The three men stood in silence on the creaking ice of the lake, shivering in the cold, fresh wind. Alexei, his usual composure ruffled by a night in a rude peasant hut, gazed irritably at the shore. Mervyn looked dubiously at the thin spring ice below his feet, which sagged noticeably as they walked.

'It's not the ice, it's what's underneath that's frightening,' remarked Alexei, seeing Mervyn's discomfort.

'Let's go out a bit further,' said the director.

Alexei finally made his offer over a lunch of *pelmeni* dumplings, Siberian fish soup and vodka at Irkutsk Airport, just before they set off back to Moscow. Mervyn had been half-expecting the question, but it was still a shock when it came. Was Mervyn prepared to work for 'the cause of international peace'?

Alexei, hunched forward at the table with a look of utmost seriousness in his eyes, was at his most persuasive. His extolling of the virtues of the just Soviet society were familiar: Mervyn was from a poor family, he had seen at first hand the fairness of Soviet life. Now, the time had come to offer Mervyn an opportunity to do something about the injustice of the world. Though Alexei didn't say the word, it was clear to both of them that this meant working for the KGB.

Mervyn, confounding Alexei's theories of class warfare, refused. He couldn't betray his country, he said. The lunch ended with accusations and petulance. For the first time since Mervyn had known him, Alexei's icy charm cracked and he harangued Mervyn for being spoiled, hypocritical, and ungrateful. Mervyn sat embarrassed and silent.

Back in Moscow, after a long, tense flight, the plane bumped to a halt on the rain-washed tarmac of Vnukovo Airport. As they stood, side by side, waiting for their luggage to be unloaded, Alexei apologized, retreating. 'Let's forget it. I was wrong. It was the wrong time. I would like to see you again in Moscow. Let's just be friends and forget this.' They parted awkwardly, Mervyn embarrassed more than scared by this not entirely unexpected outcome.

Nina from Bukhara called Mervyn at his university dorm. She was in town, she said, on an official trip, and would love to see Mervyn. Right now she was going out to buy a blouse in GUM, the state department store on Red Square, and then she would be free. They made a date for the evening.

As Mervyn put down the phone, he paused. How had Nina found his number? He made a mental note to ask her, but never did.

Mervyn was playing games. He had no inkling of the ruthlessness of the organization he was dealing with. For Mervyn, the KGB was personified in the urbane Alexei and his flattery, and the silent goons who had followed him around Moscow at a respectful distance during his embassy days.

Georges Nivat was under no such illusions. Georges and Irina's idyll quickly soured after Pasternak died of a heart attack at his dacha on 31 May 1960. With Pasternak and his international reputation gone, the Ivinskys lost their famous protector. The KGB had been itching to get them for years; they were notorious for consorting with Westerners and accepting their presents. To cap it all they were the inheritors of the international royalties from Pasternak's poisonous anti-

Soviet book. Now, Olga and her foreigner-loving daughter were to be dealt with.

Shortly after Pasternak's death, Mervyn and Georges, along with all the students in their year, were given a routine smallpox vaccination at the university clinic. Mervyn's inoculation passed without incident, but Georges soon developed a mysterious skin infection. The infection got so bad that he was bedridden in hospital on his would-be wedding day. A second wedding date was set, in July, but a guardian nurse was posted by his bedside in the small hours of the morning, frustrating Irina's plan to smuggle Georges out of hospital. Then Irina herself fell ill with the same horrible skin disease.

At first neither Georges nor Irina – nor even her mother, a veteran of the NKVD torture cells – suspected that they had been infected by the KGB in order to prevent the marriage. But it became increasingly obvious that this was the most likely explanation for their mysterious, virulent rashes. Georges was profoundly shocked by the thought; as was his prospective mother-in-law, despite all that she had seen. Georges' student visa was due to expire at the end of July, and despite his desperate pleas the authorities refused to extend it. Irina was too ill to see Georges off when he left for Paris. Mervyn drove a weeping Georges to the airport, along with Irina's mother. The old woman seemed to have shrunk, a husk of her old, vivacious self, as they saw Georges off. Both he and Irina quickly recovered, but they were not to see each other again until half a lifetime later.

Mervyn decided to take a short holiday with Vadim. They flew to Gagry, the resort on the Black Sea coast where Boris Bibikov had been arrested twenty-five years before. It was a welcome escape from the stuffiness of Moscow's brief but scorching summer, and the distress of Georges and Irina's seemingly incurable illnesses and forced separation. Down south the air was warm and fragrant, unaffected by the drabness and depression of Soviet life, and the locals were hospitable and garrulous rather than cocooned against a hostile world by shells of rudeness.

Mervyn relaxed. The whole KGB business would blow over, he hoped, and Alexei had apparently let the matter drop. He'd been careful never to mention anything to Vadim – still believing, in all apparent sincerity, that Vadim had nothing to do with his attempted recruitment. They lay around on the beaches of Gagry, Mervyn's pale skin burned red by the southern sun, or strolled the promenades. Mervyn asked a friendly, round-faced girl student to come back to his room, and she did so without demur.

But a few days into the holiday Mervyn was summoned to the telephone. It was Alexei, who announced that he was in Gagry. He arranged a rendezvous by the champagne kiosk near the round pond of a nearby park at dusk. Their meeting, among the patterned shadows and the croaking frogs, was short but dramatic. Alexei was elegant and unhurried as ever, and greeted Mervyn courteously. Was Mervyn free that evening? Good. Another rendezvous had been arranged for nine o'clock, in a room at the hotel. Alexei turned and crunched away down the gravel path with his steady step.

Mervyn was not expecting the meeting to be a pleasant one, and it was not. Alexei introduced Mervyn to his 'boss', Alexander Fyodorovich Sokolov. He was an older, heavily built man who wore a bad Soviet suit and cheap sandals. Sokolov was clearly an old-school NKVD bruiser, whose demeanour exuded contempt for his younger, foppish colleague and the spoiled young foreigner who stood before him.

Alexei launched the proceedings with great solemnity. He spoke of Mervyn's 'career' and his 'intentions', about how the Soviet Union was 'the only free and fair society in the world'. Sokolov, quoting from Mervyn's KGB file, grimly noted that his father had been so poor that he never drank wine. Surely it was time for Mervyn to strike a blow against the system which had so oppressed his parent? Evidently, thought Mervyn, the gallons of beer and cases of whisky downed by his old man had not been recorded by the KGB.

After two hours, the threats came. 'We know,' said Alexei gravely, 'that you have been guilty of immoral acts.'

'If the Komsomol were to find out,' growled Sokolov, 'there would be a big scandal in the newspapers, and you would be shamefully expelled from the university and the country.' Now that, Mervyn knew, was nonsense. In fact, there had been all too few 'immoral acts' – a single visit to a brothel in Moscow with Vadim, Nina from Bukhara, the girl at Vadim's uncle's dacha, a girl who lived in a curious, circular building near the Ministry of Foreign Trade, the student in Gagry. It was a pretty modest total, certainly compared to Valery Shein or even Vadim himself.

'The time has come to say finally, yes or no.' Alexei and Alexander Fyodorovich looked at Mervyn expectantly.

'Then the answer must be no,' said my father. 'Nothing will persuade me to work against my country.'

That night, sitting on his bed and turning over the possible consequences of his defiance, Mervyn realized that there could be no more stalling. He wasn't afraid of their threat to cause a scandal, but the KGB could get at his friends. There were sinister stories circulating about trumped-up charges, accidents, arrests for hooliganism, cancellation of residence permits. He decided to pack his bags, take the first plane back to Moscow and leave the Soviet Union, probably for ever.

Yet it wasn't that simple. Days after Mervyn returned to Moscow, Alexei made a conciliatory phone call. A decision had been taken at the highest levels, Alexei assured my father, that no further action would be taken. Alexei even insisted that they have another little dinner. He had a piece of news for Mervyn.

'That woman you mentioned, Olga Vsevolodovna Ivins-kaya,' Alexei said casually as they tucked into what would be their last cosy meal together. 'She's just been arrested. On contraband charges. She was involved in smuggling foreign currency, and other matters. She was morally corrupt.'

Alexei continued to eat as Mervyn stared at his plate, his appetite gone.

'I told you that they were a bad family,' Alexei went on. 'If I were you I'd keep fifteen kilometres away from them.'

Mervyn watched as Alexei sipped more wine. Alexei's face was blank, expressionless. Two weeks after her mother's arrest, Irina herself was taken from her hospital bed and driven to the Lubyanka for questioning. Shortly afterwards Irina, the ballet lover and aesthete, followed her mother into the unimaginably brutal world of the labour camps. Mervyn heard nothing more of them. This was not a game, it finally dawned on Mervyn. This was not a game at all. He made hurried arrangements to return to Oxford.

10

Love

Adventures can be wonderful things.
Mervyn Matthews to Vadim Popov, spring 1964

Especially when they're over.
Vadim Popov

The Moscow my father knew was a solidly rooted place, its certainties and rules as fixed as the prices in state shops and the squat Stalinist cityscape. Most Soviets of his generation spent their entire lives in the same apartment, worked in the same jobs, bought vodka for an unvarying 2 rubles 87 kopecks and waited ten years to buy a car. Time was measured from vacation to vacation, theatre season to theatre season, from the publication of one volume of a collection of Dickens novels to the next.

Forty years later, when I arrived in Moscow, the city was making up for lost time. The place was obsessed with its own thrusting modernity; it seemed to change overnight, every night. One day you'd see young men with Caesar haircuts and DKNY sweaters where previously red blazers and crew cuts had been in. Internet cafés-cum-trendy clothes shops opened in the place of old grocery stores. Gleaming new chrome and marble shopping malls sprang up with alarming speed, complete with see-through escalators and dollar-dispensing cash

machines. After a while I got so used to the pace of change
that it seemed normal – a restored church here, a new
corporate headquarters there, like mushrooms after the rain.
London seemed quaintly static in comparison. The rest of
Russia may have been quietly disintegrating, but Moscow
waxed fat on the spoils of the plundered empire.

Whenever I wasn't trawling the lower depths of Moscow's
underbelly for lurid features articles, I dedicated much of my
energy to going to parties. My father had found his fun in noisy
Gypsy restaurants. A generation later, and sudden money and
freedom had transformed the Moscow party scene into something rich and strange. At Club 13, housed in a decrepit palace
just behind the Lubyanka, dwarves in miniature Santa Claus
costumes would whip you with cat-o'-nine-tails as you walked
up the stairs. In Titanic, the favoured haunt of wealthy criminals, the black Mercedes were parked a dozen deep outside
and gangs of girls would wait at porthole-shaped tables to be
chatted up by fat-necked beaux. At Chance, naked men swam
in giant glass-fronted fish tanks, and at the Fire Bird casino I
once spent an evening drinking in the unlikely company of
Chuck Norris, the ageing action film star, and his guest
Vladimir Zhirinovsky, the ultranationalist politician.

Sometimes I would brave a visit to a bar called the Hungry
Duck. On 'Ladies' Nights' only women – and a few friends of
the owner, invited to tend bar – were allowed into the place
between six and nine. The deal was that they would be plied
with unlimited free alcohol, and as a result the place was
packed with about six hundred sweaty teenage girls, all baying
for booze as fast as we could pour it. The smell of Slavic
pheromones hung thick, and the sight of a wall of screaming
women besieging all sides of the circular bar was terrifying,
like defending Rourke's Drift against advancing Zulus. Male
strippers would strut down the bar, plucking girls from the
audience and stripping them naked over the beer taps. Doug
Steele, the Canadian owner, his face turned a Mephistophe-

lean green by the light of the cash register, would lean forward
on his brawny arms and survey the mayhem with quiet
satisfaction, like Captain Kurtz in his own private Inner
Station. By the time they let the men in at nine, drunken,
topless girls would be slipping off the beer-covered bar and
crashing on to the floor, to be scooped up by security and
dumped in a line in the foyer. Soon epic fights would break
out; vicious, eye-gouging, smashed bottle affairs with flying
beer glasses and broken bones, with the unconscious losers
joining the drunks downstairs.

I went to a party thrown by Bogdan Titomir, Russia's most
famous rapper, at his apartment-cum-disco, where the windows rattled to the sound of the music blasting on the PA and
couples sneaked out to kiss in the back of his Hummer. When
I first saw Yana she was backlit by pulsing strobes as she
snaked through the smoke, past the blondes draped over
Bogdan's electric blue sofas, past the entwined bodies in a
half-curtained alcove, towards a table piled with cocaine. She
wore a tiny miniskirt covered in printed pairs of luminous
Fornasetti eyes, which matched the strange glow of her own
under the ultraviolet light which hung over the table. She
deftly railed out a line fat as a hangman's rope, and snorted it.
Then she threw her blonde hair back and looked me straight
in the eye. And winked.

'*Polezno i vkusno*,' she said, smiling – 'healthy and tastes
good', a slogan from a TV cereal ad – and held out a rolled-up
bill.

I found her, later, sitting on Bogdan's doorstep, legs apart,
wrists draped over her knees, smoking. I sat down next to her.
She shot me a glance, taking a drag from her cigarette with the
corner of her mouth. We began to talk.

Yana was a classic child of Moscow's golden youth – rich,
smart, privileged and completely lost. Her father was a former
Soviet diplomat in Switzerland; her mother was from a long
line of St Petersburg intellectuals. Half of Moscow was in love

with her, and the more she spurned them the more they loved her. She had a talent for situations, which had served her well for twenty years of an erratic and unpunctual life. The ease with which she moved from one milieu to another, from one place, man, date, to another was staggering. Her flightiness and instability was truly irresistible. She was savagely elemental, temperamental, capricious, often as selfish as a tiny child. Yana always reminded me of someone constantly trying out a series of savage caricatures of herself on the world, adopting slightly new variants of her social persona. And as with many lonely people she had a burning desire to be loved, and to be fabulous, but loved from afar. And that was her paradox; the more fabulous she became, the more impossible it became for her to be loved for herself.

We would meet at Tram, a nouveau riche hangout near Pushkin Square with steel tubular chairs and matt black tables, where, after a light but cripplingly expensive dinner, she would drag me to various parties. One was at a set in the MosFilm studios built for *The Three Musketeers*, a labyrinth of plywood seventeenth-century balconies, archways and spiral staircases. Girls in feather jackets and hot pants danced on a horse-drawn coach while fit young men in Boss jeans and slicked hair looked on. Another was in the Theatre of the Red Army, an absurd star-shaped Stalinist building surrounded by neoclassical columns. Instead of a Victory Day balalaika extravaganza, the place had been transformed into a Day-Glo rave bacchanal populated by long-legged girls with steel bras and shaven-headed men in green fur coats. I have a vision of Yana, in a pair of wraparound shades she'd borrowed from someone, dancing maniacally on the edge of the revolving stage. She pumped her fist in the air as she cruised past me at a stately three miles an hour, screaming '*Davai, Davai!*' – an untranslatable expression of exuberance – as she went.

For all Moscow's sleaziness, I loved the energy of this bonfire of vanities. I believed that I had stumbled on something dark, vibrant and absolutely compelling. The money, the sin, the beautiful people – it was doomed, apocalyptic, transiently beautiful as a Javanese fire sculpture. The incandescent energy of the pretty, deluded party kids who frequented these places could have lit up this blighted country for a century if channelled into anything other than self-destruction and oblivion.

Yana and I saw each other regularly for about six months. Her fabulous presence transformed me, I thought, into someone better and bolder. I felt constant disbelief that this extraordinary creature was by my side. This cannot be true, I told myself. I was not even jealous as she kissed and flirted her way around parties. I waited in line with the rest for the searchlight of her charm to fall upon me, and it was enough. Every time she ignored all the rich boys and came back home with me seemed a small miracle.

There were a few rare moments when she shed the heavy burden of her persona and became meek and vulnerable, a younger and less complex version of herself. This is the Yana which endures for me now – not the fabulous Yana of Bogdan's, but the make-up-less Yana in a Russian Navy pea coat I gave her and silk combat pants stomping through Moscow in big boots, mercifully incognito.

Then, as I had always expected, she seemed to lose interest, and I didn't press it. I rationalized it by telling myself that I was better off confining my sexual energies to earth dwellers, rather than heavenly creatures like Yana.

But after Yana and I stopped seeing each other I brooded; lumpen, sagging, armchair depression. She'd make a perfect first wife, I would joke to my best friend and fellow *Moscow Times* reporter Matt Taibbi. I found my old apartment too redolent of my pre-Yana life, too grounded in adolescence. So I borrowed a friend's place for a few days while he was away, and spent days sitting on his deformed old sofa, smoking cigarettes. I felt I needed to mark the moment with some act of masochism, so I asked Matt to bring his electric hair clippers round. By the apartment's tenth-floor picture window looking on to the Kremlin, he shaved my head clean of its schoolboy locks, which fell thickly on the spread newspapers strewn around the chair.

The pain of my decision to let Yana go without a fight – to choose Later rather than Now – ran deeper than I knew. I had been unable to twist free from the straitjacket of common sense when Yana and her world of extravagant folly called, and that knowledge burned hot on my cheeks like shame. It seemed to age me – all the more so because I also knew that with time the wound would heal almost without trace, and I would go on as before. I was bitter because my teenage bohemianism had been so brutally exposed as a brittle sham, and I was humiliated because I felt acutely that the real reason that I had lost Yana was that I was not man enough to keep her. The realization was brutal, and I fled from it by returning to the more sordid habits of my old life with a vengeance, trying to obliterate the pain with sex and negate the humiliation with bragging. It worked, for a while.

After half a year or so, the intensity of my feelings for her faded into a faint pang every time I saw her photo in *Ptyuch* or some other trendy magazine devoted to the antics of the city's club kids. I was a new friend who was destined never to become an old friend – too little time, so many people and parties. But I liked to think that among a thousand discarded people, impressions, parties, somewhere in that fabulous kaleidoscope of her butterfly brain, my image was lodged.

Yana was too beautiful, too surreally perfect to live, so I was strangely unsurprised when a mutual acquaintance called late one night, in the autumn of 1996, and told me that she had been found raped and murdered at a remote Metro stop somewhere in Moscow's grey suburban hinterland. No one – least of all the police – had any idea of who would want to kill her.

Even before her death I couldn't think of her as anything but a child of her time, vibrating to the deep, doomed rhythms of a specific moment. I could never place her anywhere else but Moscow, or imagine her old, or bored, or cynical, or fat, or married. So that's why it seemed right, somehow, that Russia swallowed her in the end.

She had been so perversely bright and optimistic while everything about her lied and died. But reality finally reached up to pluck her out of her cloud, like Icarus, and pulled her down, down deep into its dark underbelly. She died broken, raped and terrified near a remote Metro station, strangled by someone – a stranger, a lover? Who knows? If she'd been a character in my novel I would have killed her off, too.

Mervyn returned to the Soviet Union at the end of the summer of 1963, three years after he had left. Through St Antony's, he had managed to arrange another graduate exchange with Moscow State University. The fact that the authorities had allowed him back was proof enough, he surmised with relief, that bygones were bygones with the KGB. Back in Moscow, Mervyn quickly picked up his old friendships – with the exception, that is, of Alexei and Vadim.

Mervyn had had enough of the high life he'd pursued in his earlier incarnations. He was thirty-one years old, and ready to settle down. Valery Golovitser told Mervyn that he knew a delightful girl who'd be just right for him. Golovitser, it seems, was a more astute student of his fellow men than his friend and cousin Valery Shein, who tried to persuade Mervyn to go out with the brassy, fashionable and pretty girls of his fast circle.

No, the girl Valery had in mind for Mervyn was as intellectual and romantic as he was himself, but brave and spirited with it. Mervyn was interested, but thought the idea of a blind date crass. He asked if he could see Valery's friend Lyudmila before they were formally introduced.

Valery suggested that Mervyn wait for them outside the portico of the Bolshoi after the end of a performance; that way he could catch a glimpse of his prospective new girlfriend. It was an arrangement that only someone from an absolutely innocent age could have contemplated, more like something out of a Molière play than the start of a real-world romance. Nevertheless, Mervyn duly waited in the driving sleet of an October evening, and indeed caught a glimpse of a diminutive young woman with a slight limp, chatting animatedly with Valery as they emerged from the theatre.

A small tea party was arranged in Golovitser's little room. Mervyn was introduced as an Estonian, to ease the exoticism and awkwardness that the presence of a bona fide Englishman would have caused. Mila remembers what she noticed most of all was the shy 'Estonian's' beautiful long back. Mervyn noticed Mila's kind grey-blue eyes. In an occasional diary Mervyn kept, written in clumsy Welsh to render it incomprehensible to the KGB in case he lost the notebook, he noted on 28 October 1963 that he'd met a girl 'of very strong character, but utterly charming, intelligent'. They arranged to see each other again. They went on long walks together and chatted for hours. Before long, my father had become a regular visitor to my mother's tiny room on Starokonushenny Pereulok.

My mother and I went to see the old place, once, thirty-odd years after she left it, during one of my mother's annual visits to Moscow. The house stood back from the street, through two archways filled with uncollected rubbish. It was in an ugly, turn-of-the-century building, squat and institutional, with thick walls and barred windows on the ground floor. The hallway smelled of sodden cardboard and mould, and the ground-floor doorway to the communal apartment was covered in flaking layers of brown institutional paint. It still had its old row of doorbells, one for every room of the *kommunalka*. I pressed the button, the same one my father pressed for the first time in 1963, hesitantly, bearing carnations, and again, for the last time, in 1969 when he came to take her away with him to England. A young woman opened the door, listened as we explained that my mother had once lived there, and let us in with a shy smile. She and her husband and the old woman with whom they shared the *kommunalka* were moving out soon, she said. The building was due to be gutted and sold off by the Moscow City Government for conversion into luxury flats.

It was not much of an apartment. There was a wide corridor lined with curling linoleum, gaping layers of wallpaper, and separate locks on each door. At the end of the passage was a squalid kitchen, its ceiling peeling from the weight of years of grease, disconnected gas pipes from defunct cookers sticking out of the wall.

My mother's room, little more than a storeroom, really, was now a nursery for a sleeping two-year-old. My mother looked round unsentimentally, peering up and down as if looking for something that remained of her. Finding nothing, she turned and we left. She seemed unmoved, and we went shopping.

At the time, I was living on Starokonushenny Pereulok myself. The house was an early thirties constructivist building, and the long, narrow rooms of the apartment had walls and windows at strange angles. It was 300 yards from my mother's old apartment near the corner of the Arbat. In the evenings I would wander the deserted backstreets, up to Ryleev Street, where Valery Golovitser used to live and where my parents first met. I'd walk down Gogolevsky Boulevard, where they had walked, arm in arm, to the Kropotkinskaya Metro, and up Sivtsev-Vrazhek Street, where my mother used to walk to Gastronom Number One for her shopping. They were streets freighted with memory for my parents, but not yet for me. I had not yet read their letters, nor taken much of an interest in their early lives; I did not, then, feel any connection between their Moscow and mine. 'Mervyn, do you imagine how I walk through the puddles of night-time Moscow to our home on the Arbat?' my mother wrote to my father, late in 1964. He did. Now I do, too.

In her little lightless room with its single narrow window, Mila made something that she'd never had before – a home. Then, when Mervyn appeared in her life, she made a family.

'In the autumn of 1963 I saw you for the first time,' Mila wrote a year later. 'I felt some kind of inner impulse, some kind of momentary, searing certitude that you were precisely the one person with whom I would finally, really fall in love. It was as though a piece of my heart detached itself and began living independently within you. I was not mistaken. In a very short time I understood you and came as close to you as if I had been your shadow since your first steps in this world. All the barriers collapsed – political, geographic, national, sexual. The whole world was divided for me into two halves – one, us (you and me), and the other – the rest.'

The minutiae of the nine months my parents spent together in Moscow survive because over six years of forced separation their conversations were all relived, in great detail, in their later letters. Almost every minute and day of their few months together was revisited and turned over, lovingly, like a keep-sake. Every little tiff and conversation and lovemaking and walk was played out in Mila's mind, replayed and discussed, words, sentences remembered and analyzed, produced like living proof that it was not all just a dream, that for a while they really had a home, had each other. 'Literally every detail of our lives together goes through my mind,' Mila wrote. 'I live for the memory of those times.'

In the winter evenings, on his way back to the university from the Lenin Library, Mervyn would stop by Valery Go-lovitser's place to chat and pick up some new records, duck into an archway to try and shake off his KGB goons, and appear at Mila's front door. He would install himself on her

divan and read while she fried sturgeon, Mervyn's favourite
fish, in the kitchen. After dinner they would go for long walks
along the boulevards and the backstreets, and sit up into the
night talking. He loved her homemade jam, served on pre-
revolutionary Gardner plates she'd bought in an antique shop
and which she took with her to London. Later, Mila's room
with its divan bed, little table and wardrobe became a lovers'
everywhere for them, while the neighbours in the next room
held rowdy parties and played the accordion.

Their romance was a homecoming for them both – two
lonely, bookish, loveless people finding in each other what
they had lacked all their dislocated lives. Mila was twenty-nine
and raised on the romantic fantasies of Soviet films and
literature. Most of her friends and her sister had married in
their teens. Mila, though she'd had affairs and was popular
with men despite her twisted hip, had never found someone
who lived up to her exacting standards.

But now, suddenly, as though by an act of God, came the
long-backed foreigner, the dreamy, shy Russophile with his
long fingers and careful vowels, so earnest and innocent
(despite those tumbles into sin in the company of Vadim
and Shein), so lost, so in love with Russia but with no home
there. She would become the embodiment of all he loved in
Russia, its passion and fire.

Mervyn was the exact shape of the gap in Mila's life. He
made sense of her existence, he was what she had been
missing to make her complete, to patch over the horror of
her childhood and the loneliness of her adulthood. She
became the intelligent mother he never had. He became
the son, the child to nurture as she was never nurtured, as
if by healing him she could heal herself, make everything all
right for both of them. After a lifetime of deprivation, Mervyn
was Mila's redemption.

'Life can't be so cruel and unfair if it gave me you,' Mila
wrote to him, later, when they were living on opposite sides of

the Iron Curtain. 'For some reason I have moved into you, and nothing will chase me out of such a warm habitation. There's so little warmth and love in the world that you can't afford to lose even a crumb of it that you've found.'

Mervyn was truly Mila's first love, and it had all the moral purity and absolute, dreamlike clarity of adolescence. Mila had all too few human reference points for her emotional life, but many literary ones. The language of love, for her, was melodramatic, naïve and slightly childish, but underpinned with a welling passion which was all her own. It was not an erotic passion, but a passion fuelled by a terrible fear of abandonment, of losing this one chance to redeem her unhappy life and cancel out all its suffering with one bold stroke.

For Mervyn it was a little different. His good looks meant that Russian women liked him, flirted with him, went to bed with him. But he never had Shein's fervour or hunger for women. Women made him shy, and he couldn't summon the cavalier charm of his Russian friends, their swagger, or their lady-killing confidence. Now, here was Mila, the woman with a crippled body but a beautiful soul, devoted, unthreatening, intellectually independent, an ally and friend first and a woman second, yet with an apparently endless supply of love to pour out to him. 'I want to make a good, healthy life for you, a home, good food,' wrote Mila later, of her vision of their future. 'It will give me such pleasure to help you with your work. I am sure that we can make a real family, bound together by love and friendship, mutual understanding, helping each other. Everything we have we have done with our own work, by our own wits. Together, we can achieve anything.'

Most important of all, perhaps, was that Mila understood Mervyn's painful past as no one had ever been able to before. 'I see your desire to get yourself out of poverty, out of anonymity into the big world,' she wrote. 'I see how you, alone and without patrons and without a clear path to follow, are pushing on with life and scaling its heights; I understand your tastes, your interests, your weaknesses.'

There was a moment, on a slushy February evening, when Mervyn and Mila left the apartment on Starokonushenny Pereulok together and walked down to Gogolevsky Boulevard. Mervyn had to turn right to go to Kropotkinskaya Metro, Mila to the left to go and visit some friends. They embraced, and as he walked away in the twilight Mervyn suddenly realized, as he wrote in his memoirs, that he was 'profoundly in love with that lopsided figure, and I could see no future for myself without her'.

He had no idea – how could he – of quite how hard they would have to fight for that love in the years to come, or how profoundly it would transform his life. His love for Mila, like his love for Russia, began as a romantic infatuation. What had gone before were adventures, free of consequences and exciting. What was to come would expel him from himself and summon all his reserves of determination.

Mila invited Mervyn to her sister Lenina's apartment on Frunzenskaya Embankment, a sure sign of the growing seriousness of their relationship. Even after all his years in Russia, Lenina's was the first family home Mervyn had ever visited. None of his friends, not even Vadim, had invited him back to anything other than a bachelor room in the university or a *kommunalka* like Valery Golovitser's.

It was a characteristically brave move for Mila to ask him, and for Lenina to accept the idea of a foreigner coming to visit. Mervyn's sporadic KGB tails were a fact of life for both of them, and they cheerfully ignored it – but his visit could prove dangerous for Lenina's one-legged husband Sasha, who was by now head of the finance department of the Ministry of Justice. Still, Mervyn came, and was fed *shchi* soup and meatballs and cake and tea, and treated as a member of

the family. He was invited back. Despite my father's dangerous foreignness and the odd formality of his manner, Lenina,
Sasha and their two teenage daughters quickly grew fond of
him.

Summer came, and Mila invited Mervyn to the Vasins'
dacha at Vnukovo, an hour's drive from the centre of Moscow
but already firmly in the Russian hinterland of infinite skies,
endless fields, earth privies and water brought in buckets from
a well. In the sunshine, Mervyn helped Sasha dig the garden
and plant potatoes and cucumbers. In the afternoons they
would feed twigs and birch bark into the samovar and drink
smoky tea and eat blackcurrant jam as the light faded. Mila
and Mervyn would go for long walks in the birch woods, he in
a short-sleeved shirt, she in a long cotton print baby-doll dress,
pinched at the waist, copied from a picture in a magazine.

I visited the dacha myself, when I was eight, on a trip to
Moscow with my mother and baby sister. I was deeply excited
at living in the little wooden house, with its creaking floorboards, filled with the smell of earth and pickles and with dust
swirling in beams of summer sunshine. The northern summer
days seemed to stretch for ever, the sky cloudless and vast. But
however hot the day was, the wheat fields were always damp
and filled with frogs and snails. There was a small pond full of
miniature perch, one of which I once caught in a jam jar and
brought home. My little fish died overnight, and I was so guilt-
stricken that I buried it ceremoniously in the garden, digging
the thick earth with my fingers.

The garden ran riot, despite the efforts of my uncle Sasha to
tend it. Lenina used to say scornfully that he'd planted three
sacks of potatoes and harvested two. This may have had
something to do with the fact that we boys – oddly enough
I remember no awkward period of shy integration with the
other village boys, we were immediately a gang – would
surreptitiously dig them up in the afternoons while the

grown-ups were having their naps, replace the potato plant carefully in the ground and repair with our haul to the woods, where we'd bake the potatoes in the ash of our camp fire.

In the late afternoons we would sometimes go into the forest to collect berries and mushrooms. This ancient habit seemed part of the Russian psyche; everyone in the village did it obsessively. After the breezy summer heat in the fields and dusty lanes the forest was dark, still and musty. It was a classic Russian birch forest, endless and disorientating and silent. I was always afraid of clearing away the dead leaves to expose the mushrooms at the foot of the trees after a huge millipede ran on to my hand. The Russian spirit was here, it smelled of Russia. Out of sight of the path it seemed primeval, full of shadows and whispers, unlike any English wood.

The old samovar was there from my father's day, and I would collect dry pine cones to stoke the fire, which never quite seemed to boil the water as it was supposed to. As we drank warm tea and ate homemade jam, I would ask Sasha about the war, and his tank. He was a good-natured man, and answered my questions patiently. An old local woman known as Babka Simka, who helped my aunt about the house, chastised me for my awful ignorance of the history of the Great Patriotic War, but I persisted. Later, my village friends and I would play at Civil War, Reds versus Whites. The greatest honour would be to pull a wooden model of a Vickers machine gun made by one of the village boys' grandfathers on its little trolley. As we trundled it down the rutted main street past my aunt's dacha, Sasha would sometimes shout, 'Peace to the land of the Soviets!' in encouragement as we passed.

Back in Moscow, on the evening of 27 March 1964, Mervyn was having dinner with Mila in her room. He was a methodical man, and had resolved to wait for a while before proposing to her. But as they went into the kitchen to put the dirty dishes into the sink, he suddenly blurted out, 'Let's get registered!'

'Oh Mervusya,' said Mila, using the diminutive of his name she had invented. They embraced in the greasy warmth of the kitchen. But she didn't say yes. Instead, she said Mervyn should think about it, in case he wanted to change his mind. They kissed goodbye in the corridor, and Mervyn walked to the Metro.

The next day Mervyn stopped by, and Mila accepted. Immediately, they went to the mansion on Griboyedov Street which housed the Central Palace of Weddings, the only place foreigners were allowed to marry. In the secular Soviet Union, couples were married not in the name of God but in the name of the State, presided over by busts of Lenin and accompanied by a taped burst of Prokofiev from a machine manned by a scowling old woman. Mervyn and Mila waited in line outside the director's office during the busy lunch hour to put their names down for a wedding date. They were told that the earliest slot was nearly three months away, on 9 June, and they took it. They left with an invitation form certifying their marriage date, and were duly issued with vouchers for champagne which they could redeem in special shops. On the street they parted, my father taking the trolleybus to the Lenin Library and my mother going back to work.

The long Moscow winter was drawing to its end. Mervyn would sit at Mila's tiny table, making notes from his books in a pool of lamplight, while Mila sat on the bed and knitted. She bought Mervyn records and books on her way home from work, where all the girls were curious and envious of her tall, shy fiancé. Most nights he would take the last Metro home to his room in the university, but sometimes he would stay, the two of them squeezed on to the tiny bed like teenagers, and Mervyn would tiptoe out before the neighbours rose. They had both, at last, achieved happiness.

*   *   *

Their idyll was bitterly short. In May, after a tedious meeting with his supervisor at Moscow State University, Mervyn noticed an unusually heavy KGB team had been assigned to follow him. He had an appointment with a university friend, Igor Vail, that afternoon, but because of the goons Mervyn called and suggested they meet another time because, Mervyn explained in unmistakable euphemism, 'I don't like to come round under certain circumstances.'

Mervyn was nervous because Vail had bought a red sweater from him a few weeks before. Mervyn was due to collect the money, which Igor hadn't been able to pay him straight away. Mervyn had also given Igor an old brown suit to give in to the *kommisionka*, or second-hand shop, which only a Soviet citizen could do. Technically, both actions were illegal, as was all private commerce in the Soviet Union. Igor had taken the suit, saying he could get a better price from an African student at the university. Igor sounded unnaturally tense when Mervyn telephoned, but insisted that he come round anyway.

Vail shared a room in a communal apartment on Kropotkinskaya Street with his mother. He greeted Mervyn over-warmly at the door. His mother was not there, but two middle-aged men in suits sat on the divan. 'My two friends,' blurted Igor, 'are interested in buying that brown suit that you wanted to sell, remember?'

'Yes, we are interested in anything you want to sell,' said one of the men stiffly.

There was a silence. Mervyn turned to leave. This was obviously a hideously amateurish set up, and with rising panic he realized who must have organized it, and why. Igor continued to smile, desperately. The man who had spoken got up from the sofa and produced a red police identity card. Mervyn, he said, was under arrest for the crime of economic speculation.

The detectives drove Igor and Mervyn in silence to the nearest police station, the Sixtieth Militia Precinct on Maly

Mogiltsevsky Pereulok, just behind Smolenskaya Square. After a short wait Mervyn was shown in to the office of the duty investigator, a Captain Mirzuyev, who painstakingly composed a long account of the incident, dwelling on Mervyn's crimes as a corrupter of Soviet youth and a capitalist speculator. But the accused refused to sign, and asked the militiaman to show him to a telephone. Mervyn knew perfectly well who was behind the whole incident and could, at least, feel a little superior at the fact that the calibre of his persecutors was higher than that of a mere police captain.

'I need to call the KGB,' he told Mirzuyev, who took him immediately to the front desk phone.

Mervyn called a number Alexei had given to him years before, which he had in his notebook. An unknown woman answered, who seemed unperturbed by the news that Mervyn was calling from a police station. She took his details and told him to wait.

Half an hour later, Alexei walked into the interview room in a sharp suit, dapper as ever. They had not seen each other for nearly three years. He eyed Mervyn disapprovingly and went through the pretence of asking what had happened. Mervyn, deciding it best to play Alexei's game, told him the details of what had happened. 'You realize it's a very serious charge, Mervyn,' Alexei said coldly. 'Very serious.'

There were few formalities. Alexei simply led Mervyn out of the police station and into a waiting car, a ZiL. Alexei has come up in the world, thought Mervyn as they drove up into the Lenin Hills and back to the university. Alexei tried to make small talk, politely asking about Mervyn's mother. Mervyn replied that she was ill, but would be a lot worse if she knew what trouble her son was in. 'Oh yes, Mervyn,' said Alexei. 'You are in trouble.'

They had little else to say to each other as they sat side by side on the ZiL's wide back seat.

*　　*　　*

Later, alone at night in his room at the university looking over the lights of the city, Mervyn thought hard about what to do. He assumed that Alexei would soon renew his old offer to work 'for the people of the Soviet Union'. There were six weeks to go before his planned wedding day, and the Soviets could very easily expel him or imprison him for up to two years if he played his cards wrong. He was on borrowed time.

Mervyn told Mila the next day that the KGB had staged a 'provocation' against him. Mila, who could be so unreasonable over trivialities, was calm in crisis. She poured Mervyn a cup of tea. 'Well that's life in Moscow,' she said, and served him some of her jam on a saucer to eat with a spoon. Somehow, Mervyn hoped that he could continue stalling the KGB long enough to marry Lyudmila and carry her away to England for ever.

Unfortunately, the KGB had other plans. There were a series of tense meetings in the Metropole Hotel with his old antagonists, Alexei and his boss, Alexander Fyodorovich Sokolov. Mervyn tried to prevaricate, telling them of his great love and sympathy for the cause of international peace and understanding of peoples. The KGB men were getting impatient and pressed hard for a straight answer. Sokolov, for one, had been brought up in an era when such caprices were customarily dealt with by the simple application of brutality. He cut acidly through Mervyn's floundering – would he work for the KGB or not? He became aggressive, banging the table, infuriated by my father's increasingly desperate evasions. At the end of what was to be their last meeting, it was very clear that the KGB's patience was fast running out, if it had not done so already.

For as long as I have known of it, my father's defiance of the KGB has struck me as a noble and principled act. But on another level I also find it incomprehensible. It has occurred to me, as I write this, that if I had been forced to choose between being separated from the woman I loved and signing a paper saying I would work for the KGB, I would have unhesitatingly signed on the dotted line. Whatever my private feelings for the KGB, I would have considered the cause of my personal happiness supreme above all others. I cannot decide if this is a difference between my and my father's generation, or one of temperament between us personally.

My father was born into a generation whose fathers had walked in good order into withering machine-gun fire for King and Country. He grew up in a conformist age, and though much in his life was remarkably individualistic, the idea of betraying his country and capitulating to the blandishments of the KGB, never mind how delicately phrased, was something he could not countenance. But his refusal wasn't a question of choosing conformity over the extravagant folly of treachery. His deeply held sense of personal honour simply would not let him do it; despite a lifelong cynicism about politics, he never had doubts about his love for his country. He was to pay a heavy price for his principles.

A note arrived, on thin official notepaper, announcing that my parents' wedding date had been cancelled because 'a criminal case has been opened' against Mervyn – which wasn't actually true, as the police case was still at the investigation stage. The KGB had also called Valery Golovitser in for a long series of interrogations, on condition of strict secrecy, but he nevertheless let Mervyn know through mutual friends that the hammer had fallen on him. My father, by now thoroughly scared of what the KGB's next move would be, realized that the consequences of his stand were beginning to be felt by his friends.

One way, Mervyn thought, to stop this spiral of revenge might be to buttonhole the Labour leader Harold Wilson, at that time still leader of the Opposition. Wilson was in Moscow for a meeting with the Soviets, who took a keen interest in Labour's chances at the next election. Mervyn took a trolleybus to the National Hotel on the evening Wilson arrived, and used his foreignness as a talisman to brush past the hotel security and find his way to Wilson's room. Wilson himself answered Mervyn's knock, but when he began to explain his predicament and to ask him to intervene personally with Khrushchev, Wilson, smelling trouble, politely but firmly refused. A visit two days later to Wilson's shadow foreign secretary, Patrick Gordon Walker, was even more firmly rebuffed. Walker advised my father, fatuously, to contact the embassy.

Mervyn and Lyudmila decided to show up at the Palace of Weddings on Griboyedov Street on their allocated date, regardless of the cancellation. Mila wore a linen wedding dress embroidered with pearls, and Mervyn carried a heavy red gold wedding ring he had bought for the occasion in his jacket pocket.

My father, in a gamble which ultimately was to do nothing but hasten the end, invited an entourage of foreign correspondents to cover his attempt to marry. Victor Louis of the *Evening News*, a mysterious character of Russian birth who was the doyen of the foreign press in Moscow, was present, as well as at least a dozen KGB goons. In the event, the wedding palace's director wisely chose to stay away from the building all day. Her stubborn deputy refused to marry the couple, saying that their reservation had been cancelled on orders from 'the administration'. Louis battled bravely on their behalf, pressing the deputy for a 'valid legal reason' for refusing to marry the couple. The bureaucrats retreated behind the old Soviet tactic of doing nothing for hours on end, and eventually their supplicants' energy dissolved into despair, and as evening fell everyone went home.

My father sensed that the inevitable reprisal after his failed publicity stunt was not far away, and went to ground in Lyudmila's flat. The foreign press, finding him missing from his room at the university, reported that he had disappeared. For two days, Mila and Mervyn clung to the illusion that a miracle might happen, trying to keep the terrible rip-tides of the world at bay outside the flimsy door of her room. Mila called in sick to work, and the two of them spent the days walking on the Arbat arm in arm, or locked in their little room reading and talking. But the shared telephone of the *kommunalka* ruined their desperate attempt to suspend time. Mervyn was urgently wanted at the British embassy.

One diplomat and one of the embassy's resident spooks stood waiting for him at the entrance to the Chancery, and took him down to the 'bubble', a supposedly surveillance-proof little booth where they could talk without being overheard. The reason for this cloak-and-dagger business was to inform Mervyn that the Foreign Office 'had reason to believe that Mila was a KGB plant'. No evidence for this assertion was offered. In what Mervyn later recalled as one of the proudest moments of his life, prouder even than his refusal to work for Alexei, he stood up in disgust and walked out of the room, and out of the embassy, without saying another word.

But though his disgust was genuine enough, the bravado was forced. Now truly desperate, his natural shyness overcome by panic and the rising sense of imminent catastrophe, my father took the trolleybus back to his little refuge on Starokonushenny Pereulok to await the inevitable. The next day, 20 June, two British embassy officials called at the apartment to deliver a letter. The presence of so many foreigners caused a sensation among Mila's whispering neighbours.

The letter informed my father that the embassy had received an official letter from the Soviet Foreign Ministry to the effect that one William Haydn Mervyn Matthews, graduate student, was now considered *persona non grata* in the Soviet Union and was to leave immediately. Minutes later, a uniformed militiaman and a *druzhinnik*, or civilian helper, rang the door bell. Mervyn had been living at the apartment without registration, the militiaman said, and he must come with them. He had little choice.

They drove quickly through central Moscow – the streets were still almost empty of traffic then – skirting Lubyanka Square, which for a nasty moment Mervyn thought might be their final destination, and instead heading up Chernyshevsky Street to OVIR, the passport and registration office. There, Mervyn was served with formal notice that his visa had expired and that he should leave immediately. A British embassy staffer present volunteered to help to find a place on an otherwise terribly crowded plane to London the next day, 21 June 1964. Mervyn was so disgusted that he refused to say a word in English, forcing the embassy man to have every word of his conversation with the officials laboriously translated.

They spent their last night together at Mila's flat. Mervyn didn't bother to return to the university to pack his things. Both he and Mila were almost dumb with grief. In the morning she accompanied Mervyn in a taxi to Vnukovo Airport, grey-faced and in shock. They embraced. As Mervyn went through the barrier to passport control and out of her life, probably for ever, Mila was overwhelmed with grief no less bitter than that she had felt when her parents had been taken away from her.

'God, what terrible minutes I spent there at the airport. I stood alone in the corner, watching your plane, overflowing with tears,' Mila wrote to Mervyn a few days later. 'The taxi drivers were trying to help, asking what the matter was; they said they'd take me for free if I didn't have the money. I couldn't leave for a long time, I hung around there, hoping a miracle would happen and you would return.'

11

Mila and Mervusya

My love is stronger than their hate.
Mila to Mervyn

Mervyn awoke to birdsong. Outside it was a bright summer morning in a neat English suburban garden. From the kitchen downstairs he could hear the clink of breakfast plates and the drone of BBC radio. As he lay in bed, the events of the last few days crowded in like the aftermath of a nightmare.

'He's a stubborn fool, and he should know better,' his forthright mother had told the *Daily Express* the day before, and she was surely right about the stubbornness. But there was more to it than that. Mervyn had fought all his life against the provincial drudgery that others had ordained for him. Now, he realized, he would have to fight for Mila too.

That morning Mervyn resolved to do everything in his power to get Mila out of Russia. This was no impulsive decision. Ever the pragmatist, he gave himself five years. Then, if it was still hopeless, he would reconcile himself to failure, and move on.

Mervyn set up an office in the back bedroom of his half-brother Jack's small house in Barnes. From there he began making calls, picking up the strands of his life. One of his first was to St Antony's. The college's warden, Bill Deakin,

had been following the press coverage of his student's antics
in Moscow with increasing concern. Deakin suggested they
have dinner at Scott's fish restaurant in Mayfair the next
evening. Deakin was a stately character, patrician to the
fingertips. He had been an associate of Churchill's during
the war, and had parachuted into Yugoslavia to make
contact with Tito's partisans alongside Sir Fitzroy Maclean.
Though Mervyn liked and respected Deakin, he was exactly
the kind of smooth establishment figure who put him on
the defensive.

Deakin had taken little notice of Mervyn before he left for
Moscow, but now that the shy Welshman had committed the
sin of putting the college's name on the front pages it was time
for a serious chat. The dinner was expensive and indifferent –
my father thought that Alexei's hospitality in Moscow had
been superior – but Deakin was charming as he downed his
whisky and sodas. His first concern as he extracted the full
story from Mervyn was to ensure that he had not been
involved in any criminal activity in Moscow which could
damage the reputation of the college. Over coffee, Deakin
suggested that my father 'have a talk with the security people'
about his experiences. Outside, Deakin hailed a taxi, leaving
my father to walk to the Tube. My father noted Deakin's
lavishness with ten-shilling tips.

Even as he was boarding the plane in Moscow, Mervyn had
come up with a plan bold enough to fulfil his urgent need to
act. Nikita Khrushchev was due to visit Sweden with his wife
the following week, and Mervyn planned to deliver them a
personal letter, pleading for them to help two ordinary young
people get married.

Somehow, either from something he'd said to the press or
to his brother Jack, Mervyn's mother got wind of his plan. 'For
my sake, Mervyn, give up the idea of going to Scandinavia to
see Khrushchev,' she wrote to her son from Swansea. 'He is
moving about with a terrific bodyguard and you might get

shot.' Mervyn ignored her advice, which was to become a
habit over the years to come.

He boarded a plane to Gothenburg, but landed just as the
Khrushchevs were leaving. The Swedish police were waiting
for Mervyn, having found out from the newspapers about his
visit, and were enormously relieved when he arrived too late.
'Khrushchev gone,' a Swedish plain-clothes policeman told
Mervyn, pointing up at the watery sunset.

Mervyn was invited to dinner by the editor of the *Göteborgs
Handels och Sjöfarts Tidning*, and gave an interview. Having
missed Khrushchev in Gothenburg, Mervyn followed him to
Stockholm, taking the train through the rainy Swedish night.
When he arrived he found himself a cheap room at the
Hellman Hotel, and set up his tea kit: an electric spiral
element, a perforated spoon for the leaves, and a mug. It
was a habit he stuck to well into my childhood. I vividly
remember the tea kit, always there on stained tables in cheap
hotel rooms wherever we stayed, in Provence, Istanbul, Cairo,
Florence, Rome. He also brought a plate and cutlery, because
he couldn't afford Swedish restaurants. Instead, he ate snacks
and sandwiches bought in grocery shops.

In the morning Mervyn made for the offices of the two big
Stockholm dailies, *Aftonbladet* and *Stockholms-Tidningen*,
where reporters told him that the security around Khrushchev was tight, and that he shouldn't try to get near the great
man. They promised to run major feature articles in the next
day's edition.

That evening, Mervyn went alone to an amusement park on
one of the islands and watched the young couples dancing.
They had to pay separately, he noticed, for each number. He
imagined himself and Mila going through the turnstiles together.

At three in the morning he was woken by a knock at the
door. It was Des Zwar, a reporter from the *Daily Mail*.
Mervyn tried to get rid of him, but Zwar was persistent. He'd

been round every hotel in town looking for Mervyn, he said. 'The office thinks there might be a good story in it, so they sent me over.'

They sat on the bed and talked. Mervyn told Zwar his story, and Zwar told Mervyn about the passions of his life, golf and beautiful women, 'in that order'. Zwar's story, a masterpiece of tabloidese which my father preserved in the first of many files of newspaper clippings, appeared in the next day's edition.

'Dr Mervyn Matthews, the thirty-one-year-old research student who was refused permission to marry a Russian girl, was in Stockholm tonight waiting for his chance to see Mr Khrushchev tomorrow. Earlier today he wandered around Stockholm's city centre with a letter to Mr Khrushchev in his pocket. He said, "I won't give up" . . . If Dr Matthews tries to break through the cordon of machine gun carrying police he runs the risk of being shot dead. Security men, nervous since the reported threat to kidnap Mr Khrushchev, are in the trees, lining the roads and even on horseback, with orders to shoot if there is a sudden move to get near the Russian leader.'

Mervyn's money was running out, and he had not succeeded in getting anywhere near Khrushchev. The next day, he flew back to Oxford empty-handed.

'I'm sitting at the window of our college thinking of you,' wrote Mervyn to Mila in his beautiful, cursive Russian script. 'This damned [postal] strike is still on, they say it won't be finished for a while, so I asked a friend to post this from Paris for me. A week has gone by and no news from you. I am waiting for your call very much.'

His language, in those very first letters, was guarded, the style formal. It is as though he was testing her reaction, her expectations of him. 'I would call myself but I don't want to interfere . . . I am still applying all my efforts to find a solution to our question. You can rely on me completely. I don't forget my Mila for a moment. I have your photos, those old ones, but I am afraid to look at them. They are in an envelope. I know that as soon as I look at your face I will be overwhelmed by such a wave of sorrow that it will be quite impossible. It's so empty, empty without you . . . The weather is hot and stuffy. A typical Oxford summer. The college is exactly the same, but I have changed. I want to know what your mood is – it will be easier for me if I know that you are not despairing. When I think of our parting my heart breaks. Do not worry – I will not leave things like this. Remember I am undertaking many steps to achieve our mutual happiness. Look after your little nerves, your health. Your, M.'

A few days later Mila's first letters from Moscow arrived in Mervyn's pigeon-hole at St Anthony's.

'Today we are starting a new life, a life of letters and struggle,' wrote Lyudmila on 24 June. 'I feel very bad without you, it is as though life has stopped . . . In the three days since you left I have lost a good deal of strength, health and nerves. I know you will be angry, but I could not do anything with myself. I am sleeping very badly, I keep on thinking that you must return, and that I should be waiting for you, I jump at every sound. My friends try and support me . . . Everybody here who is honest and sensible thinks that [our separation] is stupid, inhumane, vicious and shameful.'

Mila's friends would come by to comfort her, bringing food and dragging her out to the park to walk a little. But Mila had become 'silent around people, stupid, unable to say anything'. She refused to change the sheets on her bed because they still carried 'the smell of your body'. On the Saturday after Mervyn's departure she promised herself she'd muster the energy to go to the theatre. It was the premier of *Cyrano de Bergerac* at the Sovremennik, but for the first time in her life Mila couldn't sit through the performance, and left after the first act. She felt as though she was running around 'like a squirrel in a wheel'.

'I live only with my grief, the world outside has ceased to exist for me,' she wrote to Mervyn the next day. 'I am very sorry I let you go. We should have waited longer. Everything is a thousand times harder now, the loneliness is unbearable. At the Institute all the women feel sorry for me, but among themselves they think you deceived me. They say, "Will he go on trying?" I tell them that you certainly will, and that we love one another very much. They all run to the library to read the *New York Times*. A lot of people liked your photo . . . I try to get home as quickly as possible and not see anyone. My mother reacted very badly [to your departure]. She says she thought that would happen! You are a foreigner.'

If I have realized anything in writing this book, it is that my father is a deeply honourable man. He had promised to marry Mila, and he would keep his word. More, he would sacrifice much to disprove Martha's awful accusation that he, a foreigner, would abandon Mila to her fate, orphaning her a second time. 'My childhood and your childhood and the present all run together into one picture of pain – I so want to smash this mass and start a bright new life,' wrote a tormented Mila. 'It's so bad, so cold and orphan-like since you left.'

Lyudmila left no doubt as to the answer to the unspoken question in Mervyn's first, tentative letters – her entire existence was orientated towards the fight she had to wage, and her whole life was consumed by the pain of parting.

'Mervusya! I believe in you, will you let me down?' Mila wrote. 'I will go through with this to the end. Either way, I ask you, I implore you: if you don't want to fight to the last, write me a letter and send it with someone, it'll be easier for me that way. No prevarication – that is the most terrible, more terrible than death.'

At Bill Deakin's suggestion, Mervyn wrote a detailed report on his contacts with the KGB for MI5. He also saw a lot of David

Footman, his moral tutor at St Antony's, a tall, grave man who out of term lived in a large basement flat in Chelsea. Footman was, like Deakin, urbane and polished, with a formidable intellect and effortless social superiority. He had won a Military Cross in the First World War and, though my father did not know it at the time, had headed the Secret Intelligence Service's Soviet desk during the Second World War.

I remember Footman very clearly from various visits to his Chelsea flat in my early childhood. He was very thin and immaculately dressed, and spoke in an upper-class drawl that I had hitherto heard only on the television. His flat was filled with books and photographs of the First World War planes he had piloted (and, I was thrilled to hear, crashed, or 'pranged', as he put it), and I recall him solemnly shaking my hand as we left, though I was no older than five or six. I think Footman was the first person ever to do so.

Over weak tea in cracked cups, Footman listened sympathetically to Mervyn's story, carefully filling his pipe as Mervyn spoke. Young people were supposed to get into scrapes, he told my father; he'd been in a few himself. Footman confided that he'd always preferred to have a secretary who's had a 'tumble in the hay' rather than a prim one, they were easier to get along with. After Mervyn had finished, Footman suggested that he have a word with 'Battersby, from the Foreign Office security section – they would be interested.' He refilled his pipe and passed his hand over his distinguished brow.

'You're not reckoning on getting her out, are you? That would be a bonus. You've got to be realistic about these things.'

But Mervyn could not be realistic; it was against his nature. Also, I think he had become infected by something of the irrationality and maximalism of Russia. Not so much the superficial addiction to self-dramatization, which is undoubtedly a very Russian habit, but rather the true soaring of the spirit which thrives only when reality is impossible to deal with. Being realistic, in Russian terms, meant surrender. For Mila it would have meant going to work in a cloth mill at the age of fifteen. For Mervyn it would have meant a clerk's job in the local Co-op. Both Mila and Mervyn had always refused to reconcile themselves to what others believed was reasonable.

Soon after his conversation with Footman, a letter arrived from Moscow via Italy, where it had been posted by an Italian Communist friend of my mother's. It was Mila's manifesto, at once a challenge and a *cri de cœur*. What it emphatically was not was realistic, which makes it so magnificent – and almost unbearable – to read, even a lifetime later.

'You will get this letter on the eve of your birthday,' Mila wrote. 'I am sending it via Italy. This is the cry of my love, this is just for you and me.' Their other letters, they both assumed, were randomly checked by the KGB; this one, Lyudmila was determined, would be absolutely private.

'I have never written such letters to anyone, everything here is honest and true. My love for you may seem pathologically strong. In our time people have been taught to be content with a little, with half-measures, with the artificial. They forget feelings easily and easily part with and betray one another, they easily accept surrogates, including in love. All my life I went against the flow; all my life has been a fierce struggle against attempts to impose a way of life on me, a way of thinking which seems to me to be absolutely unacceptable. My life has been a fight to get an education, to become cultured, a fight for independence and finally a fight for love.

'From my earliest childhood I have conducted a heated running argument with life. Life told me: Don't study! Don't love wonderful things! Cheat! Don't believe in love! Betray your friends! Don't think! Obey! But I stubbornly maintained that my answer was "No", and ploughed my difficult path onwards through the debris. Life was cruel and vengeful. It denied me love, kindness, warmth. But my thirst for them only grew. Life tried to convince me that happiness is impossible, but still I believed, continued to search for it and wait, ready to fight for it when I found it and never to give it up.

'They say that you should only love someone for their good qualities – but I love everything in you, good and bad. I am not ashamed of your weaknesses, I carry them within me like something sacred, unattainable for outside eyes. I don't hear when someone speaks ill of you. I believe that only I see all of you, and from this comes my conviction that you are the best. I love you as my child, like a part of my body; I often feel that I have given birth to you. I so want to rock you in my arms, to protect you from danger, to save you from illness.

'Do you believe me, my boy, that I am willing to give up my life for you? I try, with my feeble woman's courage, to help you to refuse to fear these people, not to give in to them. Do you feel that? I still refuse to fear them, even though they are all-powerful. Truly, these dark days have shown me how much I love my mouse, how I have grown together with him in heart and soul, and what terrible surgery has been carried out on me – an operation on my heart. My aim now is to show this avenging eagle, this ravenous predator, that my love is stronger than their hate.'

How could Mervyn have refused to fight after such a soul-wrenching letter? How could anyone, after being made the object of such love and faith and hope, let their beloved down? 'Love me,' she wrote. 'Or I will die.'

'For me nothing was as it was before,' he replied. 'But you have placed a heavy moral task on my shoulders and I am not sure that I will have the strength to carry it. I am not talking about the difficulties in our marriage – you can be sure that this plan will be fulfilled by 150 per cent. No, I mean the high moral example you set me, the necessity of perfecting myself. Your praise embarrasses me. It suggests that I am better than you. But for the most part I can only learn from you. You gave me a completely new outlook on life exactly when I needed it.'

His Russian, for all the years they corresponded, was as stiff and formal as hers was fiery and passionate. It is almost as if he is struggling against his upbringing to find words to express feelings too big, too powerful to fit into the narrow confines of polite letter writing. My father signed the letter just quoted with a flamboyant flourish; a small thing, perhaps, but it was a more extravagant signature than he'd allowed himself on any previous letter.

Mervyn managed to book a telephone call to Lenina, and told her to pass on a message to Lyudmila to be at the Central Telegraph on Gorky Street later in the week. Mila was electrified by the first long-distance conversation since their separation. 'As soon as I heard your voice the blood rushed around my body like a rocket,' she wrote. 'I want to kiss your voice.' Lyudmila couldn't use the communal phone in the corridor of her apartment because of her nosy neighbours, so they set up a system of fortnightly phone calls. The calls had to be booked in advance, and they had to be short because of the cost. But the few minutes of conversation in a cramped booth at the Telegraph became a lifeline for Mila.

'Little Mervyn! I miss you so much, I so want to kiss your little head, your neck, your little nose, but what am I to do, eh, my little boy?' she wrote soon after their first phone call. 'How are we to overcome this obstacle which divides us so absolutely? It's so cruel, so hard, to have a loved one and not be able to see him, to be near him. Sometimes hope blossoms in me, belief, I want to be so courageous and strong, but more often I feel such despair, such frustration, such a terrible pain in my heart, so bitter, that my strength leaves me and my nerves can't bear it, I want to cry out to the whole world. I still can't believe it's true, that you aren't by my side. So cruel, so unfair! But who will you prove this to, who has time for our pain, our injustice? A machine doesn't feel, it doesn't think, it only sweeps people underneath it, this evil juggernaut of history.'

Mervyn was just beginning to learn about the ways of the juggernaut of history. Despite all that had happened, he still had the mad idea that he could take it on and win, in spite of the wise counsels of his mentors and the imprecations of his mother. Mervyn stood before a decision to pursue something fine and beautiful and probably impossible – or to reconcile himself to something ordinary and banal. He chose the extraordinary. In that decision there lies a moment of great courage, bright enough to light a whole lifetime.

Lenina also showed her mettle in a small but life-affirming act of bravery. She wrote to Mervyn to assure him that she would support their struggle to marry. 'Mila is my first child and I love her very much, especially now,' wrote Lenina. 'All I think about is your affair, wherever I am. We all love you. You are a full member of our family. Of course another in my place would not have loved you, seen you as a thief who in broad daylight tore a piece out of my heart. But because I want Mila to be happy and to be loved I love you too, difficult as you sometimes are.' Lenina's daughter Nadia wrote, too, hoping that Mervyn would be back for the winter and the mushrooming season.

In mid-August, Mervyn made another attempt to buttonhole a Soviet leader and pass them a letter about his plight. He took a plane to Bonn to try to meet Khrushchev's son-in-law, Alexei Adzhubei. Since the press fanfare in Stockholm had got him nowhere, he decided this time to approach Adzhubei as unobtrusively as possible. Through a college friend he got in touch with Carla Stern, a well-connected West German publisher, who gave Mervyn details of Adzhubei's movements, and an invitation to a private reception he was due to attend.

Mervyn, in his best suit, made his way through the crowded drawing room. Adzhubei was surrounded by a group of German businessmen, all eagerly discussing breaking into the Soviet market. There was almost no security. Mervyn shook hands with Adzhubei, and gave him a letter. Adzhubei looked faintly embarrassed, nodded curtly at Mervyn, handed the letter without comment to an aide, and turned back to the businessmen. My father left immediately, and the same evening returned to London. It had hardly been an auspicious meeting.

'The only thing which comforts me – and I hope you too – is the understanding and sympathy of everyone who knows our unhappy story,' he wrote to Mila on his return, not mentioning his failed trip. 'In the end I am sure that the evil which occurred will be cancelled. I am undertaking many steps to achieve our mutual happiness.'

At Bill Deakin's prompting, Mervyn called a Mr Battersby from MI5. They had an inconclusive chat. The only thing Battersby revealed was that his colleague Sewell in Moscow had no evidence for telling Mervyn that his fiancée was a KGB plant; it had just been a 'precautionary presumption'. As far as British officialdom was concerned, that was the end of the matter.

A few weeks later, in early September, MI5 sent an officer up to Oxford to interview Mervyn in person. M.L. McCaul was plump, middle-aged and very deliberate, with the manner of a sergeant major. He drove Mervyn out to the Bear in Woodstock for dinner and went over the details of Mervyn's earlier report, checking if there was anything he'd left out. McCaul referred to Alexei and Alexander Sokolov as 'your friends' and 'that pair'.

'We liked your phrase, "using an aura of friendship for

purposes of recruitment'', in your report,' McCaul told my father. 'So we put it in one of our things.' He did not elaborate as to what piece of MI5 literature Mervyn had unwittingly contributed to. A few days later McCaul sent Mervyn two photographs to see if he could identify them. One was of a Russian research student who'd been up at St Anthony's two years previously, and had nothing to do with Mervyn's case. The other picture was of a man Mervyn had never seen. He remembered Alexei's sarcastic comments on how ineffective MI5 was, and found himself in full agreement.

MI5 did, to Mervyn's surprise, finally come up with the goods on 2 March 1966, when a man met him at Charing Cross Station to show him a photograph of an elegant figure with a broad, handsome face and a distinctive streak of grey hair over his temple. It was Alexei. The MI5 man told Mervyn his surname was Suntsov, the first time Mervyn had ever heard it. In Moscow he had never dared ask Alexei his surname.

In Moscow, for Mila, Mervyn was everywhere, appearing like the ghostly overcoat in Gogol's haunting short story. At the theatre she saw some 'long-necked, long-fingered countrymen of yours, and I became so sad, so bitter, that I decided not to stay for the performance,' she wrote. 'My Boy! Where am I to find the strength to wait for so long?'

Mila's life was slowly being suffused and taken over by the virtual presence of Mervyn. She covered one wall of her little room with photographs of her fiancé, and in the evenings she would walk alone down Gogolevsky Boulevard to Kropot-kinskaya Metro and look at the people streaming out, watching for Mervyn to appear. 'If only I could meet you now at the Metro; we would walk home together, breathe the summer night air. The Arbat backstreets would seem beautiful, the people kind, the evening soft. But now it seems that everyone looks at me judgmentally. The trees seem old and yellow – with you they were young and alive. I look enviously at women who have a man's hand on their shoulder.'

On the large boards by the Metro where the day's newspapers were pasted up, she would stop and read stories about mods and rockers fighting on Hastings beach. Then she'd go back home and write, leaving the apartment again late at night to post her letter in the postbox on the corner of Starokonushenny Pereulok and the Arbat so that it would go with the first post. The little rituals which were to rule her life for the rest of her time in Russia were forming into a comforting pattern, a routine which could assuage, at least a little, the powerlessness of her situation.

'In the morning, as soon as I wake up I write a letter, my beloved boy . . . I imagine you sleeping, getting up, bathing . . . No more letters . . . the waiting is the worst. Even if the postman brought three a day it would not be enough, and now we have a gap . . . No news, it is as though my life has stopped.'

Mervyn spent the rest of the summer working with Alexander Kerensky, the bright lawyer who had risen to head the Provisional Government of the Russian Empire in the precipitous months between July and October 1917, when he was overthrown by the Bolsheviks' coup. Kerensky was now very elderly, a spidery little man with a shock of grey hair and thick glasses. Mervyn helped him with his research, which was devoted to trying to unravel the events in which he himself had played a leading part. Mervyn told Kerensky his story. The old man was sympathetic, but for him Russia was a distant and hostile country which he had fled half a century before and would never see again. They talked about the Revolution and the ruthless men it had brought to power.

'Rasputin? Oh, yes, he was very strong, very strong!' Kerensky would mutter. 'Lenin! I should have had him arrested when I could.' Mervyn nodded in sincere agreement.

My father began writing to sympathetic MPs and dignitaries who might be able to help his fight. Professor Leonard Schapiro of the London School of Economics gave him a list of names and addresses, and Mervyn began a tireless correspondence which eventually grew to fill an entire three-drawer filing cabinet. He wrote to Bertrand Russell, the philosopher, who was in the Soviets' good books for his anti-nuclear campaigns; Selwyn Lloyd, the former Conservative Foreign Secretary who had 'got on well' with his Soviet counterpart, Andrei Gromyko; Sir Isaiah Berlin, the Riga-born philosopher of All Souls College; George Woodcock, Secretary of the Trades Union Congress and a well-known fellow-traveller. All replied with polite expressions of concern, but offered little real help.

By now most of Mervyn's time was spent writing letters, making phone calls and visits. His academic work was falling by the wayside. Mervyn paid a visit to the Soviet ambassador's private secretary, Alexander Soldatov, but to his disappointment the meeting yielded nothing beyond polite platitudes. My father, with perverse persistence, kept filing Soviet visa applications; with equal persistence, the Soviets kept turning them down.

Mervyn had little hope that a visa would actually come through. Mila, on the other hand, seemed to have formed a firm belief that her own application for a Soviet exit visa, a rare privilege usually granted only to the most politically trusted, had a chance of being approved. When she learned on 18 August that her exit visa had been refused 'at the highest level', she was distraught.

'The last two months with the help of my friends and family I have lived in hope that my suffering will end but yesterday I discovered that my hopes are in vain,' she wrote, the writing paper stained with tears. 'All night I wandered in the heat, unable to sleep, and today I am still bathed in tears, as though in front of my eyes a piece of my heart has been torn out. I am once again in terrible despair. I beg you, my darling, don't let me down, I am on the verge of death.

'I am sitting at home like a bird in a cage, I slept badly, in a terrible mix of love and pain, but I will have to live, bear it, wait. It seems one more minute of waiting and my heart will tear itself to pieces and blood will pour from my mouth. Together with you I am ready to bear any tortures, but alone it's terribly hard . . . Some people are rejoicing: there is nothing they love more than to see the blood dripping from souls they have torn apart with their claws. They think they have saved me from a fiery Gehenna. They think you are a devil incarnate, and they themselves are saints. Keep knocking at the gates of heaven, listen and you will hear my voice calling to you from behind them. Even though the gatekeeper won't let you through, don't let him sleep.'

A few days later her mood seemed to have lifted. Mila apologized for her desperate letters of the previous week. 'If only you knew how your decisiveness is like oxygen to me. Please, Mervusya, never tell me that you have given up beating your head against the wall. Don't retreat! Storming the walls doesn't always work first time. I can never bear to hear that you have given up hope, faith in your own powers.'

In Moscow the summer was ending. Mila harvested the potatoes and cucumbers which Mervyn had planted. Berrying season had come, and Mila and her nieces spent days in the woods with iron buckets collecting wild strawberries, bilberries and cranberries in the marshy clearings. Sasha picked fruit, and Mila and Lenina boiled up vast pots of jam in the dacha kitchen. Mila kept some jars aside, which she planned to eat with Mervyn just as soon as he came back.

'Please tell me all the details of your life, the little curry house in the centre of town,' wrote Mila to Mervyn, calmer

than she'd been in months after her spell in the country. 'All
these things are vital to me. In them I see my real live little
person, my beloved boy.' At the end of the letter Mila drew
some little sketches of a shirt she was sewing. 'Here's a funny
poem for you,' she wrote a day later. 'Mervusya – happiness,
Mervusya – bottom, Mervusya – joy, For Mila – sweetness . . .
Is your room warm, your blanket? Do demons of temptation
come to you?'

'The postal workers are demanding 7½ per cent, the government is offering 4½ per cent, and until this argument is
settled we must suffer,' Mervyn replied. 'I think the government is quite wrong on this question, but I do not advertise
this viewpoint. The last few nights I have slept badly, and
dream of you often. I often think of those wonderful dinners
which you made me. I try not to overeat here. I bought myself
a new pair of slippers, Hungarian ones, and have begun
playing squash. Don't be sad, dear Milochka, everything will
go well for us in the end. I hug you. M.'

It was only a matter of time before Mila's scandalous love
affair with a foreigner who had been expelled from the
Soviet Union collided with her position at the Institute of
Marxism and Leninism. Behind her back, she knew, there
was a lot of gossip. Some of her colleagues clearly sym-
pathized; many others looked at her askance as they passed.
Mila did her best to be alone, so as not to embarrass
anyone. She tried to bury herself in work, only to find
that she had 'grown stupid from the pain, it is bothering me
so much'.

The blow fell after a specially convened meeting of the
Institute's leading Party members, as dour a bunch of zealots
as Mila had ever encountered. 'This week has been a nightmare, constant nerves, tears,' Mila reported. 'At work there's a
huge furore. A few days ago there was a Party meeting. They
demanded a report about "My Case". They wanted blood.

They shouted, "Why didn't we know earlier? Why didn't you tell us everything?" (This is all in the style of the Party Secretary.) "We need to find out more through the Organs [of State Security]. And what does she say for herself? She denies it. You see! If the government made a decision, that means it's a correct one. She must be punished! She put personal interests before society's! He will surely use her for anti-Soviet propaganda and then abandons her." '

A few of Mila's colleagues, bravely, tried to defend her, urging leniency and saying that falling in love didn't make her an enemy of the people. But mostly, 'the clever ones stayed silent, the bastards shouted with all their might'. This hypocrites' court was the worst sort of pressure, a perfect weapon for the conformity obsessed Soviet society. And not only Soviet society: defying authority is one thing, but few human beings can withstand a chorus of disapproval from those whom they know and trust.

Mila didn't give them the victory of seeing her break down in tears. But the experience shook her deeply. For all her spirit, she was a Soviet woman, daughter of a Communist, a child brought up by the state. Never, before now, had she been confronted with the prospect of outright dissent. And she was all too aware that the taint of rebellion might follow her through her whole life.

'I think that even if I do leave, they will immediately telephone my new work or someone will inform on me, in the old fashioned way, and they'll fire me immediately in turn,' wrote Mila. 'Nevertheless, I must leave. The atmosphere is vile, a lot of gossip, little talks "of an instructional nature", which are enough to give me a heart attack.'

Despite Mila's public disgrace, the Institute's director was sympathetic. He arranged a transfer to the Central Library of the Academy of Sciences at the same status and wage, where Mila was to translate scholarly articles from French academic journals. To Mila's huge relief, her new colleagues turned out to be young and independent-minded. The library was in fact a 'den of dissidents . . . it was like throwing a fish into water,' Mila remembered. The room where she worked was decorated with large, surreal, pencil caricatures of various wan-faced historical figures which the director had allowed some wag to draw directly on to the walls. She and her fellow workers amused themselves by snapping a series of comic photos – one shows Mila and her friend Eric Zhuk posing as the Worker and the Communal Farm Woman, a classic 1937 statue of Soviet youth. He holds a hammer, she holds a sickle, and they stand back to back in a mock-heroic pose. Another shows the young librarians parodying Rodin's sculpture of the Burghers of Calais, standing in a row with their heads tragi-comically bowed. The liberal atmosphere of the library allowed Mila to have heated arguments with the senior researchers over whether Soviet power would fall in their lifetimes. Mila argued that it would; Professor Faigin, an expert on Peter the Great, argued that it would survive for centuries. 'The Russian pig lay on one side for three hundred years,' the sprightly old professor joked. 'Now she's rolled over on to the other and will lie there for another three hundred.'

On 19 October 1964 Mila went with two new girlfriends to greet the returning cosmonauts Vladimir Komarov, Konstantin Feoktistov, and Boris Yegorov. They had gone into space when Nikita Khrushchev was still in power; by the time they came back to earth he had been quietly removed in a politburo coup, to be replaced by Leonid Brezhnev. For the wider Soviet public, the transition passed with barely a ripple, but Brezhnev's harder line was to bode ill for my parents' case. Mila and her friends waved frantically as the cosmonauts cruised down Gorky Street in an open car in a fine drizzle. Then they went to a crowded café and talked till the evening.

But despite her new job and the support of her friends, the pain of separation would not let her go. 'I hope so much that our love will not die, I so want to be with you, that it seems that if I were offered a choice I would rather die than never be with you again. Honestly!' Mila wrote, alone in her room one autumn evening. 'I miss you. I suffer terribly. I can't see or listen to anyone or anything. I want to cry out to the whole world from love, from despair, from such a cruel and unfair fate!'

As I read my parents' letters, sitting by the fire of the dacha where I lived with the woman who is now my wife, I felt a strange thing. As Xenia sat on the sofa and read the difficult, cursive script, and I took notes, sitting on the floor, I could not shake the terrible feeling that both my parents were dead and lost to me. Their voices were so distant, the details of their intimate lives and suffering so moving, that it seemed to me that I was rooting through lives already lived and gone. The letters were powerful as much for what they didn't say as what they did, and I found myself unable to break the spell, even when I called my mother and heard her familiar voice on the telephone. We spoke of reassuring banalities, and I could not bring myself to say what I was feeling – that I was over-whelmed by admiration and love. And sorrow, for the knowledge that though my parents would eventually be reunited, their unspoken belief that they could erase their traumatic childhoods through prodigious self-sacrifice and struggle in the name of love would ultimately fail.

'I so want to tell you my feelings, about my unending, deep, warm and eternally sad love for you,' my mother wrote. 'My letters seem dry because it's impossible to say in words what is happening – something wonderful and terrible at the same time. It's light and beautiful but burningly painful.'

Winter closed in on Moscow, and, later and with less vehe-mence, on Oxford. Mervyn continued to write to whomever he thought might be of some help. But it was becoming clear that there would not be a swift resolution. He and Mila

continued to speak by telephone for ten minutes once a fort-
night, at ruinous cost. They agreed to alternate the calls – Mila
would pay 1 ruble 40 per minute after filling in a complex
system of forms and bank slips to book the call at the Central
Telegraph on Gorky Street. Each call cost 15 rubles 70, a
considerable chunk of her salary of eighty rubles per month.
Yet to Mila it was worth every kopeck. She prepared herself for
her twice monthly telephone 'date' with Mervyn at the Central
Telegraph as meticulously as if he'd really be there, instead of
being a distant voice on the crackling line. She made sure not to
wear shoes that Mervyn didn't like. She would ask her cousin
Nadia to do her hair in a beehive, and she'd put on her new
raincoat and take her new handbag. It is this vision of my
mother that comes back to me most powerfully when I think
about the letters: a small, limping figure in her handmade best
outfit and carefully coiffed hair, walking alone to the trolleybus
stop on Gogol Boulevard, proud that she is on her way to a date
with a beautiful man of her very own.

In between campaigning, Mervyn had been putting the finishing touches to his first book, a sociological work on Soviet
youth. He'd been working on it, on and off, since 1958, and
now it was in galleys, ready for final correction. The work,
Mervyn hoped, would give his sagging academic career a
boost, and prove to be his passport to the permanent college
fellowship he had coveted all his adult life. But now, as the
battle lines were being drawn for a war of attrition, he had
qualms. Could the book, mild stuff though it was, possibly
offend the Soviets and harm his chances of getting Mila out?
    After weeks of agonizing, he decided not to risk it. Mervyn
called the publisher, Oxford University Press, and asked to
withdraw the book from its list. There was much consterna-
tion at the press, and at St Anthony's. It was a fantastic
sacrifice to make, and Mervyn probably knew at the time
that he was doing his chances of academic success irreparable

harm. 'From one point of view this is good,' he wrote to Mila, telling her of his decision. 'But so much effort, so much nervous energy, all for nothing . . .' As I sit, finishing my own book after five years of effort, my father's sacrifice seems unimaginably vast. For weeks afterwards, Mervyn could hardly bring himself to believe what he had done.

On 26 April 1965 Gerald Brooke, a young lecturer who Mervyn had known while they were both exchange students at Moscow State University, was arrested by the KGB. He was picked up at the Moscow apartment of an agent of the Popular Labour Union, or NTS, a small and hapless CIA-funded anti-Soviet organization. The organization was so hopelessly compromised, it later emerged, that there were almost as many Soviet informers as real, misguided agitators. Brooke was caught delivering propaganda leaflets to a pair of unfortunate NTS agents who had themselves been arrested a few days before. When Brooke arrived at their apartment, the KGB were waiting.

The NTS had once tried to recruit Mervyn at Oxford. Georgy Miller, an elderly Russian émigré, tried to persuade my father to deliver a package of papers to a contact in Moscow. My father had wisely refused; Miller, it seems, had had more success persuading Brooke. But it had been a close call. There, thought Mervyn as he read the news of Brooke's arrest, but for the Grace of God go I.

Brooke was put on trial for anti-Soviet agitation and sentenced to five years' imprisonment. The Soviet press used the case to launch an anti-Western campaign. Mervyn's old Moscow University friend Martin Dewhirst had also been accused of anti-Soviet activity during Brooke's trial, as was Peter Reddaway, another friend of Mervyn's who had also been expelled from the Soviet Union. But, mercifully, Mervyn's name was not mentioned at the trial or in the press. Why, he never found out.

Soon rumours began to circulate that the Soviet authorities were offering to swap Brooke for Peter and Helen Kroger, a pair of American Communists who had worked as Soviet spies, first as couriers to the Manhattan Project spy ring in the United States in the 1940s and then in lesser roles in the UK. The Krogers were serving twenty-year sentences for espionage in England after having been caught running a spy ring at Portland, Britain's nuclear submarine facility. Brooke, a mere graduate student, was by no means in the same league as the Krogers, and Mervyn and others suspected that he was simply a pawn in a larger game. The Krogers themselves confirmed this in a BBC interview in 1990. Brooke had been arrested specifically for use as a trading card to get the Krogers back, they confirmed, after intense lobbying in Moscow by their KGB controller in London, Konon Molody, a.k.a. Gordon Lonsdale, who had escaped arrest and made it home when the spy ring was rolled up but dedicated himself to securing the release of his old agents.

Mervyn hatched the idea that Mila could be included in any possible spy swap. 'There is already talk of a Brooke–Kroger exchange,' Mervyn wrote to Frederick Cumber, a business-man with good relations with the Soviet embassy. 'Which means two Ks for one B. I personally think there are a number of excellent arguments for getting Mila tagged on to this. The Russians would regard it as a negligible concession, and they are certainly anxious to get the Krogers out. The months of separation are weighing very heavily on both of us, and not a day goes by without my giving a great deal of thought to the problem in hand. We live, so to speak, by letter. I have now received some 430 from Mila, and sent her about the same number (not to mention postcards).'

The glimmer of hope of a deal, however, soon dwindled after the British government announced that they would not countenance such an exchange: the Cabinet flatly refused to yield to Soviet blackmail.

In Moscow, Mila would pass her days listening to English language learning records. She repeated the simple stories about Nora and Harry and their lost dog, who was returned by the butcher along with a bill for the sausages the dog had eaten. Some of Mervyn's letters were posted in error in her neighbour Yevdokia's box, and Lyudmila picked the lock with knitting needles and a pair of scissors to retrieve them. Prey to growing paranoia, she asked Mervyn to send a list of his letters, suspecting her neighbours of stealing them. 'They are sharpening their knives,' Mila feared. She slept badly, plagued by nightmares of separation shot through with long-suppressed memories of her own childhood.

'Last night I dreamt a horrible dream. I screamed and cried and my sister thought I was ill. I can't believe the dream wasn't real, it was so vivid. So now everyone is asleep and I am still crying. My sister says the dream is a very bad omen. It seems I was born to this unhappiness . . . such burning pain, such perverse sophisticated torture. All my strength and thoughts are put into our love. There is no way back for me.'

The Foreign Office were now taking no pains to conceal their irritation at Mervyn's harangues. Howard Smith, the head of the 'Northern Department' which handled Russia, seemed to consider Mervyn, at best, a troublesome ne'er-do-well, and took his calls with increasing exasperation, bordering on rudeness.

'Dr Matthews' case is one with . . . which we are very familiar,' wrote Michael Stewart, the Foreign Secretary, to Laurie Pavitt, MP, who had written on Mervyn's behalf. 'He has been told repeatedly in correspondence and interviews with officials and Foreign Office ministers alike the reasons why we do not consider it right to single out his case for official representations. In view of the past history of the case there is really no possibility of a favourable reaction to official intervention.'

By the Isis in Oxford, 1958.

The young don. Mervyn shortly after he got his
junior fellowship at St Antony's, 1957.

Mervyn on a day trip to Kuskovo, near Moscow, spring 1959.

Narrow lapels, knitted tie, Gauloises from the embassy commissariat shop: Mervyn about town in Moscow, 1959.

'A wonderful coincidence.' Vadim Popov, Mervyn's first KGB 'friend', eating kebab at the market in Bukhara, Uzbekistan, 1959.

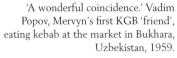

'It's what's below that's frightening.' Mervyn on the spring ice of Lake Baikal with the director of a local collective farm during his jaunt with the KGB, March 1960.

'Matthews, that ungrateful boy.' Alexei Suntsov, Mervyn's KGB case officer, who took him on a tour of the wonders of socialism but was unable to persuade him to betray his country. His widow, Inna Vadimovna, gave Mervyn this photo in 1997.

On the margins: Mervyn (*far right*) in St Antony's class of 1964. His adventures in Russia were soon to prove fatal to his Oxford career.

'It was like throwing a fish into water.' At the Library of the Academy of Sciences after Lyudmila was fired from the Institute of Marxism and Leninism. Lyudmila and her colleague Erik Zhuk in mock-heroic pose as the Worker and the Collective Farm Woman, as Rodin's *Burghers of Calais*, and at her desk.

26 июля, воскресенье, 1964 г.
Москва.

Сладкий мой, любимый мальчик!

Вчера так ждала 10 часов, чтобы услышать твой голос, голос моего дорогого именинника. Хотелось, безумно, поздравить тебя лично, крепко=крепко расцеловать, сделать прекрасный обед, испечь тебе пирог с яблоками. Но что поделаешь? Счастье еще, что можем писать и звонить ...... миллионско

расстроен
Очень я
вчера гу
ца, хорош
вать в т
отстаивал
у тебя
действуй
все делал
грустно,
делал,
хорошо.
ты помн
свой дол
хочется
любимо
му: сл
своего д
вкусом
Но если
немного
предло
или
случа
за те
что у

London,
Monday, 17th Oct 1966

My most kind, gentle and marvellous Milochka,

I am writing to you in English today, instead of yesterday, for reasons which I explained in yesterday's epistle. My little hot cross bun! (Do you know, incidentally, what a hot cross bun is?) Once again you have delighted me by sending me a couple of letters just when they were needed, nos dated 9th and 10th October). They were rather sad, because you had not received any of my letters when you wrote them, however, I hope to detect a big improvement in your mood when the next lot comes, — and I sincerely hope that will be tomorrow.

I was of course disappointed to learn that N. has not been keeping her word, chto podelaesh. She is a very mature girl, in my opinion, perhaps a little too much so to develop a profound love of learning. But perhaps I am wrong. As you say, education is vitally important in these matters. I also think that O. will do much better at French than at the other thing.

You ask me how comprehensible Chaucer is to the average man. Of course, it must be admitted that the average man would never think of reading him, but apart from that I would say that his (Chaucer's) language is very difficult at first. With a little application, however, one can soon learn to read it. I enjoyed the Canterbury Tales very much at school. There has not been any advance in the question of the landing cupboard. The owner of the house (who is in fact not the owner at all, but a lessee himself) told me that he would think about it and let me know. So far I have not heard from him. I mentioned the matter to my fat friend a few days ago, but he said that it would be wiser not for me to do anything for the time being, I must let the man have a few weeks at least to come to a decision.

I told you in one of my letters that I had sent a cheque for £50 to the former owner of the flat, because she would not reduce her prices on the articles I was buying from her. I thought that she would probably reply in a nasty sort of way, and sure enough I was right. This morning I received from her a politely worded letter thanking me for the cheque and returning three rather dirty pound notes, which she said I certainly did not owe her in any case. (You will remember that she had reduced her demand by the derisory amount of five pounds, and asked me to pay

'These letters are written with the blood of my heart.' Mila to Mervyn, 1963.

What about our Russian fiancées Mr. Ambassador?

by BRIAN PARK

TWO ENGLISHMEN who have waited four years to marry Russian women had a face-to-face confrontation with the Russian Ambassador, Mr. Mikhail Smirnovsky, in a London street.

Five days ago university lecturer Mr. Mervyn Matthews, 36, and car-worker Mr. Derek Deason, 38, who have become close friends because of their joint problem, were walking down South Audley Street, Mayfair, London, talking about their fiancées still in Russia.

Mr. "we usine ding Arab tic sian and ber

from the sky, tion

fter red ssy, f a top ood

SOUTH WALES — EVENING POST – 20 JUNE 68

Swansea man's 'surly' reply from Russians

By EVENING POST REPORTER

was the description given today by **Mr. Mervyn** a man and lecturer in Russian at the University of tion he has received from the U.S.S.R. embassy in London.

Mr. Matthews visited the embassy three weeks ago and left a letter pleading with the Ambassador to intercede in Moscow on his behalf so that he can marry Ljudmila Bibikova, whom he began courting when doing research work at Moscow University.

It was shortly after their attempt to marry in 1964 that Mr. Matthews, whose mother lives in Aberdyberthi-street, Hafod, Swansea, was ordered out of Russia.

'POST' CUTTING

Mr. Matthews said today that three days after his visit to the embassy, he received a telephone call to say that he could expect an acknowledgment of his letter. But now he has had the acknowledgment, which was bitterly disappointing.

It came from the consular department of the embassy and in the envelope was his "open" letter delivered on June 4, the envelope in which it had been contained, some press cuttings about the letter which Mr. Matthews had sent a couple of days later, and a short letter in Russian.

Among the cuttings, said Mr. Matthews today, was the 'Post' Man's Diary report in the Evening Post dated June 4, which had had pride of place on top

"I find this negative and surly response of the embassy both puzzling and distressing.

"It is indeed strange that the embassador hedged when he was asked why his Government would not allow the men to marry their sweethearts. He said: 'You must not create difficulties.'

Mr. Matthews said: "I don't know how he would feel if he'd been kept apart from someone he loved and I told him we would have to see about that."

The doors of the Chaika car—a Russian version of a Rolls-Royce—slammed shut and it drove off.

Mr. Deason—whose fiancée, Eleuora Ginsburg, 38, is a Moscow schoolteacher—said: "It was one of the most heartening things that has happened for a very long time. At least it proved the Russians are well aware of our continuing fight to get married."

The fight is a two-capital affair.

'Swansea man's "surly" reply from Russians', from the *South Wales Evening Post*, and 'What about our Russian fiancées, Mr. Ambassador?', from the *Sunday Express*.

Reunited in Moscow. Mervyn and Mila shortly before their second wedding day, October 1969.

Married. Mila, Mervyn and Eleonora Ginzburg pose by the Kremlin following celebratory drinks at the British embassy the day after their wedding, 1 November 1969.

'I visited fairyland.' The author with Lyudmila and Martha Bibikova in London, summer 1976. She brought her own sheets.

At the Vasin dacha, 1978. Babka Simka (*top left*), Lyudmila, Lenina, Sasha, the author and his cousin Masha.

Mervyn and Lyudmila, London, 2006.

The low point in Matthews–Foreign Office relations came when Howard Smith came to dinner at St Antony's. Mervyn asked Fred, the College Steward, to ask Smith to come up to his rooms after dinner. When Smith appeared in the doorway, Mervyn lost control of himself and, as he put it later, 'expressed an earthy view of his person'.

'Smith came back into the Common Room visibly shaken,' Mervyn's friend Harry Willets told him later. 'He told everyone in hearing that you had been sprawled in an armchair and called him "the shit of Smiths" when he opened your door. His cigar had gone out.' Mervyn's recollection is that he only called Smith 'a fart'. Perhaps he called him both.

It was the last nail in the coffin of Mervyn's Oxford career. His research had ground to a halt and his book had been withdrawn, he'd been on the front page of the *Daily Mail*, and now this. Deakin summoned Mervyn to his house for an admonitory glass of sherry. 'Rude and totally unacceptable,' said Deakin in clipped tones. 'And he was a guest of the college, too. We cannot possibly put up with that sort of thing. Have you heard anything more about the job going at Glasgow? Perhaps it would be better for you to go up north and get away from things.'

Oxford, my father's most cherished dream after Lyudmila herself, was over. Harry Willets confirmed that Mervyn's research fellowship was being terminated over a pint in the Lamb and Flag on St Giles' Street. Being thrown out of Oxford was a fall from grace which was to scar Mervyn more profoundly than anything else in his life; it was a blow which was to poison his every subsequent achievement.

12

On Different Planets

I have gone mad with love.
Mila to Mervyn, 14 December 1964

Moscow, I found, seemed to attract people who were ferociously smart, but often hungry and damaged, fleeing failure or trying to prove something to the world. Like a traumatic love affair, it could change people for ever. And like a love affair, or a drug, it would be exhilarating at first, but then as it wore on it reclaimed the buzz it had given, with interest. 'What, you thought all that was for free?' my *Moscow Times* colleague Jonas Bernstein would cackle whenever I showed up for work complaining of a hangover or nursing strange bruises. I suppose the answer was yes, we all did.

Moscow reached the apogee of its self-congratulatory hubris in late summer of 1997. The city's mayor, Yuri Luzhkov, decided that Moscow's 850th anniversary should be turned into a celebration of the capital's wealth and success, decreeing a massive public celebration. On the day, Luzhkov rode in triumph past the old Central Telegraph in a motorized Grecian wine bowl as five million revellers packed the centre of Moscow. Luciano Pavarotti sang on Red Square and Jean Michel Jarre performed a *son-et-lumière* on the Lenin Hills, projecting his lasers on the soaring bulk of Moscow State University. I have a memory of staggering among a pile of debris behind a row of vodka kiosks near Park Kultury looking for a place to pee, and discovering a couple copulating among the discarded beer bottles and crisp packets. It was a night of misrule; as Jarre's lasers blossomed over the city, crowds of youths rode on the roofs of packed trolleybuses and let off firecrackers in the crowd.

Yet at the same time Moscow had a filthy underbelly which people like Mayor Luzhkov wished didn't exist. I spent two days at Kursky Station, below the platforms in a warren of dingy cubby holes inhabited by homeless people who had fallen as far as it was possible to fall. As the evening rush hour died down, the station's secret dwellers would cautiously emerge from their underground world below the underpasses and reclaim the station as their own. Clambering down on to the railway tracks, I found families of tramps who lived in nests of cardboard and litter beneath the platforms. I shared beers with a gang of teenage pickpockets who handed half their takings to the police as protection money. A thirteen-year-old prostitute with a face that was plastered with white make-up and dirty hair held up with a shiny plastic clip tried to chat me up. I bought her a can of gin and tonic, and she explained that she had run away from a remote village where her alcoholic parents had beat her. 'But now I'm here in the big city,' she said, brightening, surveying her concrete world of litter and neon. 'I've always dreamed of living here.'

I found other runaways hiding in a maze of underground heating ducts on the outskirts of the city. These kids scratched a living by picking pockets, fetching and carrying for the local market traders, all to fuel their habit of sniffing a cheap brand of glue called Moment. They were scruffy and emaciated but irrepressibly friendly and cocky, even though under constant threat from marauding homosexuals who tried to rape them, the police who periodically rounded them up, and American missionaries who brought them food and made them pray to Jesus. They were cunning and cynical as rats, but they lived like a family, helping the youngest ones who were just eight or nine, feeding and instructing them in the hard ways of their little world. They invited me into their den with great pride and asked me shyly to buy them hot dogs, the greatest treat they could imagine.

In August of that year, I moved into a new apartment on Petrovka Street. My landlady on Starokonushenny Pereulok, caught up in the frenzy of the economic boom, tried to hike my rent by 50 per cent with two days' notice. I promised to pay, then did a late-night runner.

My new flatmate was a delightful Canadian flower-child turned stockbroker called Patti. Patti, like the thousands of expatriates who crowded into Moscow at that time, was riding high on the back of a giant boom which had followed Boris Yeltsin's re-election the year before. Good times were rolling, for those who positioned themselves to take advantage of the sale of the century.

Moscow's rich young foreigners were the conquistadors of capitalism, living in vast apartments once occupied by Stalin's ministers, throwing epic parties in what had been the Politburo's most luxurious dachas, scooting off for weekends in Ibiza, taking their pick of the conquered land's womenfolk and generally reaping the fruits of a hundred billion dollars' worth of Cold War NATO military spending which allowed them to be there. By day they would trade stocks, buy companies and peddle FMCGs – Fast Moving Consumer Goods – to the Russian masses, making fortunes selling Tampax, Marlboros and deodorant. By night they cruised around Moscow in polished black SUVs, guzzling cocaine and accumulating an entourage of astonishingly beautiful girlfriends.

One acquaintance of mine made millions through a cosy relationship he had going with the Russian Orthodox Church. The Kremlin was allowing the Church to import alcohol and cigarettes duty free, the profits supposedly going to the reconstruction of churches. Another friend made his cash doing audits for a major American consultancy company. The arrangement was simple enough. However doomed or decrepit the factory, he'd recommend that they lay off half their workforce, draw up a creative version of their accounts to sell to gullible Western investors and split the profits of the resulting share flotation with the management.

Russia certainly had a definite appeal for anyone with a dark streak of gross irresponsibility and self-destructiveness. And if you had it, there was nothing to stop you indulging it. It was a weird, Godless world, where values went into permanent suspended animation and you were terrifyingly free to explore the nastiest recesses of your own black heart.

But despite the good times Moscow got its revenge on its new masters, insidiously screwing with foreign psyches. You'd see young men who had arrived as cheery, corn-fed boys assuming within a year that hardened, taciturn look one usually associates with circus people. Selfish young hedonists quickly turned into selfish psychotic monsters – too much sexual success, money, vodka, drugs and cynicism in too short a time.

Patti, however, somehow always managed to keep her hippy cheerfulness, despite it all. I have an enduring image of Patti from that time. It was early in the morning, a summer dawn, and I woke to find Patti in my room, rooting in my desk, stark naked, looking for leftover amphetamines. She had an early flight to catch, scooting off on another business trip to Siberia to buy up factories. I stumbled to the bathroom, looked in the mirror, and saw Nosferatu looking back at me. Patti, now pepped up by her chemical wake-up call, cheerily clacked down the hall in her Prada sandals, dragging her Ralph Lauren bags, and called goodbye.

'Patti, darling, when are you going to buy me a factory?' I called from the bathroom.

'Soon, honey, very soon, when we're all verry verry rich! Byeee!'

As autumn 1965 approached Mervyn prepared to leave his rooms at St Antony's for ever. He had accepted a teaching post at Nottingham University; by his own assessment, a place 'towards the bottom of the second division' of universities. Fourteen months of effort and he had got nowhere with Mila, and the loneliness was eating into him. In his last weeks at Oxford, he would drive out to Wytham Woods and wander alone through the trees.

'I am very sad this evening, so I am writing to you, it helps,' Mervyn wrote. 'I was struck in your letters by what you said about your lonely walks. Do you really talk to me, call out to me? I thought all evening that I could hear your voice, low and sweet and sing-song, even though I could not answer. I think of you often and you are with me always . . . I thought how good it would be if you were here, we would sit in the garden in the sun or be doing something together. My sorrow is almost unbearable, but it goes after a time and I can pull myself together and work.'

With the end of his Oxford career came desperation. Conventional tactics were clearly not working, so Mervyn began thinking of something more unorthodox. In a final gracious gesture, St Antony's offered to pay for Mervyn to go to a conference in Vienna, even though he had done no research and had no paper to present. The only condition was that Mervyn was to get up to 'no funny business', as Theodore Zeldin, one of the fellows of St Antony's, warned him.

The conference was a lavish affair, with banquets and endless speeches. Mervyn slipped away and ate alone at a Russian restaurant called the Feuervogel, owned by a huge sweaty Russian who also waited at the tables and poured vodka even if it hadn't been ordered. A Bulgarian guitarist sang melancholy songs and bickered with the owner.

Mervyn was indeed planning some 'funny business', which involved slipping into Czechoslovakia unnoticed on the day the conference ended, to send a confidential letter which he hoped would transform his fortunes. Though at that time no visa was required and the train ride to Prague was only three hours, Mervyn spent a sleepless night before his departure, fearing that he might be snatched like Gerald Brooke. But the journey was without incident; the border guards scowled at his passport but stamped it.

Mervyn arrived in Prague on 6 September 1965 and checked into the run-down Hotel Slovan. He found Prague livelier than Moscow, and even discovered a dingy nightclub where he had a solitary glass of wine. That night he sat down to write a long, frank letter to Alexei. Mervyn spelled out the propaganda advantages of letting Mila out, and offered a 'substantial' sum of money if this were to happen. He cited cases of Poles and East Germans buying their way out, unofficially but legally. He would be helping Russia, and though he was not rich he could find benefactors. The money could go to 'charitable causes' in the Soviet Union. 'We are about the same age, Alexei, and we can talk seriously and honestly. Please help!' Mervyn pleaded.

Unlike Mila, Mervyn seemed still to harbour illusions about the fundamental decency of the KGB, or at least of Alexei personally. What he did not include was an offer to cooperate – but by this stage such an offer probably wouldn't have been accepted in any case. He sent the letter by registered post in the morning from the Central Post Office just off Wenceslas Square. He never received an answer.

Perhaps my parents found something in their separation which resonated with an emotional barrenness they each carried with them from childhood. But there came a point, quite early in their epistolary relationship, when they began to put so much of their lives into their letters that the recording of the experience overtook the experience itself, the material became too huge, the process of turning it into history began to rob them of their present.

In Moscow, Mila was settled into the private rituals of her long-distance love affair. As she left for work she would kiss Mervyn's photo. On her way home she shopped for records for Mervyn, so he and his friends could listen to Russian music together. She consulted her doctor about Mervyn's minor ailments. In almost every letter she refers to Mervyn's diet, her obsession with food a hangover from her childhood.

'Do you listen to your Mila? Please Mervyn, don't eat too much pepper, vinegar and other spices. Do you drink your milk? I drink half a litre every night. Eat properly, as I taught you, eat fresh things.' When Mervyn tried to object that he was partial to a curry from time to time, Mila would have none of it. 'I respect your tastes, but I fear some of them hurt your health – I mean what I mentioned to you in Moscow, your passion for Eastern, Caucasian and Indian food. It's too spicy for you, you are a person from a maritime climate. This is food for people with strong stomachs, but you are a delicate northern flower, you need to eat delicately.'

Mila asked for clothes, which Mervyn would buy in London (jokingly grumbling in his letters at the expense) and send to Moscow through Dinnerman's, the only authorized parcel handler to the Soviet Union. Mila would buy books and send them to Mervyn in London in brown paper parcels tied with rough string. Soon there were hundreds on his shelves.

Mila's virtual relationship with Mervyn was spiralling into a full-fledged obsession; she was plunging deep into an imagined world of her own creation. 'It is as though I live entirely in a complex mechanism called Mervyn, I see all his bolts and wheels all around me,' she wrote. 'You are the point, the aim of my life . . . Soon I will begin practising a new religion, Mervusism, and I will make everyone believe in my God of joy and warmth.'

In many ways, it seemed to her that the life represented by

the stream of letters was more real than her interactions with the live people around her. 'I have no present, only a past and a future if I can believe in it,' she wrote. 'Everything around me is dead, I wander through the ruins, onwards towards some goal, towards you.' She lived for Mervyn's letters; 'everything else, I invent just to fill in the time.'

Mila describes sitting in the courtyard at Starokonushenny Pereulok in the warm drizzle, laughing out loud as she reads Mervyn's latest letters while a hatchet-faced old babushka peers out from a cellar window. 'It was as though wings had sprouted from my back,' she wrote. 'All your soul, in the form of paper and ink, poured into me like a clear stream and filled my body and soul with strength. This is the best medicine I could have. Your letters are getting better and better, soon I will cry not from sorrow but from joy.'

At the weekend she went to the dacha. Olga read Chekhov while Mila knitted; a late summer hailstorm rattled on the house's iron roof. When the storm cleared, Mila went for a long walk through cornfields, calling out Mervyn's name. The burden of grief was taking its toll on her. 'Mervyn, sorrow is sucking the life out of her . . . surely she's suffered enough in her life. I am truly worried for her,' Lenina wrote. 'Probably because she never felt or saw the love of parents she suffers twice as much now. Our house is in mourning, literally . . . She has stopped smiling, laughing, she has tears in her eyes all the time. I ask you to write more often, she lives for you.'

Mila's periods had stopped from worry, but her doctor told her not to be concerned. 'In wartime women didn't have them for years,' she told Mila. Nevertheless she prescribed daily injections 'for your nerves', as well as a course of 'magnetic therapy' – evidently some kind of pseudo-scientific quackery of the kind beloved by the hypochondriac Soviets.

For a few months in 1965, Mila seems to have become preoccupied with the fear that her good-looking fiancé might be stolen from her. It even pervaded her sleep. Mila dreamt that she was at the Bolshoi with Valery and caught sight of Mervyn down in the stalls with another woman. She called and shouted, and was seized by an uncontrollable desire to throw herself over the balcony down to him.

The pain of separation had shaken loose all Mila's deepest fears – of abandonment, most profoundly, but also lesser insecurities about her appearance. Mila felt acutely that she was no beauty. 'This is the most painful question for me, and I never speak of it to anyone – but I am terribly sorry that I will not please your friends and acquaintances in this respect,' Mila wrote. 'I am so afraid of that, I worry about it. Though I do have one comfort – all my life I have had lots of friends, including pretty ones, and they all loved me and were attracted to me. I know that you like beautiful women, like any man. I love beauty too. I hope very much that you will see beyond this and see what others do not see. We will look at beautiful women together. I am not so insecure that I cannot acknowledge the beauty of other women if they are not bitches or fools. All my life I had very few photos taken of me – you know why, but if something comes out I'll send it to you. I feel shy when you show my photographs to people.'

At work, Mila would show Mervyn's letters around. She had a man, which in turn made her fully a woman. 'I want someone to love me – I want people to know that I am not such an unfortunate.' But the pain, and perhaps an obscure sense of shame and guilt at having lost her lover, kept her behind late at work so that she would not have to see other girls being met by their husbands and boyfriends.

In late September 1965, Mervyn saw a hopeful story in the *Sun*. Secret talks on swapping Brooke for the Krogers had got further than Mervyn had suspected. Wolfgang Vogel, a mysterious East German lawyer, represented the Soviet side. Vogel had a good track record – he had brokered the 1962 spy swap of the American U2 pilot Gary Powers for the veteran Soviet spy 'Rudolph Abel'. Abel, whose real name was William Fischer, had, ironically enough, been the Krogers' controller when they worked in the US in the 1940s, running messages for Moscow's atomic spies in the Manhattan Project. Vogel was also rumoured to have arranged the 'purchase' of East Germans by their relatives in the West.

'The British government has bitterly rejected all suggestions of a swap, now or in the future,' said the *Sun* on 22 September 1965. 'They consider Gerald Brooke, jailed in Moscow for subversion, is being held to ransom. But this reaction has not apparently deterred Herr Vogel . . . On Monday night his green and cream Opel was waved through Checkpoint Charlie without the usual close scrutiny of papers for a meeting with Mr Christopher Lush at the British HQ in West Berlin.'

Four days later Mervyn was on a train trundling eastwards through Germany. The heating in the carriage had been switched off, and he passed the guard towers and barbed wire around West Berlin at dawn, shivering cold. He stayed, as usual, in the cheapest hotel he could find, the Pension Alcron in Lietzenburgerstrasse. Mervyn telephoned Jürgen Stange, Vogel's West German lawyer contact, and made an appointment for the next day. He spent the rest of the day in East Berlin sightseeing. Wartime ruins were everywhere, and the place was tense and drab. Later in the afternoon he visited the Zoo and watched the monkeys staring at him gloomily from their cages.

Mervyn explained his case in detail to Stange, who promised to arrange a meeting with Vogel the next night. Their rendezvous was the Baronen Bar, a small and expensive place frequented by businessmen where Vogel often stopped for a drink before returning east from his regular trips. As Mervyn waited he noticed that the tall barman wore extravagant cufflinks, intended, Mervyn supposed, to inveigle the customers into giving him larger tips.

Vogel was round-faced, bespectacled and friendly. Mervyn's German was poor, and Vogel had no English; Stange had explained that his knowledge of foreign languages was confined to Latin and Greek. But Vogel was upbeat, and made a lot of optimistic noises about improving relations. He suggested that maybe Mila and perhaps one other person could be exchanged for one of the Krogers, something that Mervyn thought highly unlikely. But he was heartened by the German lawyer's enthusiastic tone.

As Vogel stood to leave, Mervyn sprang to his feet and offered to carry a small suitcase Vogel had brought with him into the bar. The case was impossibly heavy, and Mervyn could barely lift it. He staggered after Vogel and heaved the suitcase into his Opel, and waved as he drove off in an easterly direction. Mervyn never found out what was in the case, and never dared ask.

The next day Mervyn met Christopher Lush of the British Foreign Office at Western Allied Headquarters, and asked him to contact London for an official response to the idea of an exchange. Lush was dismissive. 'We don't want to become a channel for this sort of thing,' he told my father. 'We don't want everyone coming here.'

Vogel never contacted Mervyn. It was another blind alley.

Soon after he returned from Berlin, Mervyn heaved his Oxford trunks into his battered Ford and drove north to his new academic quarters at Long Eaton, near Nottingham, doubtless sitting up straight at the wheel after Mila's admonitions not to 'slouch as though you are carrying buckets'.

Mervyn found Long Eaton a place of profound dreariness, a grimy industrial town which reminded him powerfully of the miseries of his childhood in South Wales. Nottingham University's lecturers were accommodated in very much less style than he had been used to in Oxford. Mervyn did not like drinking in pubs, which left sitting at the laundromat watching the clothes whirl around as the only alternative local entertainment. After Moscow and Oxford, Nottingham was a fall from grace indeed, but at least he now had the time to devote to his campaign. Despite having an epileptic fit in the station cafeteria at King's Cross – the first he had ever suffered – Mervyn resolved to stay optimistic.

'From that day on, regardless of the news from Russia, I always made a point of going into the classroom with a cheery smile on my face,' he told Mila. 'I'm not in the least bit worried about the cancellation of my book.' A photograph from that autumn shows Mervyn at his desk at the university, a tinny radio I remember him still using in the mid-1970s in front of him, books piled on sagging bookshelves behind. The room is small and poky, and he is earnestly reading a letter. He looks strangely childish and dislocated, among the unruly piles of his possessions, but quite content.

Mervyn's mother, during one of his rare visits to Swansea, harangued him about giving up his self-destructive obsession with his Russian girl. 'This morning my mother tiger showed her claws – leopards, to change the metaphor, don't change their spots,' wrote Mervyn as he sat in his Ford in the car park of Nottingham University sports club, where he took his daily swim. 'She says I'm home so rarely and make her suffer so much – she said that the recent events in Russia nearly killed her. "And when I think of what's happened to your career I am filled with horror," she said. "Shut up," I said, "or I'll leave the house – the car's just outside," so she went quiet.'

Mervyn considered other options. One was for Mila to apply to visit another socialist country, meet him there, and somehow escape. The problem was that Mila would have to get a reference from her employers to travel, even to a friendly state, and no one at the library would dare risk giving her such an endorsement. She could also arrange a fictitious marriage to an African student, who could then take her abroad – but that idea, as well as being distasteful, was impractical since it required KGB permission, and would cast a shadow on their campaign if it failed.

He thought of bribery. A new car for a bent embassy official, perhaps? But again, with the case so politicized it was unworkable. He even explored forgery, spending days leafing through his heavily stamped passport studying the details, collecting printing sets and experimenting with producing false Soviet official stamps. Two of Mervyn's friends, middle-aged ladies of the utmost probity, agreed to give him their passports. One applied for one even though she had no intention of going abroad, the other claimed to have lost hers. But after a few days the dangers of forgery began to dampen Mervyn's enthusiasm. There was the problem of getting a one-way ticket out of Moscow, and Mila would have to risk years of imprisonment if passport control discovered that the exit visa Mervyn intended to manufacture was forged. He abandoned the idea.

In a newspaper article he found a reference to the story of a Russian who had decided to walk to China before the war, but had (seriously) misjudged the direction and ended up in Afghanistan. Mervyn began looking at maps of the southern USSR; perhaps there were areas where there was no border guard? In December 1965 he read of another young Russian, Vladimir Kirsanov, who had walked over the Soviet border into Finland. Could Mila do the same? Mervyn tracked Kirsanov down and went to see him in Frankfurt am Main in March 1966. But after listening to Kirsanov's story for a few minutes Meryvn realized it was hopeless. Kirsanov was young and fit, and an experienced hiker and climber. Mila, with her disabled hip, could never hope to trudge through bogs and climb over barbed wire fences. Again, the idea was abandoned.

Two years had passed, and the separation gnawed. Nottingham was depressing Mervyn even more than he'd feared. By the summer of 1966 he decided that he had to be nearer to London in order to continue his campaign. He took a post at

Battersea Polytechnic, which had just received a charter as the University of Surrey, and was then housed in a disused warehouse in Clapham. He bought a small flat in Pimlico, turning down other job offers because the Battersea job gave him a lot of free time to harass the Soviet embassy, the Foreign Office and Fleet Street. He never had anything other than contempt for the University of Surrey, its students and its academic standards, and he would criticize the institution where he ultimately spent most of his career with a kind of bitter self-loathing.

Mila, too, was sliding into morbid depression. She was losing weight, her ribs standing out on her chest 'like a tubercular babushka', and grey hairs appeared on her head. 'Without you my life has stopped, hardened to stone – this is not just a first impression but a totally serious conclusion, irreversible,' Mila wrote. 'Why don't we just build a hut for ourselves at the end of the world far from all the evil and cruelty and hatred? I could never be bored if you were there. Oh God, oh God, oh God, surely our sufferings aren't in vain? I see what a short and fleeting thing life is, and how stupid, how perverse it is to lose these days.' Mila paraphrased Konstantin Simonov's classic wartime poem, 'Wait', which had so poignantly caught the fate of millions of Soviet women, condemned to wait for years with no news of their loved ones. 'Wait for me, but only wait very hard, wait until the snows have gone, wait until everyone else has stopped waiting, wait . . .'

During a chance conversation with a friend in London, Mervyn learned that it might be possible to visit the Soviet Baltic states for a one-day trip without a visa. On further investigation at the Finnish tourism bureau on the Haymarket he was told that a Helsinki tourist agency called Haleva ran one-day tours to Tallinn, Estonia, and short trips to Leningrad, which also did not require a visa. They were meant for Finns, the girl at the counter told him, but she didn't think there would be any problem if an Englishman were to buy a ticket. Estonia was part of the Soviet Union, and Mila would be able to travel there without difficulty.

Mervyn located an 1892 map of Revel (modern Tallinn) at the British Library and a pre-war German guidebook. He picked the town's highest spire, St Olaf's church, Oleviste Kirik, because it was the obvious place to meet, and not too far from the docks. In a series of letters in early August he dropped hints to Mila – did she plan on taking a holiday in the Baltic? Tallinn was very nice, he'd heard. Maybe Mervyn would have to be in Scandinavia on the 26th or 29th. Had Mila heard of St Olaf's church? Mila took the hint and indicated that she would be there.

The plan was risky. Before Mervyn set off to Finland on 22 August, he left a letter to be delivered to the Foreign Office in case he did not return.

'At the end of the month I am going to make one or two attempts to return to the USSR, in order to see my fiancée,' he wrote. 'I shall almost certainly try to go over to Tallinn. There is some chance that I may end up in a Soviet prison . . . I wish to make it clear that if I am seized by the Soviets I do not wish to have any assistance from any FO employees in the USSR, and I must tell you categorically that none of your people are to make any attempt to contact my fiancée. I hope that statement leaves no uncertainties in your mind . . . I regret having had any dealing with your office, and want no more.'

He posted the letter to a friend, to be sent to the Foreign Office if he didn't return by mid-September.

Mervyn took a cheap flight to Copenhagen, then a night ferry to Stockholm and another to Helsinki. The next morning, a Thursday, he walked to the Kaleva Travel Agency office and booked a ticket to Tallinn for Saturday. He spent the rest of the day walking around Helsinki, sitting on old Russian cannon at the fort and writing to Mila, asking her to send her replies poste restante to Helsinki.

'I just can't find the words to describe the local beauty,' he wrote. 'The open sea with great bays and islands, smiling in the sun, and lovely white yachts sailing in the calm sea.'

On Friday he went back to the travel agency, and was given his small pink ticket without fuss, despite his not being Finnish. Mervyn and his fellow passengers arrived at the southern harbour the next morning at nine and boarded the SS *Vanemuine*. It sailed on time an hour later.

The day was sunny and blustery, perfect Scandinavian weather. Soon after they set sail a dour-looking Russian in a dark suit went around collecting passports in a box. As Mervyn gave his in he got a quizzical look from the plain-clothes border guard. The crossing took two hours, and Mervyn stood on the open part of the bridge, staring across Soviet waters as the spires of Tallinn came into view. As the ship docked, the Russian re-emerged with his box and began calling out the names of the passengers to return their pass-ports. Mervyn waited, a knot of anxiety in his stomach. But his name was called, the last on the list, and the Russian handed him back his passport with a blank look.

As he walked down the gangplank, Mervyn heard a woman's voice, not Mila's, call his name. It was Nadia, Mila's niece, and she was beaming, and incredulous. She and Mila had been expecting Mervyn the next day, and she'd only come to the docks for a practice run. Mila was waiting at the Oleviste Kirik. Nadia had checked for goons, and seen none.

They walked past the customs house and bastion into the Old Town. As they approached the church, Mervyn saw a woman in a kerchief sitting on a bench, and called out. To his embarrassment, it wasn't Mila. 'Mila's over there,' said Nadia, pointing to a small, familiar figure by the entrance to the church. They embraced.

'I cannot describe my emotions at that moment,' Mervyn wrote to Mila later. Even after two years of separation, he felt an immediate closeness, 'the same kind eyes, sympathy, common concerns'.

For a few hours in Tallinn, my parents lived in the strange exhilaration of stolen time. They were not meant to be there; the rulers of the ordinary world had ordained, in their peremptory way, that they should be apart. Yet there they were, wandering arm in arm around the Old Town, talking about plans for the future as Nadia followed them at a distance, looking out for the KGB. A chink in the wall had let Mervyn through, and that small victory was to give them the hope that the hours could turn into a lifetime. I do not think that they could have borne what were to be six years of separation without those moments in Tallinn when they proved to each other that they were truly still flesh and blood, not just words on paper, and that the battle could be won.

They dropped in on a girlfriend of Mila's for tea, and sat on park benches in the watery northern sun. As they wandered back towards the port, they heard the ship's horn blare. Mervyn looked at his watch – it was much later than he had thought.

They broke into a run, Mila limping as fast as she could. The ship was just casting off, but the gangplank was still down, and there were a couple of seconds for a brief hug before Mervyn ran on board. As the ship pulled away he watched Nadia and Mila on the quayside, waving, her small figure fading away as the ship pulled into the fairway. Mervyn was engulfed in grief, and hope.

The Lomamatka Tourist Bureau in Helsinki also offered a trip to Leningrad – two nights at sea, one in Leningrad, staying aboard ship. Again, no Soviet visa was required. On the evening of 4 September Mervyn boarded the SS *Kastelholm*, a small and venerable steamer, and set off for Leningrad. He admired the old reciprocating steam engine. A genial Finn collected the passports, and Mervyn slept more easily in the knowledge that there were no Soviet officials aboard.

The next morning as he went on deck he found that they were already steaming up the Neva towards Leningrad docks. Mervyn went ashore with the other passengers, and saw Mila waiting for him by a parked truck. They did not embrace, in order not to attract attention, and walked to the city centre. Mila was alone, this time, without Nadia to keep watch. They spent the day wandering the city, going to the Russian Museum, where for a few alarming minutes they lost each other in different halls.

Mila had booked a room in a student hostel, and managed to smuggle Mervyn in for a few hours in the early evening with the connivance of her fellow students. They were disturbed by a banging on the door, but it was a false alarm. It was someone who had mixed up the rooms, not the KGB coming to haul Mervyn away to jail. In the evening, after a greasy duck meal in a restaurant, Mervyn had to return to spend the night on the ship.

The next day was much the same – with no cosy place to stay and talk, they just wandered the squares and streets, holding on to each other. This time they returned to the docks in plenty of time. They said a quick goodbye among the parked lorries, and Mervyn walked to the ship alone. The parting was less sad than at Tallinn, but still the brief meeting had made the emptiness which followed all the sharper.

'So, I'm on my way back to Helsinki, over the darkening Baltic waters,' Mervyn wrote on the ship as he sailed westwards down the Neva. 'I have spent the happiest two days ever during our two years of separation. It was wonderful, mentally and physically. I hope I did not say anything hurtful while we were together. I looked back as I was getting on board, and I saw your slight figure and legs disappearing. I felt very, very sad. I still love you and we will continue our struggle for happiness. Now I have the impression that everything will move quickly. You'll see.'

From Stockholm on 8 September he wrote, 'After our meetings in these northern towns my life has again begun to acquire a meaning . . . I think that things will never again be as bad as they were.' Mila avoided mentioning the meetings directly in her letters. She had a bad scare when she read that a Norwegian ferry had sunk in the Skagerrak, but looked at an atlas and convinced herself that Mervyn could not have been on it.

My father decided to return to his old idea of applying for a Soviet visa in another country, in the hope that one would be issued in error. On 12 December 1966 he took a night ferry from Southend to Ostend, then a train to Brussels. On the first night he stayed in a cheap but clean hotel near the Gare du Nord, which turned out to be a busy brothel. A fat African guest in the next room kept him awake with his snoring. Mervyn found an agency which did tours to Moscow – Belgatourist on the rue des Paroissiens – and booked a five-day trip. Mervyn filled out the application using a different spelling of his surname to the usual, taking advantage of the fact that 'Matthews' can be transliterated at least a dozen different ways in Cyrillic. As he had hoped, the passport and visa came back a day later; his name had gone unnoticed when the Soviet embassy checked it against the blacklists.

Two days later he was in Moscow, once again staying at the National Hotel. It was strange to be back, and deeply worrying to be around so many goons who were busy watching the foreigners at the hotel. Because my father hadn't been sure that the plan would work, he hadn't warned Mila. He called her the evening he arrived from a public phone booth on Mokhovaya Street. She was amazed to hear he was in Moscow. Because he would surely be under routine surveillance in any case, he decided not to use any subterfuge. The next morning Mila came running up Mokhovaya to greet him as he waited outside the National Hotel. They went back to Mila's room off the Arbat, which was unchanged. Then they telephoned the Palace of Weddings, and were told that Efremova, the director, would be in on Monday. The next day was Christmas, which Mila and Mervyn spent locked in Mila's room. In the afternoon they walked to the Central Telegraph to send Mervyn's mother a seasonal telegram.

On Monday they went again to see Efremova at the Palace of Weddings, who was plainly terrified to see Mervyn without official notification. She mumbled something about the 'normal procedures', and showed them out. But at least she had received them. Mervyn phoned the embassy, and the duty vice consul seemed surprisingly eager to help when the embassy opened for business the next day.

The next morning, however, as he stepped out of the National Hotel, Mervyn felt silent alarm bells ringing like a discordant note in a horror film – the goons were out in force, and keeping him under close surveillance. It was now just a question of time. That afternoon there was a message for him at the desk to contact Intourist at once. At the Intourist office he was told that his visa was being annulled and he had to leave immediately. Mila was distraught when she heard the news. 'But Mervusya, we can't do anything now,' she sobbed.

At four that afternoon Mervyn was summoned to the gloomy OVIR office once again. The deputy head was waiting, and said just one sentence, twice: 'You must leave Russia as soon as possible, today or tomorrow, on the first available plane.'

There was no option but to go. If the KGB turned nasty Mervyn could very well end up in jail along with Brooke, another useful bargaining chip to be weighed against the Krogers. For the third time in five months, Mila saw him off from Soviet soil – except this time it must truly have seemed like the last. To be caught again in Russia would mean prison for sure.

There was some press coverage of Mervyn's second expulsion. The Foreign Office had received an official note of protest at Mervyn's visit from the Soviet Foreign Ministry, but neither Mervyn nor the press knew it at the time. Des Zwar contacted Mervyn, asking for his cooperation on a big piece for the *People* on how to enter Russia illegally, which Mervyn emphatically turned down.

The press coverage did have one unexpected result. Mervyn got a phone call from Derek Deason, who had himself been expelled from the Soviet Union in October 1964, and had also left a fiancée behind. Mervyn suggested they meet at a pub near Victoria Station, the Albert – a dingy place near my school where, thirty years later, I was often to be found drinking illicitly with fellow sixth-formers. Derek was Mervyn's age, and worked as a scaleman – a checker of scales – at the Dagenham Ford motor works. He had a broad, honest face and Mervyn immediately took to him. While on holiday on the Black Sea coast in the summer of 1964 Derek had met Eleonora Ginzburg, a Russian-Jewish English-language teacher from Moscow. They had fallen in love, and he had proposed to her. The marriage date was set for October. Derek arrived in Moscow with some days to spare, and because Eleonora lived with her sister in a cramped flat he decided to go to Sochi for a few days before the wedding. In Sochi he fell in with some Russians who organized a stag night for him. Derek, unused to vodka, got drunk and obstreperous, and the police were called. They bundled him on a plane to Moscow, and then he was put on another to London without having a chance to call Eleonora. The first she heard from him was when he called, in tears, from London. Derek had applied for an entry visa nine times since, and been refused.

Mervyn found Derek a spirited and intelligent companion

in arms, and they met regularly in the Albert and another quiet pub called the Audley to plan their campaign. Unlike Mervyn, Derek had no history of confrontation with the Soviet authorities, and he had more to lose by associating with Mervyn than vice versa. Still, for both of them, having at least one ally was a great comfort. They exchanged Mila and Eleonora's addresses so the two could meet in Moscow.

Return to the Soviet Union was now too risky; even Mervyn realized that he could not push his luck any further. But the Soviet Prime Minister Alexei Kosygin was due for a state visit to London, and would be a perfect target for Mervyn's by now well-practised lobbying. Mervyn decided to hand him a letter, in time-honoured tradition. He wrote to the Queen, who was to receive Kosygin, beforehand to ask her to raise the matter, but received only a formal reply saying that his letter had been noted by Her Majesty. He contacted the Special Branch to try and arrange a time and place to hand Kosygin his letter without causing embarrassment. The officer he saw was noncommittal, and Mervyn found, to his grim amusement more than anything else, that he was being followed by the Special Branch on the streets of London. He went to Downing Street and waited opposite Number 10, but KGB goons guarding Kosygin warned him to stay away. At the Houses of Parliament he joined a crowd and told a plain-clothes police inspector that he was planning to hand over a letter.

'You can't do that,' the policeman told him.

'But I'm not breaking any law.'

'If you step out from the crowd,' said the inspector, shattering Mervyn's lifelong trust in the British police, 'we'll take you to the station and pin something on you.'

The third and last attempt to get to Kosygin was at the Victoria & Albert Museum, where he and Harold Wilson were visiting an exhibition devoted to Anglo–Soviet cooperation. Again, he could get nowhere near Kosygin. But as the Soviet

Premier was driven away Wilson was left standing for a few
moments at the curb, waiting for his own car to pull up.
Mervyn pushed forward, and said, 'What about our fiancées,
Mr Wilson?' Wilson turned, a flash of recognition in his eyes.

'I know you!' said the Prime Minister, and got into his car.
The letter stayed in Mervyn's pocket, undelivered.

Mervyn came up with a new idea. Perhaps he could get his
hands on something valuable to the Soviets which he could
barter for Mila's freedom? Perhaps some undiscovered manuscripts by Vladimir Lenin – known in the trade as Leniniana –
of the sort Mila's colleagues at the Institute of Marxism and
Leninism had spent much of their working lives translating
and acquiring? The Russians had an insatiable appetite for
Lenin's writings from the periods he'd spent in western
Europe from 1907 to 1917, fomenting revolution and bick-
ering peevishly with his fellow Communists. Maybe, for once
in Mila's life, dead papers could become a life-giving thing.

Mervyn, his imagination fired, rushed to the British Library
to get some samples of Lenin's handwriting. He ordered up
Lenin's application for a reader's ticket, in the name of 'Jacob
Richter', and studied the formation of the Latin letters, taking
notes for future reference in case he ever got hold of any
Leniniana which might be for sale. As he returned the papers
to the Library desk he reflected that he could be holding the
keys to Mila's freedom in his hands.

Mervyn trawled his émigré contacts for possible undiscovered archives. In Paris he tracked down Grigory Aleksinsky,
who had been a socialist deputy for St Petersburg in the
Second Duma of spring 1907. He had known Lenin and
corresponded with the Russian Marxist economist Georgy
Plekhanov. Aleksinsky's son, also Grigory, or Grégoire, was
affable enough, in his mid-forties, and worked as some kind of
plain-clothes functionary of the French police or security
services. Mervyn took him out to dinner.

'First we drank an aperitif together,' Mervyn wrote to Mila, without telling her the real purpose of the meeting. 'Then we went to have a meal at a "cheap" restaurant, (but the bill for the two of us was nearly three pounds!) That was with wine, which made my head spin. After that he took me to his home, where his wife was waiting with tea and gateaux. Their apartment was luxurious, and they had three magnificent samovars. There was lively conversation but my host kept switching from Russian to French in each sentence, so in the end I did not know which language I was supposed to be speaking!'

Aleksinsky senior was produced, a frail old man who mumbled his greetings. They showed Mervyn the archive, in boxes, but didn't allow him to open any. The Soviets had shown considerable interest, but the old man was passionately anti-Soviet, and refused to sell. But to Mervyn, they might be prepared to sell the archive for just 50,000 francs – 3,700 pounds, or about a year and a half of Mervyn's salary.

Despite the huge cost, Mervyn was excited. He wrote to Mila's old boss at the Institute of Marxism and Leninism, Pyotr Nikolayevich Pospelov, without mentioning the reason for his interest in Leniniana.

'I know that Soviet historians make great efforts to seek out manuscripts of Lenin in western Europe and return them to the homeland of the Great Leader of the Great October Revolution,' wrote Mervyn in his best Marxistese. 'I have recently discovered that the valuable archives of Grigory A. Aleksinsky, a member of the State Duma and close acquaintance of Lenin, are in Paris. At the present time Mr Aleksinsky's son, whom I know well, is giving me the opportunity to buy his father's archives. I personally consider that Moscow is the proper place for Lenin's documents, and I would like to assist in passing them to Soviet historians.'

The Soviets were enthusiastic. Pospelov's successor, Pyotr Fedoseyev, asked for more information. It was a ray of hope.

*   *   *

Mila took a holiday trip to Mikhailovskoye, Pushkin's estate, and wandered through it looking admiringly at the English furniture. The air was cold and snowy, and she bought Antonovka apples by Pushkin's grave in Sviatogorsk. She walked alone around the estate's famous park. 'Need I say how passionately I wanted to have you near?' she wrote. 'I asked the old trees, the forest and the birds and the air to grant this wish, then I began talking out loud with you, very, very gently I recited Pushkin's poems. Mervyn, my dear, so much love and tenderness has accumulated within me, how can I give it to you? I love you more and more every day.'

On her return to Moscow, she spoke to Mervyn at the Central Telegraph. Not wanting to raise false hope, he said nothing of his plans. Still, she must have felt some optimism in his voice; walking home from her 'phone call of life' Mila sang, 'Sweetheart, remember when days are forlorn; It is always darkest before the dawn.'

'We are two pendulums swinging at the same rhythm,' she wrote that night. 'I kiss the dear end of your pendulum.' She drew two stick figures with giant hearts on the letter.

Mervyn began writing to friends and acquaintances for money. Isaiah Berlin replied that he knew no one in Oxford 'with a large bank account and a generous heart'. Rauf Khahil, an old Oxford friend whose family owned so much of Egypt that Rauf would claim that he 'couldn't bear to think about it', had inconveniently dropped dead at his lectern a few years before while lecturing in Africa. Another friend, Priscilla Johnson at Harvard, was persuaded to ask Stalin's daughter Svetlana Alliluyeva, who had defected to the West in 1967, to part with some of her handsome book royalties in the cause of Mila's liberation, but to no avail. Lord Thompson of Fleet, the press baron, with whom Mervyn had managed to wangle a two-minute meeting, gave no money, but offered good advice. Ask the sellers to give you an option, Thompson said as he gave Mervyn a lift in his big grey Rolls-Royce, 'it won't cost much and it'll leave your hands free'.

But without money, Mervyn's plan could get nowhere. Worse, when Mervyn went to the Maurice Thorez Institute of Marxism in Paris to see their Lenin expert, M. Lejeune, he firmly pronounced the notes in the Aleksinsky archive not to be Lenin's writing.

Autumn fell in London, and the great paper chase seemed to be fizzling out. Mervyn's meetings with Derek grew more despondent. The Finns had stopped their trips to the Baltics, and visits to Russia were out of the question. The Lenin papers had proved a flop, and his bridges were well and truly burned with the KGB. He had no money, and the end of the five years that my father had given himself to get Mila out of the Soviet Union loomed. The sharp desperation of their early love letters had worn down to a dull ache; Mervyn's optimism became more and more forced. Truly, it seemed as though the end of the affair was near.

There was another lead – and though my father refused to admit it to himself, it was a last-ditch effort. A friend put him in touch with Pavel Ivanovich Veselov, a Stockholm-based Russian émigré who called himself a 'juridical consultant'. He specialized in getting people out of the Soviet Union and had had eleven successes so far. His methods were unspectacular – careful documentation, campaigns in the Swedish press, string-pulling, much the same as Mervyn was doing already. It was a faint hope, but Mervyn had few other options.

Veselov wrote from Stockholm. 'I am a hunter rather than a fighter, a strangler rather than a boxer,' he told his prospective client. Mervyn was impressed. He was also poor. At the end of term, he took a boat from Tilbury to Stockholm. The smorgasbord dinner cost thirty shillings, and Mervyn went hungry rather than pay the money. His third-class cabin had four berths in it and was noisy and cramped. He continued to write to Mila, but through his friend Jean-Michel in Brussels in order to conceal his whereabouts from the KGB censors. In Stockholm he checked into the Salvation Army Hotel. Mervyn's great crusade was becoming a distinctly threadbare affair.

Veselov turned out to be a dishevelled fifty-year-old with high Slavic cheekbones who lived in a tiny apartment on a nondescript street in a working-class area of the city. He introduced his young Swedish wife, who spoke no Russian, and then, with more interest, his black cat, Misha. They sat down to talk in the apartment's single room, dusty and stuffed with furniture, Russian-style.

He described his past triumphs with great animation to Mervyn; one of his greatest successes had actually been released from a prison camp. Producing a large roll of what looked like wallpaper, Veselov walked to the end of the room and dramatically unrolled it. The wallpaper was covered with press cuttings from one of his cases. Mervyn admired his skills, both at collage and at getting people out of Russia.

Veselov spoke little of himself, but did tell Mervyn that he was an Old Believer, a schismatic sect of Russian Orthodoxy renowned for its traditionalism, which had been persecuted in Russia for centuries. He also said that he had served as a colonel in Finnish Intelligence in the war. Mervyn suspected that Veselov had deserted from the Red Army during the Russo–Finnish war of 1939–40. He had a heavy Volga accent, smoked strong cigarettes, liked company and was passionate about honesty. If the press ever heard that he had lied, Veselov said, they'd never accept another story from him again. He was also an enthusiastic amateur novelist, and was working on an epic about ancient Rome. His heroine was a lusty Roman courtesan, who resembled, Mervyn thought, a Volga whore. Late in the evening, Veselov treated Mervyn to a lengthy and passionate reading of his manuscript. Every so often its creator would pause and say, 'Oi, Mervyn! What a girl, what a girl!' When Mervyn finally plucked up the courage to cut him off and go home, in the early hours of the morning, Veselov seemed deeply offended. 'Oh, that's enough is it?' he sniffed.

In July, after a long period of silence, the spirit, or rather the news that Alexei Kosygin was due in Stockholm on an official visit, moved Veselov to contact Mervyn. There was press interest, and Mervyn should try once again to get to the Soviet Premier and give him a letter. Mervyn was sceptical. One more letter, after all the others which had no doubt gone unread, would probably do no good. But the publicity might be helpful.

Expressen, the Swedish daily, was delighted when Mervyn called. A love interest was just what was needed to pep up the rather dour story of Kosygin's visit. The paper agreed to pay some of Mervyn's travel costs. My father's expenditure on constant travel was by this point so far ahead of his income that he was considering selling the Pimlico flat and getting something cheaper in the suburbs.

Mervyn arrived in Stockholm on the eve of Kosygin's visit, and put up in the Apolonia Hotel. The next morning he was met at the hotel by an *Expressen* car, a journalist and two photographers, armed with a detailed plan of Kosygin's itinerary. The plan was to hand Kosygin a letter as he drove to the Haga Palace, the government residence. As he sat in the park he had time to write a letter to Mila.

'As you probably guessed I've come to Stockholm to see Alexei Nikolayevich [Kosygin] and if possible give him a letter . . . Just now I'm sitting in the quiet park surrounding the government residence. He should be here in an hour. The residence is very large, with a beautiful lake in front. There's a police boat on it at the moment. A typical corner of Scandinavia, rather sad. I'm glad they don't charge you for sitting on the benches, but I am sure that the day will come when they fit coin boxes.'

In the event, the massive police guard kept Mervyn and the

Expressen team far away from Kosygin's speeding car. The *Expressen* men left immediately afterwards, and Mervyn wandered around uselessly in Kosygin's wake, and in the late afternoon decided to ask the Swedish police if they could help him deliver his letter to Kosygin and his daughter, but he was arrested and put in a cell till the evening. He was finally released without explanation, and made his way back to Veselov's, tired and indignant. Veselov was filled with joyous outrage.

'Terrible! And this is a so-called civilized country! But it's just what we needed. We might be able to win the case through this! Come on, we've got to get down to the *Expressen* office, perhaps they can still get something into tomorrow's edition.' Veselov's jaw was set hard, spoiling for a fight. 'The police officer will have to be disciplined, and we'll write to the Interior Minister about it.'

The next day the story of Mervyn's arrest appeared in *Expressen*, and also in the *Aftonbladet* and *Dagens Nyheter*, with a photo of a haggard Mervyn talking on the phone. Mervyn was quoted somewhere as saying that Sweden was like a police state, which evoked a solitary letter from an indignant Swedish reader telling Mervyn that he should have more respect for the laws in a foreign country.

But all in all he had got nowhere, and ended up dropping his two letters into a postbox. There had been about a dozen small pieces in the British press, and a two-page spread in the German *Bild*, but in truth Mervyn realized that after four years he was still no closer to getting Mila out.

In December 1968, as Derek and Mervyn emerged from the Audley pub in Mayfair, they spotted a Soviet diplomatic car, registration SU1, parked outside the Mission of the United Arab Emirates. They got chatting to the chauffeur, who told them the Soviet Ambassador Mikhail Smirnovsky and his wife were due to come out shortly. Mervyn and Derek waited on the pavement till they emerged, and Mervyn accosted them. They both recognized Mervyn immediately, and Smirnovsky's wife looked alarmed.

'Mr Smirnovsky, why cannot we get married?' Mervyn demanded.

'We are well aware of the case,' said Smirnovsky, flustered, as he pushed past Mervyn into his waiting car. 'You must not create difficulties.'

Derek told the *Evening Post* that the encounter was 'one of the most heartening things that has happened for a very long time. At least it proved that the Russians are well aware of our continuing fight to get married.'

Mervyn kept busy. One project, inspired by the Smirnovsky incident, was to write to all 110 heads of diplomatic missions in London pleading his case. He bought a second-hand manual rotoprinter to produce leaflets and circulars which he planned to distribute around London, but the machine just created mess in his tiny bedroom, covering his bed sheets in printer's ink. In early April Mervyn designed a leaflet featuring juxtaposed pictures of Mila, Eleonora and Mrs Smirnovsky with the caption 'Three Soviet Women', with a brief summary of the story on the back. He had them printed professionally, despite the cost. Mervyn and Derek were threatened with arrest as they stuck the leaflets under windscreens of diplomatic cars in Kensington Palace Gardens.

Mila, in Moscow, was also beginning to feel her energy and optimism fade. She wrote a despondent letter in late December. On New Year's Day, 1969, Mervyn replied in an indignant tone: 'The situation may seem hopeless to you, if you really think so you should either say so outright or believe in me even more . . . In the course of the last nine months of 1968 about fifty articles have appeared in the newspapers of several countries on my attempts to sort things out. Apart from that please don't criticize what you don't understand, the point is that you have hardly any facts by which to judge my activities. And remember that today nothing could hurt me more than assertions that I am trying in vain. Today I am busy with our affairs, but I also started to prepare for term.'

On 2 January, in better spirits, Mila sent a telegram: 'Best New Year greetings to my dear Celt, I love him faithfully, believe, and await our happiness, longing for you, kisses, Mila.'

Mervyn decided that he could risk writing a new book about Soviet society, since Mila was apparently safe and had suffered no further reprisals since her sacking from the Institute four years before. The project might even redeem the wreck of Mervyn's academic career. At the very least, the prospect of researching another book energized him, and he began looking for funds. He took short holidays in Morocco, Turkey and the Balkans.

For good measure, Mervyn and Derek were also lobbying for a motion of support in the House of Commons; a Private Member's Bill was tabled, calling on the House to 'Urge the Secretary of State for Foreign and Commonwealth Affairs to take up again the cases of Derek Deason and Mervyn Matthews, both of whom wish to marry girls who cannot get a visa to leave the Soviet Union, both on humanitarian grounds and in order to remove what is becoming an increasing obstacle in the way of better Anglo-Soviet relations.'

The book idea soon paid off. Colombia University in New York offered my father a three-month visiting fellowship. Mervyn was overjoyed. It would be a welcome change from the disappointments of London, and because Manhattan was home to the United Nations, it offered a whole new field for campaigning.

13

Escape

Zhit ne po lzhy! – Live not by lies!
Alexander Solzhenitsyn

Mervyn arrived in New York at dawn on 20 April 1969. He took a yellow cab to the Hotel Master on Riverside Drive, where he checked into a large but dingy room. Mervyn cared more about the phone lines, and went straight down to talk to the elderly switchboard operator, Grace. She assured him that he would probably be able to get through to Moscow. Satisfied with the communications, Mervyn went out for a ninety-nine-cent breakfast in a diner.

The next week brought important news. Derek sent him a small clipping from the *Guardian*: 'The FCO yesterday asked the Soviet ambassador, Mr Smirnovsky, if he could confirm reports that Gerald Brooke, aged thirty, a lecturer, serving a five-year prison sentence in Russia for alleged subversive activities, was likely to be re-tried for espionage . . .' Brooke had been due for release in April 1970; the Krogers still had over a decade of their sentences left to serve. *Izvestia* had suggested as early as 1967 that Brooke might be re-tried because of alleged involvement in espionage. Now the summoning of the Soviet ambassador meant the rumours were well-founded. But how Wilson's government would react to Moscow's renewed blackmail was still unclear.

Mervyn wrote to U Thant, Secretary-General of the United Nations, and penned two indignant articles for the Russian émigré newspaper, *Novoye Russkoye Slovo*. As previously arranged, he exchanged long letters and audio tapes every week with Derek, the phone being too expensive except for urgent news.

More news on Brooke appeared in *The Times* on 16 June: 'A Foreign Office spokesman has said that the negotiations on Mr Brooke's case (not necessarily on a transfer with the Krogers) have been proceeding. There, it appears, the matter still rests. A spokesman did, however, yesterday deny reports of a visit to Britain by Herr Wolfgang Vogel, an East German lawyer, as being in any way part of the exchanges.' If Vogel was involved, reasoned Mervyn, something must definitely be afoot.

My father fired off terse telegrams to the Foreign Office: 'Brooke–Kroger Exchange Must Include Soviet Fiancées Bibikova, Ginzburg. Watching Developments Closely. Considering Public Action,' he wrote to Michael Stewart, who was now serving a second stint as Foreign Secretary. 'Brooke Negotiations Include Bibikova And Ginzburg, No Other Course Acceptable,' he telegraphed Sir Thomas Brimelow, Deputy Under-Secretary of State at the Foreign Office and one of Mervyn's most hated FO mandarins.

On 18 June he followed up with letters. 'Dear Brimelow [sic], It has just come to my attention that you may be considering a Brooke–Kroger exchange. Both Derek Deason and I will expect our long-suffering fiancées to be included in it . . . The disastrous events of 1964 are still fresh in my memory, and it is not my intention to allow the FCO to make more blunders at my expense. A Brooke–Kroger exchange [without the fiancées] would be another collapse on your part . . . Frankly, we will require an undertaking that any further exchange negotiations will also include our fiancées. Otherwise we shall have no alternative to take every possible step, public and private, to prevent our interests being ignored after so many tearful years. Copies to the Prime Minister and the Director of Intelligence.'

There was a heated row over the proposed exchange in the Cabinet on 20 June 1969. The arguments in favour of getting Brooke out of Russia were strengthened by the testimony of a British sailor, John Weatherby, who had been briefly interned in Russia and had met Brooke in prison and confirmed that his health was deteriorating. Harold Wilson had firmly opposed the swap since it had been first suggested in 1965, but finally allowed himself to be won over. Perhaps he remembered the persistent young Welshman who had buttonholed him in his Moscow hotel room and on the street in London. More likely, he wanted the seemingly endless saga of Brooke to disappear, and the addition of the Soviet brides to the deal would help to sweeten the bad publicity and charges of giving in to blackmail which would surely follow. Citing humanitarian grounds, the Cabinet formally authorized the exchange. Negotiations on the practicalities would be opened with the Soviets forthwith. Finally, the 'juggernaut of history' of which Mila had written so bitterly had shifted its course.

As Mervyn returned from New York on 20 July, the American astronaut Neil Armstrong clambered down from the Apollo 11 lander on to the surface of the moon. 'We are on different planets,' Mila had written to Mervyn in 1964, in the first days of their separation. 'For me to fly to you is as hard as to fly to the moon.' But now someone had flown to the moon – and, just as unexpectedly, it seemed that Mila's dream of leaving the Soviet Union wasn't so impossible after all.

Mervyn was summoned to the Foreign Office. Sir Thomas Brimelow was at first reluctant to admit that Mervyn had finally succeeded. My parents' case had given the most trouble in the negotiations, Brimelow told my father, and the Russians had wanted to exclude it from the agreement. Mervyn's tireless campaigning had certainly hindered his case, and it was only with the utmost difficulty that the Soviets had been prevailed upon to overcome their distaste for the gadfly Matthews. Nevertheless, they had given their consent, and Mervyn could finally expect a Soviet entry visa as soon as the Krogers were free. Mervyn drove home to Pimlico, not daring to believe the news. He decided to mention nothing to Mila, for fear of raising false hopes.

Brooke arrived back in England four days later. His release was on the front pages of the evening papers, with brief mentions of Mervyn and Mila. The same afternoon Michael Stewart made a statement in the House of Commons. Mervyn got a place in the Diplomatic Gallery; Derek was in the Strangers' Gallery. Stewart announced that it had been agreed to release the Krogers on 24 October. 'It has been arranged, as a separate matter, that three British subjects who have for some years been endeavouring without success to marry Soviet citizens will be granted visas to enter the Soviet Union to register their marriages . . .' Derek and Mervyn, on differ-ent sides of the House, raised a small cheer.

The next day's *Times* carried full details. Apart from Derek and Mervyn, a third person, Camilla Grey, an art historian, was to be allowed to marry her fiancé Oleg Prokofiev, son of the composer. Camilla had wanted nothing to do with Mer-vyn's campaign. There had been some other, more shadowy, side deals. Bill Houghton and Ethel Gee, two Ministry of Defence employees who had been recruited as KGB agents by Peter and Helen Kroger, were to be paroled early.

Most of the papers were disapproving. 'The higher a value you put on human life, the more vulnerable you are to inhuman blackmail,' editorialized the *Daily Sketch*. 'There is nothing but contempt and a very great concern for future relations after this example of blackmail, applied to a man who had obviously committed no offence that would be regarded as an offence in a democratic society.'

'Mr Stewart was asked in the Commons, what is to prevent

an innocent British tourist being seized in Moscow to set up a sinister package deal for a Russian spy? Mr. Stewart's reply: "I think one can say with reasonable confidence that a British citizen who goes to the Soviet Union and carefully observes their laws is not at risk." This is obviously true at the moment while the Red spies Peter and Helen Kroger are still held in Britain. But once they are freed in October?'

Mervyn, though he had benefited from Wilson's deal, felt his patriotism stung. Britain had indeed got a terrible bargain.

Now the news was official, my father booked a call to Mila in her Moscow apartment, and just caught her as she was preparing to go on a motoring holiday in northern Russia with friends. He told her the news that the spy exchange had begun, and that they were part of it. Yet the imminent prospect of an end to their epic struggle seemed to give neither of them any great joy.

'I had not expected exclamations of delight, nor tears of joy, and there were none,' my father wrote later. 'We had both gone through too much, and had been disappointed too often.'

There seemed to be a hint of distance, and sadness, in Mila's voice. Apart from all the bureaucratic obstacles still to be overcome, she would have to face leaving her family, friends and homeland. There seemed little prospect that she would ever be allowed to return to see them. She would soon be irrevocably parted from everything she knew and loved – except for Mervyn, who had become an almost mythical being to her.

'Mervusik, my dear,' Mila wrote the next day, as the news of Brooke's release broke in the national papers. 'Today, the 25th, is your birthday, sincere congratulations, I wish you good health, success at work, personal happiness. And I love you very much. I am in a spin. Victor Louis started looking for me from the morning onwards. I didn't say anything, but

they'll make things up, anyway. He wanted me to say something for his readers. Perhaps I should have, but I refused. He
uttered some banalities about our being brave, heroes, and
lucky. Then Lena, who's on holiday in the Baltic, rang. Valery
[Golovitser] and my friend Rima called in. Journalists rang
from the *Daily Express*, but I put them off as well. Friends
called and congratulated me, they're all overwhelmed . . . I
can hardly stand up.'

Mervyn's mother wrote with congratulations, the phone in
the Pimlico flat began to ring incessantly. Reporters began
turning up on the doorstep. Des Zwar sent a telegram. A few
days later Mervyn received a letter from the Inland Revenue,
on which an unknown hand had written, 'Glad to hear the
good news yesterday.'

Derek and Mervyn met at the Albert to plan the details. The
Soviet consulate had been unhelpful to the last, saying that their
visas would only be issued in October, and then they would be
able to see their fiancées and register for a date at the Palace of
Weddings. They would then have to leave, the official claimed,
and come back to Russia a month later when the statutory
waiting period had passed and the ceremony was due. In the
event, that turned out not to be true – the gruff vice consul was
simply exacting his own little piece of revenge on the young
men who had, somehow, beaten the system.

Derek signed a deal with the *Daily Express*. The paper paid
for his air tickets and hotel in exchange for an exclusive
interview. My father preferred to pay his own way and avoid
publicity now that it was no longer needed. 'Everyone enjoys
being famous, but my own public image, in so far as I had one,
was too coloured by misfortune and failure. I appeared to be
more of a victim than a hero,' he wrote in his memoirs.
Mervyn also hoped to re-launch his academic career with his
book, and maybe even get back into 'one of [Britain's] two
venerable universities', something notoriety in the press might
damage.

The Krogers were due to leave Heathrow for the Soviet Union at 11.15 a.m. on 28 October 1969. Mervyn heard later that their release had provoked a patriotic demonstration in Parkhurst Prison, the prisoners rhythmically banging their tin plates in protest at the spies' early release.

Derek and my father went to the Soviet consulate the same morning to collect their visas. The Soviet vice consul put on a broad official smile, told them they'd have to wait, and disappeared. As they sat nervously Mervyn came up with an explanation for the delay – the officials were probably waiting for the Krogers' plane to leave British airspace.

The consul eventually returned with the familiar blue visas. They were only for ten days, and Derek protested that they were too short. 'Ten days is enough to get married and divorced,' said the consul, and laughed.

They arrived at a near-deserted Vnukovo Airport in Moscow well after midnight, and took a taxi into town. They pulled up to the double arch of Mila's apartment block on Starokonush-enny Pereulok. It was bitterly cold, though it was not yet snowing. Mervyn went up the familiar four steps to the ground floor landing and rang the bell. There was no answer. He rang again, and again, with increasing trepidation. He had called Mila from London to tell her that they would be arriving that night. Surely she hadn't been taken away in some treacherous KGB double-cross?

He decided to try and telephone before jumping to dark conclusions. Leaving Derek in the taxi, he walked to a public phone on the corner of the Arbat. Miraculously, he happened to have a single two-kopeck piece on him, the only coin accepted by Moscow phone boxes. The phone worked, didn't swallow his coin without connecting, and Mila picked up the phone, a further series of small miracles. She sounded no closer than she had in London. Mervyn recalled the conversation in his memoir.

'Hello, Mila?'

'Yes, yes? Mervusya? Is that you?'

'Is everything all right?'

'Yes?'

'Why didn't you answer the door bell, then?'

'I didn't hear it. I was afraid that I wouldn't sleep, so I took a sleeping tablet.'

'Oh, my God. A sleeping tablet? Tonight of all nights? Anyway, Derek and I are here, on the Arbat. We'll be there in two minutes.'

Mila met them at the door, 'a small figure in a colourful Russian dressing gown, sleepy, but with an expectant look on her face'. They embraced 'warmly', my father wrote later, recalling that he felt 'no great romantic surge, only a deep contentment that we were at last together'.

In the books of my mother's childhood, or in a play by her beloved Racine or Molière, the story would end here. A great love is thwarted; the lovers fight back against the forces of evil, and finally triumph over adversity. In the final act, the two soulmates are united. The sleeping pill would be a tragicomic flourish before the two lovers, hand in hand, turn to the audience and bow before the final curtain. Did my mother, subconsciously, not want the romance to end? Did she take pills in order not to dream on that, the last night of her old life, the life of innocent passions and of living for an imagined future? Now the future had, at last, arrived, ringing insistently at her door. It was time to open it to a new life.

On the morning of Thursday, 30 October 1969, Mervyn and Mila woke early. It was their second attempt to get married, hopefully to be more joyful than the last. But over breakfast they decided, in an impulse of rebellion, or perhaps resignation, that all the misery of the last five years did not justify their dressing up. So instead of donning his suit Mervyn put on an old tweed jacket and trousers he usually wore in the lecture room. Mila set aside the dress my father had brought from England and wore a workaday skirt and blouse. They took the gold ring which had been bought five years earlier, and found a taxi to take them to the registry office. They had already decided to forgo the usual champagne celebration.

The wedding party met on Griboyedov Street just before ten – Mila, Mervyn, Mila's niece Nadia, Nadia's husband Yury, a couple of Mila's friends, and Derek, Eleonora and Eleonora's sister. Lenina and Sasha did not come – it would have been too risky for Sasha, given his position at the Ministry of Justice. A large crowd of reporters had also gathered, including Victor Louis. Inside the palace, the formalities went smoothly. Mila and Mervyn handed in their passports, then went into a large red-draped hall with a white bust of Lenin where a portly matron read the Soviet marriage vows. After five years and five months of unremitting efforts, Mervyn finally placed the ring on Mila's finger.

'And you are our least attractive bride!' the woman who stamped their passports told Lyudmila with classic Soviet tartness. Mervyn was 'glad our gesture of protest had been noticed'. They had a few photos taken in the corridor, inadvertently using the entrance to the gents' lavatory as a backdrop.

Outside they were bombarded with questions, but none of the party were in the mood to say anything. Mila and Mervyn were tired of all the fuss, Derek and Eleonora had to keep silent because of their deal with the *Daily Express*. The press followed them down the street as they walked away, and Yury took a swing at one of the photographers and shouted 'Bastard!' at them.

In his story the next day in the *Evening News*, Victor Louis, piqued at having been denied the sugary ending he thought he deserved after covering the story faithfully for so many years, attributed Yury's remarks to Mervyn. 'After the ceremony, which was surprisingly short, taking about five minutes, they realized they had been unwise to dismiss the taxi in which they had arrived,' Louis wrote. 'While waiting for another, Dr Matthews and his bride were photographed by a newsman. In fact the couple had been doing their best to avoid the press, and tried to hide their faces behind the bride's bouquet of white chrysanthemums. The bridegroom tried to discourage the photographer with shouts of "Bastard".'

They next day they were invited to the British embassy for a quick glass of wine and good wishes. They took photos of each other outside the embassy on Sofiskaya Naberezhnaya, opposite the Kremlin. In the photos a fine drizzle is falling, and the sky is a miserable grey, but my father wears an almost childish grin as he poses with my mother, his arms around her shoulders as she buries her hands deep in the pockets of her mackintosh and leans her head against his shoulder.

Mervyn had hoped to stay on a few days after the wedding to work in the library and buy books, but OVIR informed them that they were to be out of Russia as soon as possible. A sour-faced official at OVIR took Mila's internal passport away and handed her a foreign travel one, all without saying a word to the woman who was turning her back on the Motherland.

The last evening in Moscow was one of the saddest of Mila's life. Dozens of Mila's friends came round to her tiny room to say goodbye, sitting on low stools and crowding on the bed as they filed in and out. Valery Golovitser stayed throughout, silent and mournful, brooding on the departure of his closest confidante, taken away by a Britisher he had once befriended. Most of Mila's friends were delighted. But my mother was frightened, and found the prospect of being wrenched away from her dissident friends achingly sad. 'I was like an old prisoner who's been set free,' she once told me. 'I didn't want to leave my cell.' The crush got too great and Mervyn left for a solitary midnight walk on the Arbat. The street was silent and deserted.

On 3 November Derek and Eleonora left Moscow for London for a triumphant homecoming, courtesy of the *Daily Express*. Mila and Mervyn, to avoid publicity, took a plane to Vienna. As they walked into the arrivals hall Mervyn felt, with a huge flush of relief, that at last it really was all over. Mila's eyes widened at the neatly uniformed bag handlers. In Vienna they spent an afternoon and evening's honeymoon before going on to London the next morning.

At Heathrow, because they had arrived from Vienna not Moscow, there was a small delay as officials sorted out the paperwork. Mila and Mervyn stood briefly on different sides of the barrier. But soon they were on their way, collecting their luggage, pushing their trolley through the arrivals hall along with the other travellers.

Mila and Mervyn had spent more than half a decade living for a future they only half-believed would ever arrive. Now they were finally reunited, it was time to face another challenge – the unheroic one of dealing with the present, and of living with each other as real human beings.

But that was all a beat in the future. Mervyn and Mila, my parents, had won their battle to be together, against the most formidable odds their times could range against them. This was their moment. The moment I imagine when I think of my parents at their best and boldest; two young people *contra mundi*, their love all-conquering, alone at last and together after all the efforts of the world to keep them apart.

14

Crisis

He is born of this country where
everything is given to be taken away.
Albert Camus

When I think of it now, hearing someone mention it on the radio or seeing the dateline in a paper, Moscow conjures a sense of wilderness, of the wreckage of expended energy. I left after the great bubble of the 1990s had imploded, and the hangover was at its deepest, the pendulum back at its midway low point between an infatuation with wild capitalism and what proved to be a deeper longing for authority and order.

The unruly but free Russia which Boris Yeltsin had created began to topple in the summer of 1998. I was a correspondent for *Newsweek* magazine by then, doing a very different job than the one I had done at the *Moscow Times*. Instead of searching the city for tales of the underworld, I was driven from Duma to Ministry in a blue Volvo, and wrote wise and excruciatingly polished articles about high politics.

In my new capacity I had a grandstand view of the unravelling of the old order. Nervousness was mounting in the impeccably carpeted corridors of the White House, the seat of Russia's government. Deputy premier Boris Nemtsov, Russia's leading reformer, insisted that everything would be fine and scribbled spidery graphs all over my notepad to prove his point. Tax chief Boris Fyodorov, the reformers' heavyweight bruiser, gabbled about the irreversibility of Russia's reforms with a manic energy. But in all the government offices I visited the smiles were rigid, the confidence forced. Everyone feared, deep down, that sometime, very soon, the whole rotten edifice would come crashing down. It was time for a reckoning after all the years of asset-stripping, embezzlement and theft which the country's new masters had unleashed – and when it came, it would be cataclysmic.

The first signs that the end was near appeared in Moscow as miners from across the country set up a picket of the White House and invaded the Duma, pounding their helmets on the pavements of the capital and the marble banisters of the parliament. You could hear the hourly tattoo of dull drumming from inside the White House. It sounded like distant thunder beyond the tinted, Swiss-made windows.

In St Petersburg Yeltsin emerged from hospital to bury the remains of the last Tsar and his family, murdered by Bolshevik revolutionaries in 1918. I sneaked into the Peter and Paul Cathedral with a group of Romanov mourners, admitted because I alone among the journalists present had thought to wear a black suit and tie. There was a moment of intense pathos as the undersized coffins containing the family's bones were brought to the altar. Yeltsin, wooden and swaying slightly, intoned a speech which claimed that Russia had come to terms with its past. I had always been a fervent admirer of Yeltsin, but now he seemed a tragic figure, a tottering bear of a man lost in a maze of corruption and as bewildered as his people by the superhuman forces of capitalism that he had unleashed. The parallels between the mistakes that led Russia's last monarch to his sordid death and the seismic tremors gathering under Yeltsin's own regime were painfully clear.

Moscow's nightlife took on a strange intensity. Like rattlesnakes who feel earthquakes brewing deep in the bowels of the earth, the party people were seized with frenzy. Wherever the doomed rich gathered, in Galereya, the Jazz Café, Titanic, you could catch a glimpse out of the corner of your eye, through the dry ice and the strobes, of a phantom hand writing on the wall – 'You have been weighed in the balance and found wanting.'

Supernatural warnings of apocalypse came biblically, with a blight which wiped out much of Russia's potato harvest and incessant August rains which flattened the wheat fields, spelling disaster for the huge numbers of Russians reduced to subsistence agriculture to survive while the government withheld their wages. A freak storm toppled the golden crosses from the domes of the Novodevichy Convent and broke the crenellations from the Kremlin wall. Lightning struck the Russian flag which flew from the roof of the Kremlin's Senate Palace. Even NTV television became an unwitting mouthpiece of the Armageddon, scheduling *The Omen* and its sequels on successive weekends. Russia's babushkas, the country's pathologically pessimistic watchers of signs and portents, clucked knowingly.

Then the deluge came with the ferocity of a natural disaster. After a panic meeting on the evening of 16 August 1998, the government devalued the ruble and defaulted on all Russia's domestic and international debt repayments, destroying the stock market and wiping two-thirds off the value of the ruble in a single, disastrous week.

The new bourgeoisie, who before the crisis were planning their winter package holidays in Antalya, scuffled in crowds outside failing banks as they scrambled to recover their savings. All the old, savage reflexes of self-preservation surged back. Moscow housewives who thought that they could at least 'live like people' (as the Russian saying goes) scooped expensive macaroni off the shelves of Western supermarkets in a desperate bid to spend their fast-devaluing rubles. Their poorer counterparts emptied the city's markets of siege-goods such as matches, flour, salt and rice.

The half-forgotten mental furniture of peasant *nakhodchivost*, or resourcefulness, was dusted down and thrown into the breach. Newspapers began publishing home economics tips with headlines like 'Which foods can be stored for longest?', advising readers not to stock up on frozen meat in case of power cuts. Harassed shop assistants at the Moscow branch of British Home Stores abandoned the price tags and added up the rapidly escalating ruble prices on calculators. The luxury boutiques in Moscow's vulgarly opulent Manezh shopping mall looked like a museum of the old regime.

Within two months, the devastation was complete. Perhaps it was my imagination, but I felt that Moscow had become darker as the autumn of 1998 set in, physically darker, underlit, as though the flashy neon heart of the city was fading away. I called my landlady to say I was going to unilaterally halve the rent on my $1,500 a month apartment. She sighed in relief that I was not leaving, and thanked me.

I went to a lot of leaving parties thrown by my expatriate friends, who suddenly found their stock portfolios had evaporated and business models imploded. One was thrown at the Starlite Diner by a glamorous, silicone-chested Californian girl who had marketed Herbalife across the Russian provinces. She had hired a troupe of tragicomically inept Russian circus performers who danced on broken glass and pushed skewers through their cheeks for our entertainment. Someone played the Beatles' 'Get Back' and 'Money' by Abba on the jukebox.

At the turn of that year, the start of the last year of the twentieth century, I reached a dead end in myself. I felt great tiredness, but sleep came fitfully and brought no relief. The black dog of depression which had periodically stalked me throughout my life took hold. I thought often of the dead

Yana, and felt mediocre and spent. I passed long, empty evenings staring out of my apartment window at the falling snow, listening to the muffled noise of passing traffic.

I met Xenia Kravchenko at a dinner party thrown by a Belgian friend in her apartment in the backstreets near the Arbat. Xenia was tall and willow-thin, with a tomboyish haircut and worn jeans. What I remember most vividly about our first meeting was not her appearance or anything we said, but an overwhelming, almost supernatural realization that Xenia was the woman I was going to marry. That sounds foolish, but I felt it, powerfully. 'Suddenly, he realized that all his life he had loved precisely this woman' – I quoted the line from Bulgakov's *The Master and Margarita* to a mutual friend that very evening. A few days later, Xenia and I kissed for the first time on a park bench on Patriarch's Ponds, not far from where Woland, Bulgakov's devil incarnate, first appeared in Moscow.

Xenia was intelligent and beautiful. The two words go easily together. But in fact the truly intelligent, those women who are aware of their own power over men, realize that they have something of the Medusa in them. Xenia had a great cathartic force hidden behind her calm, an uncanny ability to expel people from their old selves. I felt, after my first weeks with Xenia, that I had been purged by her Gorgon presence, undergone a profound change. It was at times cruel, but it was epiphanous.

There was no great crisis or drama to it. On the contrary, I often found Xenia maddeningly diffident about life in general, and indeed about me in particular. She seemed to drift in a cloud of invincible innocence, refusing to take the world around her seriously. Yet she became a mirror on which I found my life violently dissected. My addiction to the phantasmagoria of Moscow, the voyeuristic streak which led me to seek out all that was most putrid and sordid and corrupt – all this suddenly seemed childish, and tired, and false. Though I didn't really realize it as it was happening, Xenia was shearing me away from my old, corrupt self, forcing me to think of myself as someone normal and whole. A potential husband and father, even.

Xenia's looks and self-confidence cushioned her against the harshness of the reality which surrounded her. She had somehow managed to remain aloof from the swinish, grubby life of Moscow. It was as if she and her family had survived from another, gentler age of Russia. She came from a long line of artists, and lived in a magnificent apartment which had been in the family since 1914. The old place was packed with dusty antique furniture and paintings; it had a stillness and permanence to it that I had hitherto only seen in old English country houses. The family's dacha, too, where I write these words, stood on a high bank of the Moscow River at Nikolina Gora among the country cottages of Stalin's cultural élite, just across the road from the Prokofievs, relatives of the composer, and the Mikhalkovs and the Konchalovskys, families of writers, painters and filmmakers. Her family had known their neighbours for three generations, and they all seemed to have grown as charmingly feckless as the defenceless gentry in *The Cherry Orchard*. Their charm and absentmindedness was quite unlike the iron-willed Soviet generation which my mother represented. They had been among the lucky ones; their lives had, through good fortune, not been scarred by the Soviet century.

Xenia moved into my apartment. We ate our meals in my bedroom, with its blood-red walls, as my cat rolled in a pool of sunlight by the window. Xenia would stay in when I went to work, sketching and painting, and when I came back we cooked large curry dinners and drank cheap red wine. I was as happy as I have ever been.

In autumn 1999, a new war began in Russia. Its opening shots were not bullets but massive bombs placed in the basements of apartment houses on the outskirts of Moscow and Volgo-donsk, in southern Russia. I stood among the smoking rubble of destroyed buildings in the Moscow suburbs of Pechatniki and on the Kashirskoye Highway as firemen dug through the wreckage of the very ordinary lives which lay strewn about. Cheap sofas were splintered to matchwood among the piles of bricks, and plastic toys crunched under my feet. In all, over three hundred were killed in the attacks.

Chechen rebels were blamed, and within weeks the Russian Army was rolling into the breakaway rebel republic. Foreign reporters were banned from travelling independently, except in Kremlin-orchestrated bus tours which carefully avoided the front lines. I spent much of the winter devising new ways of getting to Chechnya covertly, sometimes with the rebels, sometimes with pro-Moscow Chechens, and several times by attaching myself to Russian journalists and striking deals with local Russian commanders to spend time with their units.

On my last trip to Chechnya – the thirteenth – I and my friend Robert King, a photographer, found ourselves near the village of Komsomolskoye. The Russian Army had trapped the remnants of the main rebel force, which had retreated from Grozny, in the small hamlet and had been pounding it for three days with rockets and artillery. We arrived on the fourth day, just as the dawn fog was lifting, to find that the Russian battalions which had been dug in around the village for days were gone, leaving only drifts of litter and fields of mud churned by tank tracks. We drove into Komsomolskoye unchallenged.

Other Chechen towns and villages I had seen had been bombed flat, the houses replaced with deep, smoking craters. This place was different. The village had been fought over house by house, and every building was riddled with meti-culous patterns of bullet holes and the walls punched through by shells. The villagers' vegetable plots were criss-crossed with

the doomed rebels' shallow trenches and improvised fortifica-
tions. The place smelled strongly of cordite, of burned wood,
of fresh-turned earth, and of death.

The rebels' bodies lay in groups of three or four. The first
we saw were in the corner of a house, piled face-up among the
debris of the collapsed roof. Their hands were tied, and their
chests churned into a bloody mess by bullets. Further on, we
came across the corpse of another rebel, a giant of a man with
a bushy red beard, his hands secured behind his back with
twists of fencing wire. Buried deep in the side of his head was a
Russian entrenching tool with which he had been beaten to
death. In a narrow ditch were a row of bodies, tangled
promiscuously together, lying where they had fallen after
being machine-gunned. Robert moved among the wreckage
snapping photos, his professional instincts taking over. I
scribbled in my notebook as I walked, spilling the images
on to the page as words as fast as I could – perhaps in order
that they would not linger in my mind.

In all, we counted over eighty bodies, and this was only the
edge of the village. In all, the Russians claimed to have killed
eight hundred of rebel commander Ruslan Gelayev's men in
and around Komsomolskoye. I had little stomach to go
further. I was also nervous of mines and booby-traps. I walked
over to a breeze-block house which had been partially burned
down. The corrugated concrete roof had collapsed and shattered among a jumble of iron beds and plastic picnic chairs.
Among the shards of the roof I noticed a blanket, which
seemed to be wrapped around a body. I picked up a piece of
roofing – a foot-long fragment of tile – and began clearing the
debris. I gingerly moved the blanket to reveal a man's face, and
as I did so the tile touched his cheek. The flesh was hard and
unyielding, absolutely nothing like touching a human at all.

The dead man was an African, his skin deep black but with
European features, perhaps a Somali. He seemed to have been
one of the foreign fighters who had come to Chechnya to join

the jihad, and finally made his rendezvous with his Maker in this bleak corner of the Caucasus. He looked like a decent young man: someone you would ask directions from if you were lost in a strange city, or trust with your camera to take a photograph of you.

Later – and I was to think of him often – I imagined him standing with his cheap luggage and polyester suit in an airport on his way to the holy war, nervous but excited. And I thought of a family somewhere going about its daily business, squabbling sisters and nagging mother, not knowing that their son was lying here in the wreckage of a Chechen house where he'd died fighting someone else's war.

I had had enough of Komsomolskoye. We hurried back to our car, a battered Russian military jeep driven by a young Chechen called Beslan, who prided himself on his driving skills. We had four hours before the only Moscow flight of the day left from Nazran Airport in Ingushetia. Beslan promised to get us there in good time. He gunned the engine as we swung out on to the main road, and we careered westwards towards the border. Robert and I were jammed in the back seat with our Chechen guide, Musa, an official in the pro-Moscow government who talked us through checkpoints by waving his government ID. Two Russian policemen, whom we had hired for $50 a day as bodyguards, shared the front passenger seat. Halfway to the border, we saw a Russian Mi-24 helicopter gunship hovering menacingly over a copse, from which smoke was rising. The chopper turned slowly in the air to face us.

The next thing I remember was that the view of damp fields in the windscreen was replaced by a wall of earth. I recall bracing my arms as hard as I could against the front seats, and there was a moment of great physical stress and then relief as I felt my body yield to the overpowering laws of physics and fly forward through the windscreen. Fortunately for me the glass had been shattered seconds before by the head of one of our police escorts.

The moments that followed were filled with infinite peace. I lay on my back on the gravel of the road, spread-eagled, looking up at the clouds drifting across the big Chechen sky. I was conscious of being alive in a way I have never been before or since, and though I realized that I was probably badly injured, the signals were somewhere far away, like a ringing phone which could be quietly ignored. Slowly, I flexed my fingers along the surface of the tarmac, rolling tiny stones and bits of grit back and forth. Somewhere, I could hear voices, and I breathed deeply through my nose to check for the smell of gasoline, or cordite, or burning. I smelled only the smell of clay, and the flowering grasses by the roadside.

My mind frequently wanders back to this moment, ascribing to it different meanings as the mood takes me. The only thought that I can attribute with complete honesty to that time and that place is this: I felt a deep contentment that I had someone in Moscow who was waiting for me, and an overwhelming urge to return to Xenia and to Moscow, and never leave again.

A bearded face loomed above me, and began to speak. Something like a reflex took hold of me; I began answering, quite calmly, and issuing orders. My shoulder was dislocated, and, I suspected, some ribs cracked. I told the Chechen villager to put his foot on my collarbone, pick up my useless right arm, and pull. Shock must have blocked the pain, because I continued giving instructions until the joint popped back into place. I saw Robert kneeling by my side, and he gently unwound the scarf from my neck and made a makeshift sling. As I sat up I saw that Beslan's beloved jeep had crashed into a four-foot-deep shell hole blasted in the road. Beslan himself, I noted with some satisfaction, had smashed his head on his own steering wheel, and was dabbing away blood. The two policemen were more badly injured, lying by the roadside, concussed.

Things started to move quickly. I produced money to pay off everyone. A car was summoned from the nearest village to take Robert, Musa and myself onwards. I had only two thoughts in my mind – to get on the plane, and never to return to Chechnya. Even when our second car hit a pothole and my injured shoulder was dislocated a second time, the desire to head for home blotted out all pain, indeed everything else in the world unconnected to pushing on to Ingushetia, and safety.

Somehow, we made it. Nazran Airport was crawling with officers of the Federal Security Service, or FSB, the KGB's successor, who fingered our accreditations suspiciously and questioned us as to where we'd been. Robert and I made a suspicious pair. Both of us wore the Russian military coats and black knitted caps which were our feeble disguise against foreigner-hunting kidnappers. We were both filthy, and smelled strongly of smoke and corpses. With a superhuman effort of will, I maintained my calm, insisting that we had never left Ingushetia and never been into the forbidden territory of Chechnya. As we boarded the bus to the plane, more FSB officers rushed up, wanting to look at Robert's undeveloped photos. I cajoled and joked with them and, after an agonizing few minutes, they went away. We walked up the steps of the old Tupolev 134 in dread that they would change their minds and haul us off the plane, and back into the world of Chechnya.

Only later that evening at the American Medical Centre in Moscow, as a doctor from Ohio cut the stinking Russian Army T-shirt off my body with a pair of cold steel scissors, did I burst into tears of pain and relief. Xenia waited for me outside the Casualty Department. Never had I felt so profoundly that I had come home.

War and memory are strange things. You see disturbing things which skitter off the surface of your mind like a pinball bouncing down the board. But once in a while some memory or image or thought suddenly lodges in a hole and penetrates right into your deepest heart. For me that memory was the dead black man in Komsomolskoye, who began to haunt my dreams. My shoulder healed quickly enough, but my mind seemed to have been infected. At Xenia's dacha, we walked along the river, chatting. But when we found an empty meadow where the spring silence was broken only by the creaking of the pines swaying in the wind, I collapsed into a deep, damp snow bank and refused to move. 'Just leave me here for a few minutes,' I whispered, my eyes fixed on the grey-white sky. 'Just leave me alone.'

I became convinced that the unquiet spirit of the dead rebel I had touched had entered me. I relived the moment of physical contact with his cold cheek, and believed that somehow, like an electric charge, the man's spirit had jumped into my living body. I dreamed of the churned fields of Komsomolskoye, and imagined the angry souls of the dead men flapping limply along the ground, like wounded birds.

It was Xenia who pulled me out of it. She drove a reluctant Robert and me to a church near my apartment, where we both lit candles for the dead men. But more importantly, she helped me by making a home, a real family home, the first I had had since leaving London seven years before. I left my bachelor apartment and rented a dacha deep in the Moscow woods near Zvenigorod, not far from Xenia's parents' at Nikolina Gora. We painted the rooms bright colours. I bought Dagestani kilims and old furniture, and we dismantled the old Russian stove in the living room and used the heavy old tiles to build an open fireplace where the stove had stood. Xenia replaced the brass knobs on the grate we had bought with two small clay heads she had sculpted. One was a portrait of me, the other of her, and our little clay images faced each other across the hearth.

Epilogue

Better by far you forget, and smile,
Than that you should remember, and be sad.
Christina Rossetti

Mila and Mervyn arrived at Heathrow in a grey London drizzle. They took the bus to Victoria; a taxi would have been too expensive. As they drove down the Westway London struck Mila, she told me, as being 'very poor, very down-at-heel'. When she saw old women in woollen coats and headscarves she told her new husband that they were 'just the same as our Russian babushkas'.

Mervyn's little one-bedroom flat on Belgrave Road in Pimlico was an ascetic place, with a tatty carpet and barely warmed by large brown electric storage heaters, set low to save money. My mother remembers that Mervyn's single bed was just two foot six inches wide, and covered with thin army surplus blankets. When the newly freed Gerald Brooke called round to ask if there was anything Mila needed, the first thing she thought of was proper woollen blankets. After the overheated apartments of Moscow, Mila found the flat desperately cold. In order to warm up she would go out for brisk walks through the streets of Pimlico. Her abiding memory of that first winter in London was 'the terrible damp chill which penetrated your bones – much worse than the Russian winter'.

My parents went for walks in St James's Park, and visited the House of Lords for tea with Lord Brockway, one of the dignitaries whom Mervyn had persuaded to help his campaign. A friend of Mervyn's took Mila to Harrods, but she was unimpressed. Western plenty didn't amaze her as it did some Soviet visitors. 'We had all this in Russia – before the Revolution,' she joked as she was reverently led into the Food Halls. Mervyn drove her to Swansea, stopping off at Oxford on the way, and introduced Mila to his mother. For all her entreaties to Mervyn to give up his struggle over the years, Lillian embraced Mila warmly.

My mother immediately set to work making my father's flat as cosy as possible, setting out the old china she'd brought from Russia and putting her books on the shelves. She made a great effort to become the perfect wife of her imagination, preparing dinners from her well-thumbed copy of *1000 Tasty Recipes*, the Soviet housewives' culinary Bible. She tried to make friends with the neighbours, but most of them snubbed her and wouldn't even greet her in the hallway – whether out of British coldness or because Mila was a citizen of an enemy empire, she never worked out. Often in her first six months, the shock of dislocation would overwhelm her and she would burst into tears. She wept from the cold as she typed translations to earn a bit of money, her tears falling among the typewriter keys. Mervyn was at a loss as to how to comfort her. He chose to let her cry herself out.

'I can't say I was completely unhappy,' my mother recalled. 'But I think I had spent too much of my life in Moscow for leaving not to be a terrible trauma.'

She missed her friends, and the passion and excitement of the dissident lifestyle – swapping samizdat books, waiting for the next issue of the *Novy Mir* journal (which had even dared to publish Solzhenitsyn's *One Day in the Life of Ivan Denisovich* in 1962), being part of a devoted group of like-minded people who had become like a family to her. And though she had never been rich, even the small luxuries of Soviet life had always been affordable. But in London, Mervyn's salary barely covered his own needs, let alone Mila's. She remembers standing weeping outside a Tube station after she'd spent all her money on little presents for her Moscow friends at a haberdasher's on Warren Street and didn't have enough left over for the fare. In a fit of generosity, my father took her to Woolworth's and bought her a green wool dress for a pound. It was the only item of clothing she bought all of her first year.

For the first time in her life, Mila felt depressed, unable to summon the unconquerable will which had fuelled her fights ever since her childhood illness. She wrote to her sister in Moscow of her terrible homesickness. My mother didn't say openly that she wanted to return, but Lenina feared that was only because her headstrong sister couldn't bear to admit to herself that all her years of struggle had been a mistake. Lenina showed the letter to Sasha, who sat down at the kitchen table to compose a reply. 'Dearest Mila, there is no way back for you,' he wrote. 'You have chosen your fate and you must live with it. Love Mervyn; have children.'

After so much expectation, so much idealization, so much sacrifice and burning, high ideals, could the reality have been anything but a disappointment? What marriage, what life in the fairyland of the West could ever live up to the expectations of six years of longing? I believe that to my parents, the fight had become an end in itself sooner than either of them realized. When victory came neither of them knew how to continue the story. For years Mervyn and Mila had been superhuman creatures to each other, bounding over mountains and valleys, beating on the doors of heaven, confronting the juggernaut of history. But when they finally came together as real, living people, they found themselves having to invent something neither of them had ever known – a happy family. After a life as actors in a great drama they found the hardest thing was simply to become human again.

In the spring of 1970, as she was returning from Brighton on the train after a session teaching Russian, Lyudmila had one of her attacks of melancholy and burst into tears. Unlike in Russia, no fellow passenger came to comfort her or to ask what the matter was. But she looked up out of the window at the green English fields. 'What a fool I am,' my mother remembers thinking. 'I have been crying for six months. This Russian blackness must stop.' Slowly, Mila began to make a life for herself in London. My father was always shy of company and never had many close friends, but my gregarious mother soon made English friends who loved her warmth and wit, and with whom she could go to the theatre and ballet. They never became the close-knit, comradely surrogate family of my mother's youthful circle, but being among cultured people helped ease the pain of losing her old Moscow life.

My mother took on more translation work and part-time teaching at Sussex University. An organization called Overseas Publications offered her a job editing samizdat literature in Russian, which offered the opportunity to continue her old dissident enthusiasms. She edited *Let History Judge*, a meticulous indictment of Stalinism by the dissident historian Roy Medvedev, as well as many other books published by Overseas Publications, copies of which were sent into the Soviet Union via parcel post by a network of Russian émigrés across Europe. Surprisingly, almost all the books would get through, to be avidly circulated and copied in typescript by Mila's friends in Moscow. The organization's director told Mila that it was funded by a wealthy American industrialist; in reality it was covered by the CIA's covert anti-Soviet activities budget, as was Radio Liberty, where my mother also got work as an editor. Radio Liberty even offered her a presenting role, but she refused in case it damaged her chances of one day revisiting her homeland.

Mila was soon earning enough of her own money to subsidize secretly the tiny household budget her husband gave her to buy clothes and books. Though they'd both grown up poor, my mother enjoyed spending money in a way that my father has never been able to. She'd always loved beautiful things, and as soon as she was able she bought old furniture and pictures.

Mila followed Sasha's advice: by summer 1971 she was pregnant. I was born on 9 December 1971, at Westminster Hospital, which Mila found 'as luxurious as the Kremlin clinic'. It was a difficult delivery because of my mother's deformed hip, and I was pulled into the world with calipers. The doctors told her that she had 'a beautiful baby' – a remark which impressed her greatly, and which she often repeated to me during my childhood. Soviet doctors usually kept their opinions to themselves. My father scraped together the deposit for a £16,000 Victorian terraced house on Alderney Street, which my mother decorated with paisley patterned orange wallpaper she'd found on sale at Peter Jones. For the first time since very early childhood, Mila was finally part of a proper family of her own.

In the winter of 1978, nine years after she had left, my mother returned to visit the Soviet Union, taking me and my baby sister Emily with her. We stayed at Lenina's apartment. I remember a constant stream of visitors weeping in the hallway as they embraced my mother, who they never expected to see again. I found everything utterly different from England, from the queues in the bread shops to the vast snow banks and the palatial Metro. I thought I understood exactly what Pushkin meant about the smell of Russia. It was a distinct odour, partly cheap disinfectant, partly (though inexplicably) the smell of a certain Soviet brand of Vitamin C tablet, tangy and artificial. Russian people smelled, too, in a way that English people never did, an overwhelmingly powerful body odour which was not unpleasant, though I felt its carnality was somehow not very decent or respectable.

Though I had travelled a lot as a child to visit my father in various academic postings around the world, in Russia I was for the first time in my life overwhelmed by my own foreignness. Everyone wanted to show me how things were '*u nas*', or *chez nous*, and asked me whether English chocolate was as good as Russian Bears Wafers (answer – yes), whether we had champagne or toy soldiers or snow or even (this from a particularly moronic and patriotic boyfriend of my cousin Olga's) cars as fine as Soviet ones. Even aged seven, I could tell that Soviet cars were rubbish. But despite the vividness of Russia to my imagination, I never, even then, felt that this was anything other than a strange and foreign place.

Nostalgia for a lost homeland is a particularly Russian affliction; at parties given by my mother's émigré Russian friends, the hostesses tried to recreate a lost world of Russian-ness in suburban London. The tables groaned with sturgeon and caviar, pickles and vodka, the air was thick with the smoke of Russian papiros cigarettes, and the talk was of recent or planned trips back to the Rodina. But my mother, for all her emotional nature, was never sentimental about the Mother-land, and I don't believe that she ever really missed Russia – at least not after she got over her first, wrenching bout of homesickness soon after her arrival in Britain. Throughout my childhood she was always full of praise for what she saw as the peculiarly English virtues of punctuality, thoroughness and good taste; the only thing which irritated her was English thrift, which she saw as meanness of spirit. One thing she shared with her fellow émigrés was a deep contempt for the Soviet regime, as well as a love for the latest cynical political anecdotes from Russia. One of her favourite jokes was about Brezhnev's mother: the old woman visits her Party boss son in his luxurious seaside villa and nervously admires the pictures, furniture and cars. 'It's lovely, son,' she says. 'But what will you do if the Reds come back?'

Mila's example proved infectious. One by one, almost all her friends and relations were to either leave Russia or marry foreigners. In 1979, Lenina's elder daughter Nadia and her

Jewish husband, Yury, who had shouted at the photographers at Mila's wedding, got leave to emigrate, taking their baby daughter Natasha to Germany. Sasha cried hysterically at the airport and tried to run after his daughter as she went through passport control, hobbling on his artificial leg. 'I'll never see you again!' he shouted.

Six months later, Sasha was summoned by his boss at the Ministry of Justice, who stood at his desk and shouted at Sasha for not having informed his Party organization that he had not only a sister-in-law but a daughter in the West. Sasha collapsed with a massive heart attack right there in the Minister's office, and died that afternoon in hospital. Nadia was not allowed back from Germany for the funeral, and for ever after blamed herself for her father's early death.

My mother's shy balletomane friend Valery Golovitser, who introduced my parents, finally got an exit visa after nine or ten applications. In 1980, along with thousands of Soviet Jews, he took his family to the United States. He soon left his wife Tanya and finally came out as a homosexual, living with his long-time lover Slava in New York and organizing ballet tours by Russian artists.

Valery Shein, Mervyn's bohemian friend from the Festival, had a wildly successful career in theatre management, became rich and famous, and married a beautiful Russophile English-woman in 1987. She was famous among Valery's friends for having stood for an hour in a queue for bananas and then having bought only one kilogram – a normal Soviet shopper would have bought all they could carry.

Georges Nivat's fiancée Irina Ivinskaya was let out of the Gulag at the end of 1963. She married a well-known dissident and later emigrated to Paris. Her mother Olga, Pasternak's Lara, stayed in Moscow, where she died in 1995.

Mila's niece Olga followed her sister to Germany in 1990 by way of a fictitious marriage with an Englishman, leaving her daughter Masha behind in Moscow to be brought up by her grandmother, my aunt Lenina. When Masha finished school she, too, left, for a cancer operation in Germany, and stayed there, eventually dying of the disease. Lenina was left alone in Moscow, where she died of a heart attack in May 2008.

My father has never lost his wanderlust. Throughout my childhood he would leave for months at a time to take up visiting professorships at Harvard, Stanford, Jerusalem, Ontario, Australia. I doted on the wonderful letters he sent, illustrated with coloured sketches of Australian lizards, pirates and little caricatures of himself in funny situations – falling out of boats, driving a car on the wrong side of the road. And I missed him, terribly, and waited desperately for his letters. Several times I flew alone – as an 'unaccompanied minor' complete with a label with my particulars securely fastened to my coat, like Paddington Bear – to join him in Cambridge, Massachusetts, and San Francisco, California. Men alone, we ate pizza in our pyjamas and stayed up late watching Godzilla films on the television. He taught me to sail dinghies on the Charles River basin in Boston.

At home, the situation was less harmonious, though I never for a moment felt anything less than absolutely loved. Rather the contrary: with no epic battle to fight, my mother turned her energies to the people closest to her – her husband and children – and the result was often overpowering. A terraced house in Pimlico was far too small to contain that dynamo of emotional energy. My father's reaction to the frequent dramas of the household was to retreat into his own private world, stalking away in silence from the dinner table after a minor argument, leaving my mother in tears, and retreating into the fastness of his study. There were times when the tension in the house crackled like frost.

My father began visiting Russia regularly again in December 1988, thanks to Mikhail Gorbachev's Perestroika. He found late Soviet Moscow outwardly the same as the city he had known, but on his first trolleybus ride he noticed no KGB cars, no goons. For the first time, my father felt free on the streets of the city, anonymous at last.

Three years later, and Communism had collapsed in Eastern Europe. I spent the summer vacation of 1991 travelling there with my girlfriend Louise. By coincidence, we arrived in Leningrad on the evening of 19 August 1991 – the eve of the attempted putsch by Party hardliners against Gorbachev which marked the final death-twitch of the Communist Party of the Soviet Union. We woke to see the grim televised face of General Samsonov, head of the Leningrad garrison, warning citizens that gatherings of more than three people were illegal. A day later, and I stood on a balcony of the old Winter Palace and saw Palace Square filled with people, a rolling sea of faces and placards. Near St Isaac's Square we helped students build barricades across the street out of benches and steel rods. The following day, Nevsky Prospect was filled as far as the eye could see in both directions with half a million people protesting against the system which had shaped almost every aspect of their lives for three generations. The slogans on homemade placards carried by the demonstrators were permutations of the words 'freedom' and 'democracy'. The same day in Moscow, Boris Yeltsin emerged from the White House – the seat of the government of the Russian Federated Socialist Republic – and stood on a tank to address the crowds who had gathered to defend the building against the forces of reaction. It was an iconic moment, and though we in Leningrad didn't see it because State TV was in the hands of the putschists, it marked the end of seventy-four years of Communist rule. The coup collapsed that evening after an abortive attempt by troops loyal to the KGB to storm the White House.

In a mysterious way vast gatherings of people take on a collective personality of their own, and as I perceived it the animating force of that great St Petersburg crowd was an overwhelming sense of righteousness, a feeling that history was on our side. There was a rather naïvely Soviet sense of the invincibility of reason – that for once life was uncomplicated, we were right, and Communism was wrong. I felt an intense happiness that day. Perhaps, I thought, all the evil of the country, the poison which had tainted Russia, was finally being exorcised by these hundreds of thousands of people who had come out on to the streets to demand the end of a system which had killed millions in the name of a shining future which never arrived. In later years, most of the people who demonstrated on those August days were to be bitterly disappointed by the fruits of democracy. But for many of my parents' generation – at least for those, like Lenina, who suffered under Stalin – the fall of the Soviet system would always remain something deeply miraculous. An old friend sent a postcard to my mother. '*Neuzheli dozhili?*' she wrote, in the wonderfully terse Russian phrase which means, 'Can it be that we have lived to see this day?'

Oddly, my mother seemed rather unmoved by the upheavals of that autumn, which began with the victory for Yeltsin's democrats and ended in Gorbachev's resignation on Christmas Day. Russia was, by then, a place of the past for her; with characteristic wilfulness she'd emotionally drawn a line across her old life and become something new. She was pleased, of course, and saw it as a victory for the dissident movement to which she had, in small part, contributed. She says now that she saw the whole collapse of the Soviet Union from her 'glorious isolation' in London; she felt no great surge of emotion at the news. But there was one moment, I think, which had resonance for her: the night soon after the coup's collapse when a roaring crowd gathered outside the old KGB headquarters on Lubyanka Square, shouting for revenge for the KGB's support of the reactionaries. A steel cable was put around the neck of the sinister, elongated statue of Felix Dzerzhinsky which stood on a plinth in the centre of the square, and a crane wrenched Iron Felix into the air, where he swung above the crowd as though lynched. She'd always believed that Soviet power would collapse in her lifetime, she said, but that was the moment she really believed it had finally happened.

A year later, in 1992, my father pushed open the doors of the Lubyanka on his way to an appointment with the KGB's newly formed public relations department. Alexei Kondaurov sat in a plush office overlooking the courtyard where prisoners had once been executed. The KGB – or the FSK, as it was known in the early Yeltsin years – were interested in 'building bridges' with Western sovietologists, Kondaurov gushed as Mervyn sipped lemon tea. He even asked Mervyn to write an article on how he researched the Soviet Union from abroad for the FSK's new magazine. My father was more interested in contacting his old would-be controller, Alexei Suntsov. The FSK man made friendly noises, but nothing came of it.

We had more luck in 1998, when I called the press office of the Russian Foreign Intelligence Service on my father's behalf. I chatted to General Yury Kobaladze, their smooth press flack, and took him to an expensive lunch among the expat deal-makers in Moscow's best French restaurant, Le Gastronome. Kobaladze revealed that Suntsov had died, but that his widow was still alive.

We found Inna Vadimovna Suntsova through Valery Ve-lichko, head of the KGB veterans' club. In the club's offices behind Okyabrskaya Metro he was introduced to a plump, seventy-year-old woman with a pleasant face. She and my father shook hands warily. Neither recognized the other, though they had met twice, once in 1959 at the Ararat – no, corrected Suntsova, the Budapest, restaurant. They'd also gone in Alexei's car up to the Lenin Hills to see Moscow by night.

Suntsova rummaged in her bag and brought out a picture of

Alexei in uniform, which came as a shock to Mervyn, even though he had known that he was a serving KGB officer.

'I know that he was bitterly disappointed in you, and complained,' Inna told my father. ' "Matthews, the nasty boy, he let me down, after all I've done for him." When things didn't work out with you, it definitely had a negative effect on my husband's position in the service.'

Mervyn didn't ask who it was that had blocked his marriage. He doubted it was Alexei, and doubted Inna would know. She seemed surprised when Mervyn told her the story of his battle. Inna gave Mervyn a photo, after some hesitation, of Alexei in civilian clothes.

Mervyn's oldest Russian friend, the KGB man Vadim Popov, had disappeared. Mervyn tried to look him up at the Lenin Library, but apart from his doctoral thesis there were no other publications, and the Institute of Oriental Studies where he had studied had been amalgamated.

My father did, however, find Igor Vail – the graduate student who had been used by the KGB to entrap Mervyn – by the simple expedient of looking in the Moscow phone book. It turned out that Vail had been waiting thirty years to apologize for the red sweater incident. He had been summoned by the Lubyanka on the fateful morning, he told my father, and threatened for two hours. They had been bugging Mervyn's room, and had recorded compromising things Igor had said when he had visited Mervyn. Igor would be expelled from the university if he did not cooperate in the entrapment; he had had little choice. Mervyn gracefully forgave him. 'That was a different life, and a different world,' he told Vail. 'It's all behind us now.'

My father and I saw each other in Moscow, off and on, throughout the nineties. The meetings were rarely happy. My father certainly disapproved of my dubiously bohemian lifestyle. I, in turn, regarded him as a dour spoilsport. Anger is always so much less complicated than love, and for large chunks of my adult life I chose, for no reason I can readily identify, to be angry with my father. Angry for imagined (and real) slights during adolescence, angry at his lack of imagination and his refusal to bankroll me while I indulged mine. I think he found me spoiled, and ungrateful. 'You've had so many advantages, Owen,' he would scold me when I was a child. 'SO many advantages.'

It was only towards the end of my time in Moscow, after I had worked out much of my aggression at the world in general, that I bothered to begin to try to understand my father, whose life my own had unwittingly followed so closely. After refusing to believe that my parents' lives had anything to do with mine, I finally acknowledged that the time had come to record those moments when Russia reached into me, as it had into my father. Both of us had found something of ourselves here and that realization brought me a feeling of fellowship with the old man. The feeling was soundless, but it crackled.

My father has spent much of his old age retreating into himself, working hard to cocoon himself behind walls of solitude. It is odd that while my parents were kept apart by politics, by a seemingly unbridgeable ideological divide, some force of will, of magnetism, drew them together and gave them hope and courage through six years of separation. But now, half a lifetime later, the defining momentum of my family is a centrifugal force which has thrown us physically apart. My father spends much of his time these days in the Far East, far from anyone who knows him, travelling in Nepal and China and Thailand, pottering on beaches, living in rented rooms, reading and writing. At home in London, my parents have reached a kind of truce – founded, perhaps, on a realization that suddenly life has passed and the running series of domestic skirmishes they fought with each other could have no victor.

*   *   *

My father and I reached a kind of reconciliation, feeling our way towards each other, after I married Xenia. We moved to Istanbul, where my sons Nikita and Theodore were born, but would come back to spend every winter at Xenia's family dacha. My father came and stayed at my in-laws' rambling apartment in the backstreets off the Arbat, just round the corner from Starokonushenny Pereulok. He spent his time wandering around bookshops, amazed that the Dom Knigi on the New Arbat was filled with so much literature, and he could pay with his English credit card. On the street were advertisements for the Russian edition of GQ (the latest edition even carrying a flattering profile of his own war correspondent son) and a booth selling mobile phones.

In the last days of 2002 we drove out to the dacha. There was a hard frost, and the tall pines of Nikolina Gora stood stark against a baby-blue winter sky. In the distance, a line of trees was crisply outlined, deep black against the snowfields. The air was so cold it burned the lungs.

My father and I went for a walk on the frozen Moscow River. I lent him the heavy old overcoat he'd bought in Oxford in the fifties, and I wore a shaggy sheepskin Soviet Army coat. My father was getting visibly elderly, his hip was giving him trouble and he limped and stumbled in the snowdrifts of the riverbank. It was so cold that the thick snow overlying the river's ice creaked like floorboards under our boots.

'No great shakes, really,' said my father, of his life. 'No great shakes. When I realized I wasn't getting back into Oxford I gave up. When I look at my achievements, they're quite modest. Quite modest.'

There was a long silence, the low moan of wind blowing the snow into eddies.

'But you won. You got mother out of Russia. That was a huge achievement, no?'

He gave a dismissive nod, and a sigh. 'I thought I would be

deliriously happy when I got her out, but I wasn't. The problems started almost immediately, all kinds of tensions. I thought I'd give it a few months, to see if things got better, and they did, to a certain extent. So I just let things drift, really.'

'So did you ever think of giving up?'

'No. I never once thought of it. I'd made up my mind and given her my word, and that was that. Though I never imagined it would go on for so long. After five years we were still at square one. If she'd broken it off I think I would have got over it fairly quickly. There was this Erik . . . I never knew if anything was going on there, but I thought she might end up with him if things didn't work out.'

He spoke as if it was not himself he was describing but someone he knew – detached, without pain but with a tinge of professional regret, like a surgeon probing an infirm patient.

'I was very moved when she told me about what she'd been through, her childhood, the war. Terrible really. It struck me very deeply. She'd had such a miserable life I wanted to give her a decent deal. That was an important part of it. And then there was the physical disability.'

In the distance a snowmobile roared into view, and my father winced as we stood aside and it passed in a cloud of exhaust. Through the trees on the high riverbank we could see the pitched roofs of the dachas of Russia's new super-rich, Xenia's new neighbours, built on plots of land worth millions. The old dacha of Andrei Vyshinsky, the Prosecutor-General who had signed my grandfather's death warrant, had been rebuilt as a faux French chateau. A new world.

'Who would have thought that things would change so fast. I never, ever imagined that it would happen in my lifetime.'

That evening, in the kitchen of the dacha, my father stirred his tea with the same old perforated spoon which has accompanied him on his travels like a talisman. We had a minor row about my sister, and he stalked upstairs, waving me off with his teacup. Half an hour later he came back, we changed the subject, and spoke some more. As he stood to leave to retire to bed he stopped abruptly and hugged me as I sat at the kitchen table, and kissed me lightly on the head.

One final image. My mother, on the terrace of our garden in Istanbul, with four-year-old Nikita. She is seventy-two years old, and her hip is giving her trouble, and she walks with a stick. But as I watch from my study window, I see that the stick is discarded, and she is cutting off a piece of old rope with a pair of scissors. As Kit looks on in delight, she starts to skip, slower, faster, crossing the rope in front of herself as she counts off skipping rhymes she learned in the playground at Verkhne-Dneprovsk. Kit is delighted, and starts chanting the rhymes himself, waving his arms in the air and running in circles in childish excitement. 'One-two, one-two-three, the rabbit peeks out from behind his tree,' my mother chants, just as she had learned when she was Kit's age and one of Stalin's children. Like many Russian children's rhymes, it's wonderfully rhythmic, absurd, and violent.

> Hunter takes aim with his gun,
> Shoots the rabbit, bang-bang-bang,
> Rush him to the hospital bed!
> Seems our rabbit is quite dead.
> Bring him home, three-four-five,
> Look! Little rabbit is alive!

Select Bibliography

Amis, Martin, *Koba the Dread: Laughter and the Twenty Million* (Vintage, 2003)

Applebaum, Anne, *Gulag: A History* (Anchor, 2004)

Akhmatova, Anna, *The Complete Poems of Anna Akhmatova* (Zephyr Press, 1998)

Beevor, Antony, *Stalingrad: The Fateful Siege: 1942–1943* (Penguin, 1999)

Bulgakov, Mikhail, *Heart of a Dog* (Grove Press, 1994)

Camus, Albert, *Actuelles, III: Chroniques algériennes 1939–1958* (Gallimard, 1958)

Conquest, Robert, *The Great Terror* (Macmillan, 1968)

—— *Harvest of Sorrow* (University of Alberta Press, 1987)

Figes, Orlando, *Natasha's Dance: A Cultural History of Russia* (Picador, 2003)

Ginzburg, Yevgeniya, *Into the Whirlwind* (Harvill Press, 1989)

Gogol, Nikolai, *The Overcoat and Other Tales of Good and Evil* (W.W. Norton & Co., 1965)

Grossman, Vasily, *Life and Fate* (New York Review Books Classics, 2006)

—— *A Writer at War: A Soviet Journalist with the Red Army, 1941–1945* (Vintage, 2007)

Koch, Stephen, *Double Lives: Stalin, Willi Munzenberg and the Seduction of the Intellectuals* (Enigma Books, 2004, revised edition)

Koestler, Arthur, *Darkness at Noon: A Novel* (Scribner, 2006)

Kotkin, Stephen, *Magnetic Mountain: Stalinism as a Civilization* (University of California Press, 1997)

Mandelstam, Nadezhda, *Hope Against Hope: A Memoir* (Modern Library, 1999)

Mandelstam, Osip, *Selected Poems* (Penguin, 1992)

Matthews, Mervyn, *Privilege in the Soviet Union* (Unwin Hyman, 1978)

—— *Poverty in the Soviet Union* (Cambridge University Press, 1986)

—— *Mila and Mervusya: A Russian Wedding* (Seren/Poetry Wales, 2002)

—— *Mervyn's Lot* (Seren, 2003)

Massie, Robert K., *Peter the Great* (Ballantine, 1981)

Medvedev, Roy, *Let History Judge* (Columbia University Press, 1989)

Meier, Andrew, *Black Earth: A Journey through Russia after the Fall* (W.W. Norton & Co., 2005)

Merridale, Catherine, *Night of Stone* (Granta, 2000)

—— *Ivan's War: Life and Death in the Red Army, 1939–1945* (Picador, 2007)

Montefiore, Simon Sebag, *Stalin: The Court of the Red Tsar* (Vintage, 2005)

Moynahan, Brian, *The Russian Century: A Photographic History of Russia's 100 Years* (Random House, 1994)

Pasternak, Boris, *Doctor Zhivago* (Pantheon, 1997)

Razgon, Lev Emmanuilovich, *True Stories* (Ardis Publishers, 1997)

Remnick, David, *Lenin's Tomb: The Last Days of the Soviet Empire* (Vintage, 1994)

Rilke, Rainer Maria, *Selected Poetry of Rainer Maria Rilke* by Stephen Mitchell (Random House, 1982)

Rybakov, Anatoli, *The Children of the Arbat: A Novel* (Little, Brown & Co., 1988)

Shalamov, Varlam, *Kolyma Tales* (Penguin, 1995)

Simonov, Konstantin, *Days and Nights* (Simon & Schuster, 1945)

Solzhenitsyn, Alexander, *The Gulag Archipelago 1918–1956* (Harvill Press, 1999)

—— *Cancer Ward* (Farrar, Straus & Giroux, 1991)

—— *One Day in the Life of Ivan Denisovich* (Farrar, Straus & Giroux, 2005, new edition)

Thomas, Dylan, *Collected Poems of Dylan Thomas 1934–1952* (New Directions, 1971)

Tsvetaeva, Maria, *Selected Poems* (Penguin, 1994)

Werth, Alexander, *Russia at War: 1941–1945* (Carroll & Graf, 1999)

Acknowledgements

This book was an awfully long time in the making – in fact, fully half my adult life has passed since I first put down notes for a book I was going to call *Moscow Babylon* back in 1998. Luckily for everyone concerned, that book never appeared; instead, the project transformed over the years into the memoir it is today. I owe a vast debt of gratitude to all the friends and colleagues who put up with my writerly sufferings for all that time, and who helped me to realize that what I really should be writing about (and trying to understand) was not me, but Russia.

Most of my close friends have had the good fortune to read various bits of the manuscript over the last decade. Andrew Paulson, year after year, kept telling me that my writing was great, which was helpful even if probably in most cases untrue. Melik Kaylan flatteringly told me that he found the writing 'surprisingly good'. Charlie Graeber, Andrew Meier, Michael FitzGerald, Mark Franchetti and Masha Lipman were kind enough to edit and comment at length on the whole thing, once it had more or less taken shape; their advice and friendship has been invaluable.

Mia Foster first suggested this project: 'Why don't you write a *book*, Owen?' she said by the fireplace at Charlie Bausman's dacha at Nikolina Gora – and it was Charlie who egged me on to actually starting. But the only reason I could even contemplate writing a work of history, even of personal history, is thanks to my history tutors at Christ Church: William Thomas, Katya Andreyev and the late Patrick Wormald. Robin Aizlewood opened up Russian literature for me as an intellectual experience, rather than as the emotional, childhood one revealed to me by my mother.

In Russia, various friends and partners-in-crime deserve acknowledgement, though they'll doubtless be horrified to find themselves mentioned in a single list: Isabel Gorst, Ed Lucas and Masha Naimushina, as well as Ab Farman-Farmaian, Vijay Maheshwari and Robert King. I shared a dark fascination with – and many journeys into – the grim underside of Moscow with Mark Ames and Matt Taibbi. They turned out to be the great chroniclers of those strange and savage years.

In Istanbul, where I escaped for much of the period of the writing of this book, Gunduz Vassaf has been a wise and an unfailingly good friend, as has Professor Norman Stone. Andrew Jeffreys has been my closest confidant and sharer of post-Moscow adventures. Georgiana Campbell lent me her cottage in Dorset to start writing. Jean-Christophe Iseux has known me better and longer than almost anyone; he is one of the only people I know who truly lives a life of his own choosing, and that inspires me one day to do the same.

Marc Champion and Jay Ross at the *Moscow Times* made me a journalist, though I doubtless made their lives hell because I thought that I was so much better at the job than I really was. At *Newsweek*, Bill Powell was an ideal boss and mentor, *il miglior fabbro* of news magazine stories I have ever met. Chris Dickey has been a powerful influence and staunch ally. Mike Meyer and Fareed Zakaria made do for years with a correspondent who always had half an eye on this book, yet never complained. And now that I find myself in the odd position of doing my old boss's job as *Newsweek's* Moscow Bureau Chief, I have Anna Nemtsova as the new me – except she does the job of second correspondent far better than I ever did.

But most important of all, Mike Fishwick at Bloomsbury has shown a towering faith in this book, above and beyond the call of duty or reason. 'Wait for me, but only wait very hard,' wrote Konstantin Simonov of the Soviet women waiting for their loved ones to come home from the war, never knowing whether they actually would. Fishwick knows how they felt. Without his belief in me, none of this would ever have come to pass. Trâm-Anh Doan and Emily Sweet have been models of patience and efficiency.

On the home team, my US agent Diana Finch invested a huge amount of time and emotional energy in getting this book rolling. She, more than anyone, made me as a writer. Bill Hamilton, my London agent, has been a brick and model of imperturbability in the face of his author's alarming changes of plan, schedule and fortune.

Finally, not only is this book dedicated to my parents, but I owe them enormous thanks for their help in writing this account of their lives. I have drawn heavily on my father's two volumes of memoirs, *Mervyn's Lot* and *Mila and Mervusya*, and my mother not only spoke to me at length about her memories but also wrote detailed notes on the final manuscript. My aunt Lenina has been a dear friend and inspiration to me for years; it's a source of great sadness to me that she died in her sleep just a few days before I was able to show her the first proofs of this book. My sister Emily has made intelligent and fearless critiques of the book in all its various incarnations. My parents-in-law Alexei and Anna Kravchenko have not only tactfully ignored years of sporadic moodiness, alcoholism, despair and sundry other affectations of the literary life, but also always insisted on describing me to all comers as 'the writer' of the family. After a decade of effort, this is finally more or less true.

But by far the biggest burden has fallen on my wife,

Xenia. As long as she's known me, I have been writing this book. Two wars, two children and a move to a new country later, and I was still at it. Somehow she will have to get used to living with me alone, now that the book is finally born and out on its own in the world. I couldn't have done it without her.

Index

A NOTE ON THE AUTHOR

Owen Matthews was born in London and spent part of his childhood in America. He studied modern history at Oxford University before beginning his career as a journalist in Bosnia. In 1995, he accepted a job at the *Moscow Times*, a daily English language newspaper. He also freelanced for a number of publications including *The Times*, the *Spectator* and the *Independent*. In 1997, he became a correspondent at *Newsweek* magazine in Moscow, where he covered the second Chechen war, as well as politics and society. Owen was also one of the first journalists to witness the start of the US bombing of Afghanistan's Panjshir Valley in 2001, and went on to cover the invasion of Iraq in 2003. Owen is currently *Newsweek* magazine's bureau chief in Moscow, where he lives with his wife and two children.

A NOTE ON THE TYPE

The text of this book is set in Berling Roman, a modern face designed by K. E. Forsberg between 1951–58. In spite of its youth it does carry the characteristics of an old face. The serifs are inclined and blunt, and the g has a straight ear.